KU-285-174

SUCCESSFUL GARDENING
FINISHING TOUCHES

Published by The Reader's Digest Association Limited.

First Edition Copyright © 1995
The Reader's Digest Association Limited,
Berkeley Square House, Berkeley Square, London W1X 6AB

Copyright © 1995
The Reader's Digest Association Far East Limited
Philippines Copyright 1995
The Reader's Digest Association Far East Limited

All rights reserved

Originally published as a partwork.
Successful Gardening
Copyright © 1990
Eaglemoss Publications Ltd.
All rights reserved
No part of this book may be reproduced, stored in a
retrieval system or transmitted in any form or by any
means, electronic, electrostatic, magnetic tape,
mechanical, photocopying, recording or otherwise, without
permission in writing from the publishers

® READER'S DIGEST
is a registered trademark of
The Reader's Digest Association Inc. of Pleasantville,
New York, USA

Consultant editor: Lizzie Boyd

Typeset in Century Schoolbook

PRINTED IN SPAIN

ISBN 0 276 42098 5

Opposite: Half hidden by climbing golden hop, a wall fountain
spouts a melodious trickle of water. Cheerful pots of ball-clipped
box add the finishing touch.

Overleaf: A metal arch covered with a mass of blue-flowered
Clematis × jackmanii strikes a welcoming note above a gateway.

PUBLISHED BY THE READER'S DIGEST ASSOCIATION LIMITED
LONDON NEW YORK MONTREAL SYDNEY CAPE TOWN

Originally published in partwork form
by Eaglemoss Publications Limited

SUCCESSFUL GARDENING

FINISHING TOUCHES

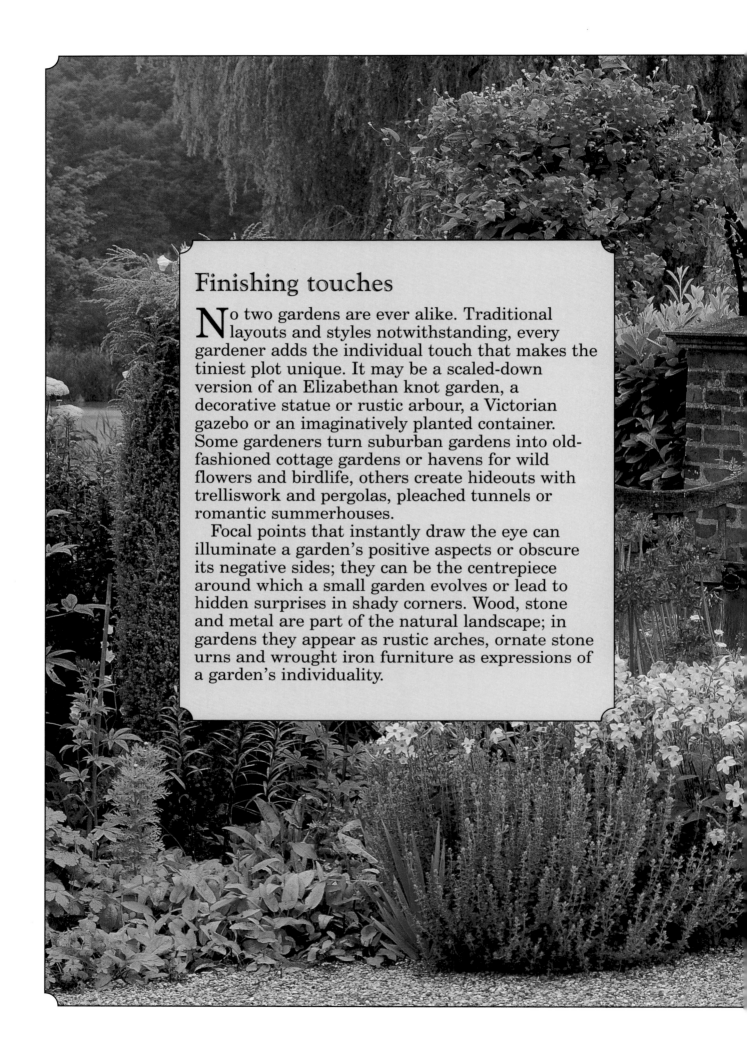

Finishing touches

No two gardens are ever alike. Traditional layouts and styles notwithstanding, every gardener adds the individual touch that makes the tiniest plot unique. It may be a scaled-down version of an Elizabethan knot garden, a decorative statue or rustic arbour, a Victorian gazebo or an imaginatively planted container. Some gardeners turn suburban gardens into old-fashioned cottage gardens or havens for wild flowers and birdlife, others create hideouts with trelliswork and pergolas, pleached tunnels or romantic summerhouses.

Focal points that instantly draw the eye can illuminate a garden's positive aspects or obscure its negative sides; they can be the centrepiece around which a small garden evolves or lead to hidden surprises in shady corners. Wood, stone and metal are part of the natural landscape; in gardens they appear as rustic arches, ornate stone urns and wrought iron furniture as expressions of a garden's individuality.

CONTENTS

Cottage garden A traditional garden is stocked with old-fashioned flowers in seemingly artless profusion.

Cottage and wild gardens

Most gardeners like to incorporate the traditional features of lawn, neat flower beds and borders in their gardens, with a paved sitting area near the house, and at the rear a kitchen garden with greenhouse, shed and compost heap. Others have visions of quaint cottage gardens as portrayed in Victorian and Edwardian prints, although true cottage gardens were utilitarian rather than ornamental. The nostalgic image of a cottage garden is one of old-fashioned flowers growing haphazardly over paths and lawn edges, beneath rustic arches smothered with scented roses and honeysuckles. Such images can easily be transplanted to modern gardens because it is the plants, rather than the layout, that determine the style.

It is also possible to adapt a working cottage garden to an ornamental feature in the style of a potager. Here, brick paving divides the kitchen garden into small geometric beds filled with food crops, scented herbs and cottage-garden flowers. Decorative vegetables can be grown among flowers and shrubs, edge conventional beds or climb up walls and fences.

An entire garden can be left as a near-wilderness, but more often a corner or section is devoted to growing wild flowers, native trees and naturalized bulbs, with few attempts at orderliness or restraint.

Wild habitats that provide food, water and a secure environment have the added bonus of attracting wildlife – birds, butterflies and small mammals – with certain types of plants and shrubs being more alluring to animal visitors than others.

Natural shelter Self-sown foxgloves, climbing sweet peas and old garden roses create a safe haven for birdlife.

COTTAGE GARDENS

**Today's cottage gardens combine
the rustic charm of old-fashioned plants
with the formality of modern garden designs.**

The traditional cottage garden, as it existed in Victorian days, would hardly appeal to gardeners at the end of the 20th century, in spite of the nostalgia and romance the concept evokes. A cottager's garden then was a working garden, essential for food production to supplement the low wages of a farm labourer.

The cottage garden was a small plot, usually square or rectangular, which surrounded a tiny house. The ground would be closely packed with rows of vegetables, fruit bushes and herbs. Flowers for the church and family gravestead would be massed between them, and at the back would be a pigsty, poultry and beehives.

There were no trees in a cottage garden, apart from a fruit tree or two, for they cast too much shade to grow the essential crop plants. Neither was there a lawn, an obvious waste of space.

Cottage garden design
A cottage garden style as such did not exist, and every plot had its own individuality within the constraints of a uniform outline. The narrow path of cinders, or beaten earth, that ran from the front gate to the house was often edged with clipped box, lavender or clumps of pinks, sometimes with bricks laid on edge or decorative ridge tiles, and sometimes with stones or shells collected from the seaside.

Behind the edging were tidy vegetable rows, interspersed with what we today call cottage-garden flowers – hardy, trouble-free perennials and biennials that could be relied upon to come up year after year or self-seed without any effort on the owner's part. There would be fragrant herbs – among the vegetables or in pots by the back door – to scent cupboards and linen presses and to flavour the stewpot.

Every inch of soil was utilized, and bore fruitfully. Farm labourers had access to rich farmyard manure, and every year the vegetable plots were double dug and manured until the soil was rich and friable. However, not all was utilitarian: the odd corner would hold flowering spring bulbs and colourful summer annuals sown every year; sweet-scented rosemary or myrtle would be planted by doors and windows, and hollyhocks would grow against the cottage walls. Rambler roses and honeysuckle would tumble over

▼ **Old-world charm** Clumps of cottage-garden favourites perfectly complement this picturesque country house. Red and pink, now as then, are popular colours, ranging from the deep hues of perennial sweet peas and low-growing dianthus to the softer shades of veronicas, double-flowered poppies and daisy-like dimorphothecas.

◀ **Path edging** Enduring favourites spill over a path and scent the air. Clumps of lavender and lady's mantle nod to tumbling ox-eye daisies and bright yellow anthemis. They need little attention and spread year by year from self-sown seedlings.

▶ **Artless profusion** More by chance than careful planning, harmonious plant groups fill the garden. The climbing red rose 'Danse du Feu' perfectly matches the elegant spikes of red-flowered penstemon, intersected by the graceful plumes of the variegated grass *Phalaris arundinacea* 'Picta' (gardener's garters).

▼ **Open vistas** Seemingly flowing into the landscape, with low hedges to mark the boundary, the garden has glorious views over rolling meadows and fields. It is open to the sun throughout the day, with few trees to screen the views or cast shade.

◀ **Rose bower** A rustic arch is draped with a double-flowered 'Aloha' rose, its pink blooms heavy with scent. At ground level, sword-shaped fans of iris leaves accentuate a brick path laid in a herring-bone pattern.

woodlands and distant hills forming a backdrop.

The use of rectangular and square beds gives the various features an overall unity, but the design is never rigid. The beds are a plant-lover's delight, an accumulation of plants in attractive partnerships that make a connected series of groupings. There are individual beds of pastel pinks, blues and mauves, cool blues and white. Brighter colours – red and yellow – are concentrated in the outer beds.

Trees, shrubs and climbers

Because so many beautiful trees are visible from the garden, few are planted within the beds and borders. But established fruit trees remain, adding a gnarled presence to the long flower borders.

In country-garden fashion the boundary hedge is a mixture of native plants – holly, hawthorn, privet and beech. An interior hedge of *Lonicera nitida* serves as a backdrop for flower beds.

Masses of roses cover walls and archways and fill mixed beds. And, in keeping with cottage-garden tradition, old-fashioned shrub roses take precedence over modern bush roses. A dwarf conifer bed breaks the tradition; its bright yellows and blue-greys are attractive all year round.

Aromatic shrubs are much in evidence, and old-fashioned lavender, rosemary, rue, santolina, sage and artemisia are planted among the perennials. A huge wisteria clothes the house wall, and trellises and arbours are covered with honeysuckle, clematis, and perennial sweet peas.

Cottage-garden flowers

Herbaceous perennials form the bulk of the planting and include typical cottage-garden types, such as columbines and delphiniums. There is an informal but careful mixture of heights and growth habits within the beds, with plants spilling over lawn and paths.

Flower forms vary, too; from dense spikes of bell-shaped delphiniums, salvias, campanulas and obedient plant, to the airy

front door porches, twine on tripods among vegetables or on arches across narrow paths. The privet hedge by the road would be neatly trimmed and often clipped into fanciful topiary shapes.

Modern cottage gardens

Today there is less emphasis on food plants, and the cottage garden has become a combination of numerous styles though with a preference for mass planting of flowering plants. There are smooth lawns and secret corners and paved areas for quiet contemplation, and while the layout is informal, clearly defined beds and borders have been introduced.

The plantings, though, are dense and chiefly limited to modern varieties of old-fashioned flowers with rustic charm and robust growth habit.

Little if any staking is in evidence; plants are allowed to grow into dense clumps and are rarely graded according to height. They tumble over edges and paths, drop their petals and hybridize with each other.

The garden described here combines some of the most popular features of traditional cottage gardens with the more relaxed attitude of modern gardeners. This garden benefits from a countryside setting, with meadows,

sprays of hostas and gypsophilas; bowl-shaped peonies and flat-headed yarrows and sedums; daisy-like asters, fleabane and feverfew; thistly sea hollies; and delicate, foaming lady's mantle and astilbes; and clumps of pink and blue crane's-bill.

There are euphorbias, day lilies, heucheras, shasta daisies and mallows overspilling the beds. And gardener's garters, a true old-fashioned favourite, pokes its grassy flower heads through rose bushes.

Other cottage-garden flowers include old-fashioned pinks (*Dianthus* species), tall-growing monkshoods and lupins, red-hot pokers and oriental poppies, the popular phlox in a range of colours, and woolly-leaved mulleins.

Annuals, biennials and bulbs
Bedding schemes rarely feature in cottage gardens, but annuals and biennials are sown to fill any gaps between perennials. Old-fashioned annuals include bellis and snapdragons, larkspurs, marigolds and fragrant sweet peas, cornflowers and night-scented stock, nigellas and sunflowers. Biennials, such as foxgloves and hollyhocks, honesty and sweet Williams, also belong,

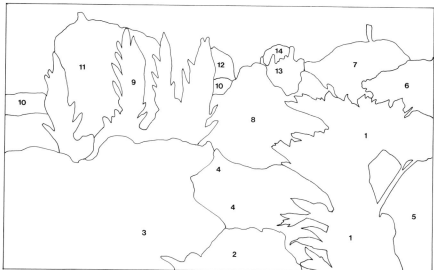

COTTAGE CHARM

The plan identifies some cottage-garden favourites shown above.

1 *Angelica archangelica*
2 Purple-leaved sage (*Salvia officinalis* 'Purpurascens')
3 Meadow crane's-bill (*Geranium pratense* 'Kashmir White')
4 Crane's-bill (*Geranium psilostemon*)
5 Feverfew (*Chrysanthemum parthenium*)
6 Variegated Russian comfrey (*Symphytum x uplandicum* 'Variegatum')
7 Honeysuckle (*Lonicera x americana*)
8 Peony (*Paeonia lactiflora* 'Bowl of Beauty')
9 Clary (*Salvia sclarea*)
10 Yarrow (*Achillea filipendulina*)
11 Bronze fennel (*Foeniculum vulgare* 'Purpureum')
12 Globe thistle (*Echinops banaticus*)
13 Delphinium hybrid
14 Giant scabious (*Cephalaria gigantea*)

along with the usual spring-flowering bulbs. And there may also be a pot or two of splendid madonna lilies.

Focal points

Ornaments and statuary are kept to a minimum in both traditional and modern cottage gardens. Highly decorative containers are also out of keeping, though earthy terracotta pots are appropriate.

Large-scale topiary was part of grand country house landscape architecture, and cottage gardeners enjoyed trying their hand at clipped topiary shapes to top the boundary hedges.

Rustic arches covered with roses or honeysuckles add to the old-world charm, and a wooden seat beneath an apple tree evokes a bygone era.

▶ **Mixed borders** Shrubs and perennials mingle happily in haphazard combinations. Ever popular lady's mantle weaves its yellow-green sprays through a large-flowered shrub rose, and self-sown, silver-leaved campions add spots of red colour to a bed of mainly foliage plants.

▼ **Quiet corner** A secluded area can easily be made into a miniature cottage garden. Shielded by hedging and filled with old favourites like poppies and blue and white crane's-bills, it becomes part of another, quieter world.

KITCHEN GARDENS

**A geometric design of small vegetable beds
looks highly ornamental, especially if filled with
colourful crops of contrasting shapes and textures.**

Home-grown vegetables and fruit are fresher and tastier than bought ones, and the gardener is in control of the amount of synthetic chemicals that are used in their production. Another advantage of a kitchen garden is the opportunity to experiment with unusual vegetables and fruits.

In traditional cottage gardens almost the entire plot would be devoted to food crops. At the other end of the economic scale, large country estates were renowned for their walled kitchen gardens, with fruit trees trained along the walls and hothouses stocked with vines and out-of-season vegetables.

As the cottage gardener became more affluent, vegetables gave way to ornamental plants, and country house kitchen gar-

dens fell into disrepair with the scarcity and rising cost of labour. Today, the vegetable garden of orderly rows is usually confined to the rear of the garden and is screened off from the ornamental area, but it is quite possible to make it into an attractive feature. Vegetables and fruits can be incorporated in mixed borders with flowers and shrubs, and low-growing colourful types can be used to edge beds and borders.

Potagers

Another alternative is to create an ornamental vegetable garden in the style of the French potager. This is a decorative arrangement of small beds or blocks set in a geometric pattern divided by paved or gravel paths.

The beds can be rectangular, square, triangular or even circular, but the pattern must be symmetrical so as to link the arrangement of the beds. The geometric shapes of the beds can be emphasized with formally clipped edgings of dwarf box or clumps of lavender. Paving should blend with the overall garden design –

▼ **Ornamental food crops** Brick paths divide small beds filled with fruit, vegetables, herbs and flowering plants. It is a pleasing design that combines the practical with the decorative, and standard roses provide the necessary vertical emphasis. The beds are easy to tend from the paths, and after harvesting, the bare look of the vegetable beds is largely concealed by the ornamental plants.

▶ **Raised beds** Adding height to small gardens, free-standing raised beds are particularly suitable for disabled gardeners. They are easy to tend, and French beans and dwarf runner beans need no staking but can be allowed to tumble over the walls.

▼ **Space savers** Vertical space is often ignored; in small gardens, especially, it should be fully maximized. Here, runner beans are trained on trellis attached to a house wall; they are fronted by tomatoes supported by canes, and marrows fill the spaces between them. The narrow bed is attractively edged with feathery artemisias.

coloured or plain concrete slabs, bricks, paving stones or gravel.

Attractive structures, such as rose-covered, curved or Gothic arches, rustic screens with espalier fruit trees, terracotta pots, beehives, a wooden seat in an arbour, and a well or sundial, make pleasing additions to a potager when placed to complement the overall pattern.

In potagers, vegetables are often grown for their decorative as well as their culinary qualities – for example, dramatically coloured cabbage varieties and lettuce with feathery foliage.

Ordinary lettuce, carrots and leeks can contribute to a potager's appearance if planted so that the shape and colour of their leaves harmonize or contrast with each other. Beds or blocks of vegetables should be of a reasonable size so that they crop over an extended period.

Space-saving crops

In small gardens, grow compact vegetables – for example, turnips, carrots and winter radishes. Dwarf varieties of French beans,

▲ **Modern cottage garden** Vegetables and flowers for cutting go well together. Here, dahlias grow between rows of leeks and beetroot, and rudbeckias, asters and a tall clump of sweet peas add more colour to the vegetable plot.

▶ **Kitchen garden** The back garden is the usual site for vegetables. This well-managed plot has orderly rows of runner beans, broad beans, Brussels sprouts, potatoes and onions – a large kitchen garden is needed to keep a family self-sufficient.

bush marrows and non-trailing ridge cucumbers can also be included, with tripods of decorative runner beans.

Crops which grow quickly give good value for space – for example, summer radishes, lettuces, salad onions, early carrots and beetroots. For winter greens grow leeks, perpetual spinach or Swiss chard which are upright and don't cover too much horizontal space.

Vegetables can also be grown in containers on a paved or concrete area, and even on a balcony or roof garden. Growing bags are another convenient way of raising vegetables in a small area.

▲ **Decorative vegetables** Newly planted dwarf box plants edge a bed of 'Red Salad Bowl' lettuces and cabbages. Cordon-trained apple trees form the background.

▶ **Classic potager** A formal design of squares divided into symmetrical triangles by brick paths creates a highly ornamental feature. The beds are planted with young fruit trees, herbs and ornamental vegetables, their shapes emphasized with edging of dwarf box.

Climbing vegetables

Decorative schemes can be created in a very small garden or mixed border with vegetable climbers, which make effective use of vertical space.

Runner beans, for example, can be grown for the ornamental value of their flowers. There are varieties of runner bean with salmon-pink, white or red and white bicoloured flowers, as well as the usual scarlet flowers. A space-saving way of growing runner beans is to train them up a wigwam of canes. Grown like this, runner beans make a fine exclamation mark in any garden.

Climbing vegetables can also be grown to form screens. Peas, for example, make a good windshield if trained up canes – a purple-podded variety could be grown for

▶ **Miniature herb garden** A red-painted cartwheel makes an eye-catching focal point in an adaptation of the Elizabethan knot garden. Different herbs grow between the spokes and rarely encroach on each other. Identification and harvesting are easy.

▼ **Herb container** Terracotta pots, specially adapted for herb growing, take up little room and make unusual features on patios and other hard-surface areas. Individual pockets hold chives, tarragon and various aromatic thymes.

decoration. The Jerusalem artichoke, which reaches a height of up to 2m (7ft), serves the same purpose.

Another idea is to train ridge cucumbers or small marrows up wire netting to provide a temporary screen of leaves and golden flowers followed by fruit.

Herbs

Growing herbs alongside vegetables is traditional. Many herbs are low growing and make delightful edgings – chives, parsley, golden marjoram and silver-variegated thyme, for example, can effectively mark the outline of beds.

Other herb varieties which add colour and combine effectively with vegetables are purple and yellow sage, golden-variegated lemon balm, blue-flowered borage, bronze fennel and varieties of mint in shades of yellow or cream.

Decorative vegetables

Several vegetables are highly decorative in their own right; they can be grown in a separate bed in a potager, or combined with general planting in an ornamental bed or border.

A selection of decorative vegetables would be ideal in small gardens for purely ornamental purposes. For example, the eye-catching ruby chard – a form of Swiss chard – has glowing wine-red stems and looks lovely and unusual in a mixed border.

Experiment with decorative and unusual leaf shapes – perhaps globe artichokes, which have huge lobed and spiny leaves and hand-

19

some purple flower heads, or graceful, feathery asparagus.

The purple-podded climbing French beans, with their purple stems, lilac flowers and purple-flushed leaves, can be trained on bean poles or against a wall or fence at the back of a border. The yellow-fruited courgette, which has patches of yellow on the leaves, is attractive scrambling between low-growing perennials.

For other colour effects experiment with Italian chicories, which have beautifully variegated shades of red, pink and white. Red and brown lettuce and red Brussels sprouts also provide colour.

Some varieties of sweetcorn are highly ornamental. There are types with variegated leaves, prominently striped with white, cream, pale yellow and pink. Other varieties have coloured seeds in the cobs – yellow, orange, red or purple; they are inedible, but they can be dried and used for winter decoration indoors.

Ornamental cabbages, known as flowering cabbages, are commonly available from seed. These reasonably hardy plants make curious and eye-catching focal points for formal late summer bedding schemes and can also be grown as edging to beds and borders.

Having the same general growth habit as their green or purple-leaved edible counterparts, the ornamental types are valued for their handsome leaves and striking colours. They are round-headed cabbages with crinkly green or grey-green leaves variegated with red, pink or white.

Ornamental cabbage seeds are available as seed mixtures and grow up to 45cm (1½ft) across. They should be treated as half-hardy annuals, sown under glass and planted out in early summer. They are decorative throughout summer, but the leaves acquire the strongest colours when the night temperature falls below 10°C (50°F). The cabbages are edible, their flavour best after exposure to low temperatures.

Decorative gourds

Ornamental gourds are related to melons, marrows and cucumbers. They produce large golden flowers and hard-skinned, colourful fruits which are suitable for drying and using for indoor winter decoration. They are not edible.

The most popular and easy-to-grow ornamental gourds belong to the species *Cucurbita pepo ovifera*. Mature fruits usually reach about 10cm (4in) in dia-

meter. Fruit colour is green at first, but at maturity well-defined patterns develop on the skin in zones of orange, yellow, cream and shades of green. Some fruits are round, others pear-shaped or elongated; and the surface may be covered in swollen warts.

Sow seeds in spring under glass at a temperature of about 21°C (70°F). Germination is more reliable if the seeds are soaked in tepid water for a couple of days before sowing.

Plant out young gourds in early summer. Provide support on which the 3m (10ft) high stems can climb with their tendrils. They need rich soil and a sunny and sheltered site. If the flowers develop when bees are not active, hand-pollinate.

Harvest the fruits when they are fully ripe and rock-hard. Wait until the fruit stalks turn buff-brown and start to shrivel. Leave the fruits to dry thoroughly, then coat them with clear varnish.

▼ **Swiss ruby chard** Decorative enough to be included in herbaceous borders, the bright red stalks and purple-green foliage of Swiss ruby chard grow up to 60cm (2ft) high. This edible vegetable also makes colourful focal points in summer bedding schemes.

WILDFLOWER GARDENS

Overlooked for years, wild flowers are once again becoming popular – and proving they can blend effectively with their cultivated counterparts.

Many native trees, shrubs and wild flowers have disappeared from hedgerows and farmlands due to intensive farming and indiscriminate use of chemicals. Conservationists, concerned with the loss of much of our native flora, are encouraging gardeners to introduce those plants facing extinction to cultivated settings.

Many of our native plants are protected; they should never be dug up nor picked in flower, which prevents the dispersal of seed.

Most nurserymen now offer seeds of wild flowers, either singly or as selections. Many wild flowers are of outstanding beauty, in flower or fruit, and attract a wide variety of birds and butterflies.

Styles of wild gardens

Wildflower gardening is adaptable to every plot, whatever its size and situation. An entire garden can be devoted to it, or a wildflower feature can be established within the garden scheme. Mini-habitats on a

particular theme are fairly easy to create – a meadow, natural pond or a woodland glade, for example.

A pond garden

On an open sunny site, a 'natural'

▼ **Wildflower beds** Borders and beds of corncockles, red valerian, meadow's crane's bill, poppies and sweet William attract butterflies and other beneficial insects such as hoverflies and ladybirds. Teasels provide a feast of seed heads for goldfinches during autumn.

pond can be constructed using a butyl rubber lining. Its edges can be concealed with paving, but a more natural effect is created if the liner is extended and covered with soil to form a wetland area. This could be planted with boggy plants, such as marsh marigolds, bogbeans, water violets and flowering rushes.

The sides of the pond should slope gently so that animals – hedgehogs, for example – have easy access to it. In the shallow water at the margins, plant colourful associations of yellow flag (*Iris pseudacorus*), bright pink ragged robin (*Lychnis flos-cuculi*), white lesser stitchwort (*Stellaria graminea*) and yellow lesser spearwort (*Ranunculus flammula*).

Some wild flowers should be planted with caution. For instance, the greater spearwort (*Ranunculus lingua*) spreads through creeping underground stems and is too invasive for a small pond. True water lilies (*Nymphaea*), fringed water lily (*Nymphoides peltata*) or frogbit (*Hydrocharis*) can float on the surface, above a submerged oxygenator like water starwort (*Callitriche*).

A flower meadow

Ordinary lawn seed is too fine for a meadow effect, but mixtures of rough grass seeds combined with wild flowers are available from seedsmen. Weedkillers and fertilizers should never be used on them. To create the effect of a really 'natural' meadow, cut the grass by hand or electrically operated scythe in early spring and again in late summer when the flowers have faded and scattered their seed.

One or two closer-mown paths can give access to other parts of the garden. Good meadow flowers include the common ox-eye daisy (*Leucanthemum vulgare*, syn. *Chrysanthemum leucanthemum*), yellow rattle (*Rhinanthus minor*), common cat's ear (*Hypochaeris radicata*) and field scabious (*Knautia arvensis*). In spring, there would be cowslips (*Primula veris*), fritillaries (*Fritillaria meleagris*) and naturalized narcissi and violets.

A woodland glade

Where space permits, a small coppice or woodland can be established, ideally a mixture of deciduous and coniferous trees. Golden yews, and trees with fine autumn colours, such as alders, birches, maples and *Sorbus* species, are particularly suitable.

Cherry laurels, hydrangeas, cotoneasters, honeysuckles, mahonias and snowberry bushes are good choices for alkaline soil. Paths of grass or shredded bark can wind through the woodland.

Grassy glades are common features on the edge of woodland. They can be planted with bulbs – snowdrops, bluebells, wild garlic (*Allium ursinum*), summer-flowering *Lilium martagon*, which naturalizes readily – and herbaceous perennials such as violets and primroses, wood anemones, Solomon's seal (*Polygonatum*), trilliums and hellebores.

Design details

The framework of a wholly natural wildflower garden rests with the trees and shrubs which enclose and shelter it. There is a whole range of native British species – such as rowan (*Sorbus aucuparia*), wild crab apple (*Malus sylvestris*), guelder rose (*Viburnum opulus*) and dog rose (*Rosa canina*).

◀ **Suburban wild garden**
Close to a busy motorway, a suburban garden has been transformed into a small natural paradise. Its focal point is a pond surrounded by a wetland meadow of rough grass and native wild flowers.

▶ **Flower meadows** Wild-grass seed mixtures often include seeds of ox-eye daisy and yellow rattle. The grass needs infrequent cutting, apart from any roughly mown paths for access.

▼ **Summer symphony**
Flourishing throughout summer and into autumn by waysides and on wasteland, common mallow (*Malva sylvestris*) raises its spikes of purple-pink flowers above sprawling clumps of white-clustered yarrow (*Achillea millefolium*). The dainty blue bells of campanulas are frequently seen in their company.

The plants in a garden of wild flowers should be compatible with those growing naturally in the area. If there are any naturally wild areas close by, one of the best ways of choosing plants is to see what is present there at different seasons of the year.

The garden itself may suggest a particular theme – a dry sunny garden may be perfect for a grass-land garden dancing with meadow flowers in high summer. Once established, such a garden has the bonus of being very labour-saving, with only mowing being necessary on a regular basis.

Wild flowers which are quick and easy to raise from seed include many colourful 'weeds' which are now rare. Poppies (*Papaver rhoeas*), cornflowers (*Centaurea cyanus*), corn marigolds (*Chrysanthemum segetum*), flax (*Linum usitatissimum*) and night-flowering catchfly (*Silene noctiflora*) are just a few of the plants which will make a vivid display in one season. At the end of the season, collect the seed and dig over the site. Most cornfield weeds are short-lived annuals, which must be sown each year.

► **Woodland garden** In early spring before the tree canopy thickens, a sunny glade sports a host of wild daffodils and narcissi among the feathery foliage of wild garlic. Later, bluebells will spread a carpet over the faded trumpets.

▼► **Flowers of the field** Silky-petalled scarlet poppies are once again a familiar sight in the fields of East Anglia and southern England. Often found in the company of wild scabious and feverfew, poppies have large round seed pods that scatter seeds far and wide.

▼ **Spring bulbs** Double-flowered narcissi and tall-stemmed, blowsy tulips mingle happily with a mini-jungle of wild flowers, including yarrows and forget-me-nots. Left to self-seed and multiply, wild flowers need little human intervention.

UNTAMED WILDERNESS

**Wild flowers and old-fashioned
cottage-garden plants, many of them sweetly fragrant,
display their greatest charm in a natural setting.**

The making of a garden is largely a matter of man attempting to tame nature by altering, shaping, tidying and trimming it to a particular style. Most gardeners work to some kind of pattern that incorporates beds and borders, lawns, paths and utility areas, around which plants are fitted and their subsequent growth disciplined and restricted within a particular space.

Whatever the style and size of a garden, human intervention is necessary in order to maintain some kind of order – shrubs must be pruned, roses dead-headed, climbers trained, weeds eliminated and grass mown. Left to its own devices, a garden will quickly lose the manicured neatness that many gardeners strive to establish. At the same time it can also lose much of its grace and become a rather sanitized version of what we perceive nature to be.

Just occasionally a garden is allowed to express itself with the minimum of human intervention. The result can be a delightful profusion of traditional perennials, old-fashioned blowsy roses, sweet scented herbs and self-sown seedlings.

Wild gardens

A near-natural garden fits especially well into a rural landscape with views over rolling fields and backdrops of woodland or hills. Boundary walls or rustic fences can provide shelter and at the same time prevent nature from encroaching too much on the garden proper.

Plants can be allowed to ramble seemingly at will to create an informal cottage-garden wilderness or you can establish a wild-garden area in a small part of a traditional garden, separated by gravel or grass paths or contained within 'rooms' enclosed by clipped evergreen hedges.

Conservation is a popular topic, and a small wild garden is a perfect way of preserving our native flora as well as those old-fashioned plants that are facing extinction in the competition with modern-day hybrid types. There is also the added bonus of providing new habitats for our endangered wildlife.

Seasonal in its appeal, a wild garden is at its most beautiful in late spring and early summer.

▼ **Cottage wilderness** A floral meadow of old-fashioned perennials spills unhindered over paths and low walls. Bright lady's mantle and tall-stemmed creamy phlomis drop their seeds to extend their territory.

Drifts of naturalized bulbs, such as snowdrops, crocuses, daffodils, anemones and bluebells, give way to wild primroses and violets before roses and summer plants burst into bloom.

Such a garden can remain attractive through the summer and the early autumn, with masses of saffron crocuses and the occasional rose still in flower in late autumn.

As in most natural landscapes, the end of autumn through winter to early spring must be accepted as being dormant. Apart from conifers, hollies and trailing ivies, little plant life will be evident, though winter-flowering jasmine, Christmas roses and Algerian iris could provide touches of colour.

Colour and form

A natural, semi-wild garden is rarely planned with particular colour schemes in mind, though the warm hues of old-fashioned roses will often dominate. Blue bellflowers, yellow daisy-like doronicums and the towering spires of great mulleins (*Verbascum thapsus*) are other natural candidates, together with brilliantly coloured foxgloves and scarlet poppies.

▲ **Rustic appeal** A wooden arch, dressed with clipped yew, spans a narrow path that is almost obscured by semi-wild flowers. Native lady's mantle (*Alchemilla mollis*) flops over the edges, and perennial sweet pea (*Lathyrus latifolius*), heavy with fragrant blooms, scrambles up any available support.

▶ **Plant companions** Natural associations rather than deliberate planning schemes often result in stunning effects. Here, the huge flower heads of angelica stand out against a backdrop of fresh green foliage. The soft blues of bellflowers and Jacob's ladder add touches of colour to a summer scene. A 3m (10ft) tall biennial, angelica dies after flowering but leaves a host of self-sown seedlings to take its place.

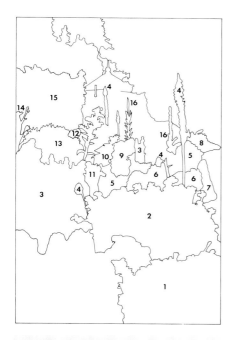

WILD PROFUSION

A wilderness corner can be established in most gardens, perhaps by an old-fashioned rustic gazebo that fits into the lush surroundings. The plan above helps identify some of the main plant groups shown on the right, where a glorious array of shrubs, roses, aromatic herbs and perennials grow in close and contented company.

1 Gallica rose (*Rosa* 'Charles de Mills')
2 Masterwort (*Astrantia major*)
3 Jacob's ladder (*Polemonium foliosissimum*)
4 Foxglove (*Digitalis purpurea*)
5 Chives (*Allium schoenoprasum*)
6 Golden marjoram (*Origanum vulgare* 'Aureum')
7 Edging box (*Buxus sempervirens* 'Suffruticosa')
8 Catmint (*Nepeta* x *faassenii*)
9 St John's wort (*Hypericum* 'Hidcote')
10 Variegated Russian comfrey (*Symphytum* x *uplandicum* 'Variegatum')
11 Gallica rose (*Rosa* 'Officinalis')
12 Purple-leaved sage (*Salvia officinalis* 'Purpurascens')
13 Pink comfrey (*Symphytum officinale*)
14 Fennel (*Foeniculum vulgare*)
15 Ivy (*Hedera helix*)
16 Mulleins (*Verbascum* species)

Coloured foliage, such as purple-leaved sages, golden marjoram and variegated mint and comfrey, can appear occasionally, but most foliage colour is in shades of green. There should be no deliberate juxtaposition of contrasting leaf shapes, as in a sophisticated foliage garden. Self-seeding of annuals, biennials and perennials should be encouraged, as the haphazard charm of a semi-wild garden gives even obviously planted perennials and shrubs a feeling of random wilderness.

Surprisingly little maintenance is needed. Self-seeded plants find optimum conditions naturally, and their lush growth keeps down the weeds. Areas of rough meadow grass need less frequent mowing than manicured lawns, and old garden roses need only occasional trimming to maintain their shape. Nor do they require dead-heading; their hips are an additional decorative feature from late summer onwards.

Most maintenance work – lifting, dividing, pruning and perhaps removing unwanted plants – can be done in winter, with the garden left undisturbed through the growing season.

Cottage-garden flowers

Traditional perennials for semi-wild gardens include lady's mantle with its soft sprays of tiny lime-green flowers, dainty columbines, catmint, campanulas with their lovely nodding flowers, yellow loosestrife, knotweed, polemonium (Jacob's ladder), the cheerful yellow ox-eye chamomile and dense clumps of astrantia and

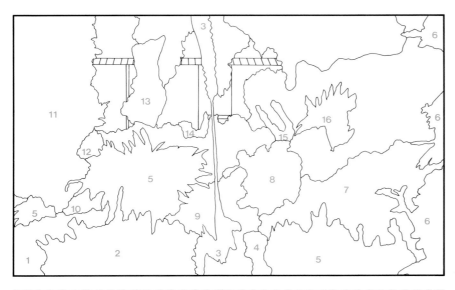

AN INFORMAL PLANTING SCHEME

The plan identifies the main plants in a typical wild garden (right).

1 Lungwort (*Pulmonaria officinalis*)
2 Catmint (*Nepeta x faassenii*)
3 Foxtail lily (*Eremurus elwesii* 'Albus')
4 Bellflower (*Campanula glomerata*)
5 Day lily (*Hemerocallis*)
6 Plume poppy (*Macleaya cordata*)
7 *Spiraea japonica* 'Anthony Waterer'
8 Floribunda rose
9 Rhododendron
10 Yellow archangel (*Lamium galeobdolon* 'Variegatum')
11 Flowering cherry (*Prunus serrulata*)
12 Lamb's tongue (*Stachys lanata*)
13 Climbing rose ('Wedding Day')
14 Peach-leaved bellflower (*Campanula persicifolia*)
15 Foxglove (*Digitalis purpurea*)
16 Yucca

purple martagon lilies. Self-seeding biennials include primulas, honesty, forget-me-not, foxgloves and mulleins.

Low-growing plants, such as thrift, bergenia and lungwort, are also suitable. In mixed and herbaceous borders they would be grouped towards the front, but in a semi-wild setting they look more natural jostling beneath the occasional taller-growing plants.

Day lilies (*Hemerocallis*), hostas, columbines, lamb's tongue, spotted dead nettle, heuchera, lychnis, bright blowsy peonies, plume poppies and the not quite hardy foxtail lily (*Eremurus elwesii* 'Albus') are other good choices for mass planting.

Herbs of all kinds belong in open sunny spots, their scents mixing with those of flowering plants and attracting butterflies and bees. Different kinds of thymes, mints, marjorams, sages and wild umbellifers, such as cow parsley, herb Robert, feverfew and tansy, should be included for their dainty flower heads. Evergreen types – rosemary and lavender – are especially fragrant in the warm and sunny micro-climates created by dense planting.

In shady but dry positions, the yellow spurges, and especially *Euphorbia characias* and the evergreen *E. robbiae*, quickly form large clumps. *Iris foetidissima*, too, thrives in dry shade, and while insignificant in flower it is outstanding in autumn when the large seed pods split open to reveal vivid orange seeds.

Trees and shrubs

Native trees – broadleafs and conifers – heighten the illusion of a natural landscape. Hazel, birch, apple and pear trees, variegated and green hedge hollies, mulberry and willows can be planted among perennials or along the garden boundaries. Bird cherries (*Prunus padus* and *P. avium*) and crab apples are delightful with their spring flowers, and lilacs and mock orange could also be included for their scent. Walls can be clothed with climbing roses, golden hop, clematis and honeysuckles.

Old roses such as Moss, Centifolia, Rugosa, Alba, Gallica, China, Damask and Bourbon are the types to grow among perennials and other shrubs. Many of the modern shrub roses, and especially the so-called New English Roses, look particularly at home in informal surroundings rather than formal rose beds.

Spiraeas and brooms, buddleias and dogwoods, hawthorns and rowans, formerly so common in hedgerows, thrive in wild gardens, and many are outstanding in autumn with blazing leaf colours and clusters of bright berries.

On acid soils, small glades of rhododendrons and azaleas can be established. Ling and heathers, too, thrive in similar conditions

and spread to form evergreen carpets that become sheets of colour for many months of the year.

Pools and ponds

Natural ponds provide a home for water plants and attract wildlife, especially birds. Man-made pools are easy to install and will soon lose their artificial appearance.

Permanently moist ground around the margins is ideal for bog plants and other moisture-lovers. Thickets of tussock grass, rushes and flag iris are natural occupants of damp sites and provide nesting sites for birds; they often attract migrants in winter.

Native ferns, candelabra prim-

ulas and single-flowered marsh marigolds (*Caltha palustris*) are other fine waterside plants. The dramatic purple-leaved *Ligularia dentata*, with branching spikes of yellow daisy-like flowers in summer, or the striking *Gunnera manicata*, with its curious cone-shaped inflorescences, look perfectly natural by large ponds and lakes. Water lilies and nuphars can float their green leaf pads and cup-shaped flowers on the water surface.

Some gardens are blessed with natural streams whose banks are natural habitats for a range of bog plants. Astilbes, rodgersias and the golden skunk cabbage

will thrive here, along with water avens, creeping Jennies and mimulus.

Features and focal points

Garden statues and ornaments look out of place in wild gardens, but rustic structures such as wooden pergolas, woven wattle hurdles, a dovecote and the odd wooden seat in a quiet corner, with roses and honeysuckles tumbling around it, can be decorative in their own right.

An old-fashioned wooden summerhouse, a brick-paved sitting area or a small cobbled courtyard square all complement a natural garden scene.

29

Perennial favourites Bluebells and azaleas belong to both humble cottage gardens and stately borders.

WILDLIFE IN THE GARDEN

The presence of wildlife adds an extra dimension to a garden, enlivening it with activity and charm all year round.

Creating habitats in a garden for attractive, interesting or beneficial wildlife is an increasingly popular hobby, as people become aware of their local environment and its ecology.

For all creatures the basic approach is the same: to provide food, water and a setting in which they feel safe. You can settle for attracting butterflies and bees, birds, amphibians or small mammals, or a range of these creatures to the garden.

A garden devoted to wildlife can be unstructured and have only wild plants, including 'weeds', such as nettles, thistles and brambles, but an orderly garden filled with cultivated species and varieties can still attract a certain amount of wildlife. A good compromise is to devote a corner or area of the garden to wildlife by growing ornamental plants that provide berries, fruits or flowers that are known to be favoured by insects and birds.

A hedgerow-type boundary hedge, a herb garden and an ornamental pool are pleasing in their own right and provide a home for a surprisingly wide range of wildlife. Even a compost heap is a rich source of worms, larvae and adult insects, which in turn attract other, larger and more interesting creatures.

Butterflies and bees

Butterflies occasionally appear on warm winter afternoons but are most conspicuous in spring, summer and early autumn, when their colour and graceful flight enliven the scene. The small white is a common urban butterfly, while suburban and country gardens can be visited by many species. Most moths are nocturnal, but there are attractive day-flying ones as well.

All mature butterflies and moths feed on nectar, and are attracted by flower colour and scent. For spring, effective plants

◄ **Tortoiseshell butterflies** These small orange butterflies with conspicuous brown, black, yellow and blue markings are common in early summer. They favour flowering buddleia shrubs.

▼ **Honey bees** The industrious bees are active from early summer through to autumn, feeding on flower nectar.

31

are yellow alyssum, aubrietia, wallflower, honesty and sweet rocket. In summer, there is catmint, lavender, thyme, valerian and sea holly. And, for autumn, grow sedums and Michaelmas daisies. Some seed merchants sell special mixes to attract a wide range of butterflies.

Buddleia, or butterfly bush, is the best all-round plant for nectar-seeking insects. You can also attract butterflies by feeding them honey, dissolved with a little sugar and a pinch of salt in water. Pour the mixture into a shallow dish and place it in the garden.

To encourage butterflies and moths to lay eggs in the garden, grow plants which serve as food

▶ **Bird feeder** A rigid wire cage is a good choice of feeder as it can easily be hung outside the reach of cats. As well as the voracious starlings, a feeder will also attract many interesting birds that fill the garden with their varied plumage, song and flight patterns.

▼ **Christmas decorations** Birds gather around a spruce (*Picea*) festooned with apples and coconut. Birds need extra food in winter and when this is supplied, they become regular visitors to the garden.

for emerging caterpillars. Nettles and brambles are ideal for many species, as are members of the crucifer family, such as honesty, sweet rocket and cuckoo-flower. Other effective plants include dock, sorrel, knotweed, holly, ivy, dogwood, buckthorn and vetch.

The nectar and pollen of many garden flowers attract bees. As well as the social bumble bees and honey bees, there are various solitary bees. The wider the range of flowers in the garden, the more bee species it will attract.

Good plants for attracting bees are members of the daisy and labiate families – comfrey, lungwort, campanulas, ragged robin, rose campion and especially borage. And lime is the traditional bee tree. In winter, snowdrops and crocuses provide nectar for the occasional bees, while in summer, poppies and roses are popular.

Birds

With their richly varied song, plumage, flight patterns and nesting habits, birds are both interesting and appealing. They also bring some practical benefits by feeding on harmful insects, larvae and snails, though they also damage flowers, buds and fruit. Urban gardens have thrushes, blackbirds, black-headed gulls, starlings and sparrows, as well as less welcome destructive birds such as pigeons and jays. Suburban and country gardens also attract bullfinches, robins, collared doves, wrens, swifts, tits, warblers, house martins, owls, nuthatches, woodpeckers, wagtails and rarer migrants.

Trees, shrubs and hedges give birds vantage points, song posts and nesting sites. Oak, fruit trees and bushes, rowan, holly, thorn, sloe, privet, buckthorn, field maple, hazel, spindle, rose, guelder rose, cotoneaster and pyracantha are all sources of fruit, berries and insects. Flower and seed heads, such as thistle, sunflower, aster and ornamental grasses, entice grain eaters.

Extra winter food, such as commercial bird-seed, oat flakes or apples, attracts birds. Once you start feeding birds, you must continue as they grow dependent.

When breeding starts, reduce, then stop, the food supply.

Ground feeding can be hazardous, but some species, such as dunnock, will not feed from a table. To make a bird feeder safe from cats, rodents and squirrels, the table should be raised on a smooth post, 1.5m (5ft) or more high, with a conical baffle under the top to keep the food dry. Narrow gaps in the table let rainwater drain through; and a raised edge prevents food from falling off.

An assortment of objects can be hung from trees to attract birds – a table-like platform, peanut-filled net bags or wire cages, coconut shells or logs drilled and filled with fat, cereals and dried fruits are effective.

Bird-baths and ornamental pools provide drinking and bath water. Birds are especially attracted to moving water. Pools with sloping or shelved margins and well stocked with water plants are preferable to straight-sided, empty pools.

Some opportunist birds nest in suitably sited containers, such as

old tea kettles and chimney pots. Nesting birds are territorial and a small garden is unlikely to attract more than a pair or two, however many boxes are put up.

Position boxes before the breeding season starts. Place them where you can see the flight path from the windows, and at least 1.8m (6ft) above the ground, on a shady wall, fence or tree trunk well out of the reach of cats. The more concealed an open-fronted box, the safer it is.

In autumn, after the last fledglings leave, clean out and disinfect the boxes against fleas. A hinged roof makes cleaning easy.

Frogs, toads and newts
Pollution and changes in land use have destroyed many natural habitats for amphibians, and it is important to create new ones. Many people regard amphibians as intriguing rather than beautiful,

▼ **Lily pads** The tough surface-floating leaves of water lilies are favourite resting places for frogs. The creatures add character and rural charm.

though male newts assume brilliant colours during the mating season.

Children find amphibian life cycles fascinating, and they make a good introduction to natural history. The croaking of male frogs and toads adds rural, if not melodious, overtones to a garden and, on a practical level, amphibians eat slugs and other garden pests.

Ideal sites for amphibians include pools with still or slow-moving water, sloping banks, a muddy bottom and vegetation, especially water lilies. Frogs and toads prefer large pools, as they form groups to mate, while newts don't mind small pools. Goldfish eat spawn and tadpoles, but if there are enough hiding places, some will reach maturity. A pool without fish becomes over-run with midge and mosquito larvae.

Amphibians eventually find water on their own, but you can introduce spawn or tadpoles. Frogs spend a lot of time in the water, but come out to feed and

▲ **Pond life** Water, densely planted around the margins, with surrounding marsh and wetland invites many insects and birds to visit.

◄ **Urban and suburban foe** A bold fox comes to drink from a garden pool. Gently sloping sides make it easy for small animals to drink in safety.

hibernate. Toads spend most of their time out of water, except when they are breeding.

Newts also live in the water, but come out to hibernate. They need hibernation sites for the winter – log and leaf piles, and hollows under rockery stones, pool-side stones or paving slabs.

Mammals

The red fox forages by day and night but is most likely to appear at dusk. It eats chickens, small rodents and wild birds in the country, and steals from dustbins and tips in built-up areas. It needs scrub or tall vegetation in which to hide, and banks or tree roots for its underground den.

Hedgehogs live in hedgerows, gardens and woods, especially near damp grassland. They are most active just after dusk and eat insects, slugs, worms and berries, but are also partial to pet food. They hibernate from mid autumn until mid spring, and a heap of

▲ Hedgehogs Inhabiting woods and hedgerows, hedgehogs are largely nocturnal. They can be encouraged into the garden by planting berrying shrubs and setting out dishes of pet food. They are partial to slugs, but also harbour fleas, which can migrate to pets.

▼ Rustic bird table Open and covered feeding tables attract a varied and interesting range of wild birds. Unfortunately, starlings are the most common visitors, and it is almost impossible to discourage squirrels and cats lying in wait.

dead branches and leaves in a corner of the garden gives them an ideal nest site.

Squirrels are a delight to watch in the garden, but they become fierce during the breeding season and they are agile at removing birds' eggs from nests and food from bird feeders. Sadly, the grey squirrel has now all but eliminated the red squirrel.

Watchpoints

☐ It is difficult to attract wildlife selectively – for example, by putting out food for hedgehogs you may also attract vermin.

☐ Bullfinches strip flower buds from fruit trees.

☐ Squirrels dig up and eat bulbs, destroy orchard fruits, strip tree bark and eat saplings.

☐ The caterpillars of large and small white butterflies can decimate brassica crops in the vegetable garden.

PETS IN THE GARDEN

Most family pets use the garden as a place to exercise, relax and relieve themselves, and some live in it for at least part of the year. The safety, comfort and well-being of a pet must be considered in a garden, and at the same time ornamental plants and crops must be protected.

Dogs

A 1.5m (5ft) high wall or close-boarded fence will keep a dog in (and unwanted dogs out), and a dog flap can give access to and from the house. The largest dog flap is for a shoulder width of 32cm (12½in) – roughly that of an Alsatian or labrador.

Some dogs like privacy, and a kennel is ideal even if the dog does not actually sleep there. The kennel should be draught-proof, weather-proof and large enough for the dog to stand up, turn around and lie down easily.

A kennel with an overhanging pitched roof will shed rain so that the walls stay dry. Some have hinged roofs that can be opened for ventilation. The front of the kennel should be hinged to give access for cleaning.

To prevent rising damp a kennel should stand on a slightly raised, hard surface, such as paving slabs or concrete. The door should face away from prevailing wind and mid-day summer sun.

Limiting dog damage

Dogs can harm plants by treading or lying on them, or burying bones in flower beds. Putting a dog in a run or on a chain and tak-

▲ **Dovecote** Positioned in a secluded, semi-wild corner, a dovecote makes a magnificent focal point. Attractive birds with delightful song, doves are a pleasure to look at and listen to. A dovecote should be sturdy and house the doves well above the reach of cats.

▶ **Bird-bath** A pedestal bird-bath encourages birds to visit the garden. Ideally, it should be large enough for smaller birds to bathe their plumage as well as provide drinking water. Keep the bath clean and the water fresh.

ing it for regular walks should prevent this happening. Raised beds will also help to keep plants safe. Temporary fencing or netting can be used, but looks unattractive.

Female dog urine turns lawns and foliage, such as low conifer branches, brown. Pepper-based sprays and dusts that repel but don't harm dogs are available, but have only a limited time-span. As a last resort grow bare-stemmed, standard trees. For dog faeces you can buy long-handled 'pooperscoopers' or chemical dog toilets.

Cats

Cats are more agile and less domesticated than dogs, and keeping them in or out of the garden is difficult. A single, taut wire stretched 5cm (2in) above a wall prevents cats balancing and deters them from going to and fro.

As cats need freedom and independence more than specific exercise, cat flaps, ideally with built-in draught-excluders, are essential. There are also electronic or magnetic cat flaps which prevent unwanted cats from entering. They open on a signal from a disc fixed to the cat's collar.

Cats are naturally clean, digging shallow holes in the soil and burying their faeces afterwards. However, they have a preference for newly cultivated areas, such as seed beds and young lawns, and are liable to scratch up plants.

Insert holly or rose prunings vertically in the soil to deter cats. They prefer dry soil, and regular watering may discourage them. Chemical deterrents are also available.

Rabbits and guinea pigs

If the garden is secure, rabbits, guinea pigs or cavies can have the run of it, provided they are safe from predators. A separate compound will ensure that dogs and cats – and even foxes – are kept out, and logs, drainpipes, hay and stones can provide hiding places and amusement.

Both rabbits and guinea pigs need a sturdy hutch. The largest part of the hutch, for the animals' daytime use and feeding, should have a mesh-netting front. The smaller part of the hutch, used for privacy and sleep, should be solid and draught-free.

Place the hutch in a sheltered position and raise it off the

▲ **Pool inhabitants** Goldfish are hardy, tough and colourful and add interest to an ornamental pool. Water lily pads give necessary shade during the summer months, and submerged aquatics provide essential oxygen.

ground to prevent damp, with a ramp leading to the ground.

In well-insulated hutches in mild districts, guinea pigs can stay outside all year round. In cold areas they should be kept indoors during the winter. Rabbits can live outside all year round if the hutch is moved to a sheltered spot and given extra insulation in cold spells. Both animals suffer from heat exhaustion; in hot weather place the hutch in a shady spot and provide extra ventilation.

Rabbits and guinea pigs enjoy a portable grazing cage, usually triangular in section and made of wire-mesh netting and wood. The cage should be partly solid for shelter against wind and rain. Move the cage from place to place as the grass is cropped short.

Tortoises

Tortoises prefer to roam freely in the garden, but as they eat lettuce, strawberries, flowers and tender young plants they are better in a pen. For one tortoise a suitable pen should be 1.8m (6ft) square, preferably on rough ground with shrubs and stones.

Provide tortoises with shelter as they dislike extremes of temperature and hate getting wet. A raised, waterproof wooden shelter, about 15 x 30 x 45cm (6 x 12 x 18in), with a sloping overhanging roof and an entrance at least 10cm (4in) square is ideal.

Tortoises hibernate from mid autumn until mid spring. Put them in a well-ventilated box with straw or shredded paper, and over-winter them in a cool, frost-free shed or garage.

Keeping fish

An ornamental fish pond is decorative and soothing, and there is a wide variety of fish to choose from. As a rough guide, a garden pool can take 15cm (6in) of fish for every 30cm (1ft) square of surface area. Alternatively, allow 2.5cm (1in) of fish per 4.5 litres (1 gallon) of water. If you buy young fish, allow for their final size.

The colourful goldfish are popular and include several types, such as multi-coloured shubunkins and comets, and tender fan-

► **Dog-proof** Raised beds can help to keep plants safe from dogs. The higher they are the better. Dogs often damage plants in ground-level flower beds by lying on them or burying bones.

tails, moors and lionheads, which need to be overwintered indoors in a heated aquarium.

Other hardy fish include koi carp, which are costly, beautifully coloured relatives of goldfish. Golden orfe and golden rudd are other attractive possibilities.

Sticklebacks, pike, perch and catfish are fierce carnivores, and unsuitable for pools. Never introduce wild fish as they can carry parasites or disease.

Water lily leaves provide excellent shelter for fish in summer. In winter, a pool heater can prevent some or all of the surface water from icing over.

Feed fish daily, from late spring to early autumn, giving them only as much as they can finish in five minutes.

Chemical safety

Chemical herbicides, pesticides and slug pellets can be fatal to animals, and chemical spray drift can kill fish. Always keep chemicals away from pets. If you suspect poisoning, take the pet and the chemical container to a vet.

Some cultivated plants and weeds, such as buttercup, lily-of-the-valley, foxglove and aconite, are poisonous. Where guinea pigs, rabbits or tortoises roam freely, the garden must be kept free of such plants.

◄ **Butterfly plants** A number of garden plants are particularly attractive to butterflies. They include buddleia, honeysuckle, lavender, golden rod, pinks, thyme, Michaelmas daisies and, as here, ice plants (*Sedum spectabile*).

Features and focal points

Used with imagination many functional garden features can also be highly decorative. Climbing plants need supports for their stems, and self-contained sitting areas and garden compartments look better if they are semi-enclosed. Attractive trellis panels, handsome pergolas and romantic arbours combine the practical with the ornamental. They can be built from plastic or timber, metal or brick, decorated with twiners and hanging baskets or stand as attractive ornaments in their own right. They should ideally complement the style of house and garden, add to the visual enjoyment and be in scale both with the garden and with the plant material in it. Wall shrubs and fruit trees become charming, space-saving features when trained over metal or timber frames, tripods and arches.

Large gardens can incorporate architectural effects; in smaller plots an artistic eye for detail can achieve similar results, with a well-placed focal point at the termination of a path or border. An inviting garden seat, an ornamental urn, a whimsical wall plaque or a handsome specimen plant can lift a garden from the mundane to the memorable. Awkward corners can become secret, sheltered settings for temperamental pot plants, miniature pools, corner fountains, dovecotes or decorative bird-baths.

A summerhouse may be the crowning touch for outdoor summer living. Again, it should harmonize with the surroundings; grand classical buildings, with pediments and pillars, belong to stately gardens, Chinese pagodas fit into Oriental styles, while timber and rustic buildings suit almost any type of garden.

Quiet retreat Trellis and an overhead pergola enclose a peaceful corner bright with summer bedding.

TRELLIS AND TREILLAGE

**Trelliswork can be imaginative as well as functional,
adding humour or grandeur to a garden, as well as a means
of supporting plants, or providing screening.**

Trellising is not new to the garden scene – the Victorians, for example, made much use of trelliswork – but it has never been more popular than it is today.

Trellising is a quick and relatively inexpensive way of dividing a garden into separate areas. It can also introduce instant height, provide privacy, support plants and bring a note of individuality.

Trellis is latticework, traditionally of light wooden battens, for screening or for supporting climbing plants. It usually has a square or diamond-shaped pattern with little or no additional decoration, and is often modest in its intent.

Treillage is French for trellis and the term is used to describe trellis that takes a highly ornate – even architectural – form, sometimes incorporating columns, pillars and pediments. It may also play visual jokes with perspective. As a rule, treillage calls attention to itself, while trellis is more unobtrusive.

Both trellis and treillage can be purely ornamental, especially if painted white, providing crisp contrast to foliage or walls, or they may be ornamental as well as functional, supporting climbing plants. Trellis painted dark green or black, or hidden by climbers, loses its ornamental value and becomes purely functional.

The smaller a garden, the more valuable are fixtures and plants that need minimal ground space to produce a good show. Trellis and treillage can be used to provide a large vertical area without encroaching on ground space.

Not only does trelliswork have two-dimensional impact as crisp, linear decoration, it can also be used three-dimensionally to form free-standing structures, such as arbours and semi-enclosures. It may play a small role or, used on a large scale, impose its character on the whole garden.

Materials

Trelliswork is traditionally made of wood, but can also be made of plastic or metal. It can be bought in panels or purpose-made to suit individual requirements.

A long-lasting, maintenance-free material is better for permanent climbers, such as honeysuckle, than one which needs painting or is short-lived and rots.

◄ **Traditional latticework** The stairway to a basement garden has been transformed into an elegant feature. Solid-wood, square-patterned trellis is mounted on the end wall and provides both privacy and support for climbing plants, without shutting out the light. Green-painted trellis complements the warm colours of the quarry-tiled stairway, enclosed on the other side by low trellis panels secured to sturdy wooden posts.

▲ **Decorative pergola** A stunning focal point, this architectural pergola is constructed from natural hardwood and fiery red trellis and treillage panels, complete with rounded finials. Sun streaming through the pergola forms patterns of light and shadows across the path below.

Most materials are more liable to rot if they are placed in the soil than if they are raised on posts or wall hung.

Hardwoods, such as iroko (which is more durable than oak), teak and luan, are expensive but long-lasting and, used in their natural state, maintenance-free. They can be stained or painted, but then need maintenance.

Softwoods, such as pine or larch, are less expensive but should be painted or pressure-treated with a preservative. Even so, they are short-lived and few softwood trellises last much longer than five years.

Wrought iron, painted black or white, is beautiful but very expensive, heavy to erect and suitable only for free-standing panels of an ornate design. It is very long-lasting and needs occasional painting.

Mild steel, painted or plastic-coated, and manufactured to simulate wrought iron, is much cheaper and lighter in weight. However, it needs regular maintenance and is prone to rust.

Plastic-coated wire and PVC trellis are inexpensive and come in black, white, green or brown. They are lightweight and maintenance-free but become brittle with age and exposure to sun. Once the plastic coating is damaged, the wire core becomes rusty. The life expectancy of these materials is similar to that of softwood.

▼ **Trellis partition** Crisp white treillage panels in open and close-weave diamond patterns are used to separate one part of a garden from another. The gateway leading to the lush greenery of a semi-wild garden beyond is crowned with an arch over which climbing roses sprawl in profusion.

▶ **Trellis as ornament** A deep window recess becomes a dramatic setting for a terracotta container of scarlet-flowered zonal pelargoniums. The small-scale, square-meshed trellis has been cut to shape and is secured to the wall with hinges that allow for easy repainting when necessary.

Types of trellis

Trellis panels come in two different patterns: the expanding lattice type, and the rigid square type. Both kinds can be made from plastic or wood.

Plastic trellis – in white, green or woodgrain – is fairly long-lasting and requires no maintenance, but it is not as strong as some timber trellis.

Timber trellis comes in a number of strengths ranging from the expanding lattice type to the heavy-duty square-slatted kind. The wood can have a natural finish, or it may be painted. Before you buy, make sure it has been pressure-impregnated against attack from insects and rot.

Plastic and wood trellis can be mounted both against and along the top of a wall. Heavy-duty, timber, square-slatted trellis provides a sturdier structure along the top of a wall (although it is also fine for mounting against a wall). The expandable lattice type is better suited to mounting flat against a wall.

Trellis panels in both timber and plastic are available in several sizes, ranging from 30cm to 1.8m (1-6ft) deep. The length of each panel is usually 1.8m (6ft).

Styles and uses

Trellis latticework can be lacy and delicate, or strong and sturdy. Free-standing panels usually need to be more substantial than wall-hung panels of trellis. Panels supporting the heavy weight of a large climber or wall-trained plant, such as an evergreen magnolia, also need to be sturdy.

Wall-hung plant supports vary from black-painted wire mesh to ornate treillage.

Tightly woven trelliswork can conceal uneven brick or rendered walls, and the patterns and shadows cast by trellis can make a dull wall look interesting.

Free-standing trelliswork can create a sense of enclosure without the heavy shade that a similar-sized solid wall often produces. The dappled light through the latticework also suits many plants which scorch in full sun.

Ornamental trellis

Trellis can be used as an ornament in its own right and does not have to be limited to its functional use

▲ **Wall decorations** Thin-slatted, diamond-shaped trellis attached to a wall creates an attractive linear decoration while reducing the glare from the white rendering. It also provides footholds for the self-clinging Persian ivy (*Hedera colchica* 'Variegata') and convenient spots for tying in the stems of climbing roses.

▼ **Patio enclosure** Rustic fencing in a dramatic diagonal pattern makes an eye-catching trellis for a patio. It creates a sense of enclosure while allowing light to filter through to a colourful collection of container plants.

◄ **Sky blue arbours** A pair of garden seats beneath pitched roofs and with airy side panels of trellis evokes a scene from the Tudor age. The cool blue and white colour scheme is emphasized by elegant, glazed pottery containers.
The floral decoration is all-white: hanging baskets of sweet alyssum and miniature roses on the seats on either side of a blue-painted wooden planter spilling over with marguerites.

▼ **Boundary fencing** A circular opening in a sturdy wooden trellis fence allows a view to the outside world. As well as playing a functional role by marking the boundary and supporting climbers, the fence also has architectural merit.

as support for weak-stemmed and climbing plants.

A trellis arch mounted around a doorway, for example, instantly transforms the entrance to a house, giving it a distinctive style. The arch can be painted to match or contrast with the door and for added effect plant containers with golden yew pyramids or clipped bay trees can adorn either side of the arch. Such arches are available as ready-made kits complete with instructions. They are generally too flimsy to support heavy climbing plants, but sweet peas, morning glory or golden hop would be ideal.

For a more formal look, narrow, square-meshed trellis can be mounted flat against a wall to break up a large expanse, and painted in a compatible colour. Floral decoration is not essential, but, depending on the house style, the odd pot or basket of annuals can be suspended from the trellis.

Even simple panels of heavy-duty, square trellis mounted along a low wall can have a decorative appeal. They can be used on front garden walls or internally in the garden to create areas of seclusion or provide backdrops for colourful planting schemes. Trellis with a natural wood finish is always a safe buy as it blends with most architectural styles and planting schemes.

Trelliswork can also create a sense of mystery, allowing tantalizing glimpses beyond but concealing imperfections.

Large panels to eye-level height or above can divide a garden into separate 'rooms'. Toughened or reinforced trelliswork can replace fences, providing privacy while allowing light to filter through.

Trelliswork panels can also be used to create three-dimensional, free-standing structures as focal points. They can form the back, sides and roof of an arbour, with or without a seat inside.

Trellis arches are also ideal for leading from one section of the garden to another, or for marking the entrance to the garden.

Trompe l'oeil treillage is used to create an illusion of depth where none exists – perhaps on the back wall of a small town garden. To be effective, trompe l'oeil treillage must be seen against a solid and reasonably simple backdrop, with or without plants. If you can see through the treillage to movement beyond, the visual trick doesn't work.

Free-standing treillage pillars

▲ **Custom-built trellis** Square white trellising, topped by traditional ball finials and guarded by a pair of ferocious stone panthers, marks the entrance to the sitting area in a long narrow basement garden. Custom-built, at a cost, the screen and cool planting schemes add light to a shady town garden, at the same time succeeding in altering the visual perspective of the narrow plot.

or obelisks can be used purely as architectural decorations, as supports for climbing plants, or for both purposes.

Adding plants

Trellis and treillage are usually combined with plants for seasonal interest, flower and foliage colour, additional privacy, dappled shade and fragrance.

Jasmine, honeysuckle or scented roses trained over a trellis arch next to a door, or covering a trelliswork arbour over a bench, are especially lovely.

The more ornate a panel is, the more restrained the planting should be, otherwise the beauty and detail are obscured. The effect of trompe l'oeil can also be ruined by too much foliage or by large-leaved foliage, such as Irish ivy (*Hedera helix* 'Hibernica').

For treillage, choose a slow-growing or moderately vigorous climber, such as passion flower, *Clematis macropetala* or *Eccremocarpus scaber*. Avoid anything too rampant that would quickly obscure decorative detail.

For trompe l'oeil, choose a delicate-looking, small-scale plant – perhaps the fern-leaved, evergreen *Clematis cirrhosa balearica* or the perennial flame creeper (*Tropaeolum speciosum*).

If a mass of plant cover over a trellis is required as quickly as possible, there is honeysuckle, *Clematis montana* and several ornamental vines. Wisteria, and especially Chinese wisteria (*Wisteria sinensis*), makes plenty of foliage quickly but does not flower until it is about seven years old.

Ivies are not especially quick, but they give year-round evergreen cover if the view beyond the trellis is unsightly.

Self-clinging climbers, such as ivy and climbing hydrangea, and tough, rigid-stemmed plants, for example pyracantha and ceanothus, are unsuitable if the trellis needs regular maintenance.

Rambling roses, which can be untied and laid on the ground during maintenance, are more suitable. Perennial climbers, such as hops, flame creeper and perennial sweet pea are even easier because they die down to ground level from autumn to spring so maintenance can take place unimpeded.

In paved gardens, large pots or tubs for plants can be placed at the base of wall-hung or free-standing trellis. Alternatively, if the containers are substantial, small supports can be inserted directly into the potting compost.

▼ **Functional trellis** A paved corner of a town garden gains additional height from sturdy timber trellis that extends above the boundary wall. It also provides support and extra space for climbing plants. The chief disadvantage of a fixed trellis is the time-consuming work involved in unscrambling the plants every few years when the wood needs re-staining.

MOUNTING TRELLIS

To estimate the amount of trellis needed for mounting against a wall as a plant support, ascertain the eventual spread and height of the plant before buying a suitable-sized trellis or number of panels. The bottom edge of the trellis should be at least 30cm (12in) above ground level to keep damp – and rot – at bay.

Trellis panels on the wall of a house should be sited away from windows, where strong trellis, which could be climbed by an intruder, could prove a security risk. They should also be kept well away from gutters and roofs – a rampant climber can block guttering or lift tiles.

The simplest method of erecting trellis is to nail it straight to a wall. In order to give plants room to grow around the trellis and allow air to circulate, it is better to fix the trellis, whether it is made of plastic or timber, to three or more timber battens. These should be fixed horizontally to give support at the top, middle and bottom of the trellis.

Trellis can be nailed to a timber fence, provided that you attach it to the posts rather than to the panelling.

Trellis above a wall

Mounting trellis on top of a wall involves slightly more work as

TRELLIS AGAINST A WALL

Tool list
tape measure
timber battens
rustproof nails
staples
drill with timber and
 masonry bit
wall plugs
rustproof screws
screwdriver
mounting plates
masonry nails
hammer

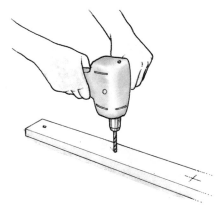

1 Drill fixing holes at 30cm (12in) intervals in three timber battens.

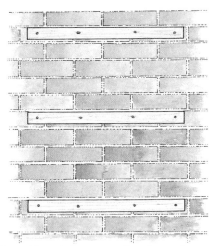

2 Hold each batten against the wall and mark the position of fixing holes. Drill fixing holes in the wall and insert wall plugs. Screw battens in place with rustproof screws.

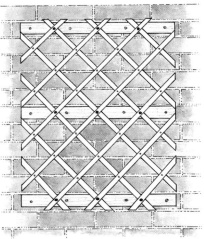

3 Nail trellis to batten framework. Fixing holes are already provided in plastic trellis; on timber trellis, drill holes at 60cm (24in) intervals around the edge. Secure with rustproof nails.

Trellis on a painted wall

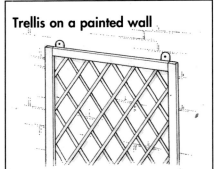

If you plan to mount lattice trellis against a wall which needs painting every few years, frame it with timber battens. Lay the extended trellis on the ground. Nail or staple slim preservative-treated battens around the edge to form a rectangular frame. Repeat on other side. Attach mounting plates to the top edge of the frame and hang it from masonry nails hammered into the wall.

◄ **Plastic lattice trellis** This may look less elegant than timber trellis, but it lasts longer and requires no maintenance. It is usually available in a white, green or woodgrain finish.

timber supports must be attached to the wall to hold the trellis panels firmly in position.

To calculate the amount of trellis that will be needed along the top of a wall, measure the length of the wall and divide this by the lengths of the panels (usually 1.8m/6ft). This should give you the number of trellis panels required.

You will also need 100 x 50mm (4 x 2in) thick wooden posts to support the trellis. Their height should take into account the size of the trellis, plus 15cm (6in) to overlap the wall, and an extra 5cm (2in) or so on top to allow for the post cap. Buy one more post than the total number of trellis sections required. The diagrams on the right show exactly how the trellis should be mounted.

Trellis above a fence

If you are mounting trellis along the top of a timber fence made up of standard-sized sections, buy as many trellis lengths as there are panels in the fence. If the fence includes any part panels – which it probably will – buy an extra length of trellis for cutting down to size.

Do not attempt to increase the

▲ **Wall-mounted trellis** When used as a plant support, leave a small gap between the trellis and the wall. This will allow air to circulate and give the plant room to grow around the trellis.

Tool list
timber posts 100 x 50mm
  (4 x 2in) thick
tape measure
timber saw
drill with timber and masonry bit
masonry bolts
hammer
wooden post caps
wall plugs
rustproof screws
rustproof nails
wood preservative

height of the existing fence by more than a third. If you do, you risk placing too much strain on the fence panels and timber supports, and as a result high winds may well cause the trellis to work loose.

Use the same method as for mounting trellis above a wall (see diagrams on the right), but make sure the supports are fixed to the existing fence posts. The fence panels are not strong enough to take the weight, and the wood from which they are made is likely to split.

WALL-MOUNTED TRELLIS

1 Cut the required number of lengths of 100 x 50mm (4 x 2in) timber to match the height of the trellis, allowing for a 15cm (6in) overlap at the bottom plus 5cm (2in) on top for the post caps. Cut supports – one more than there are panels.

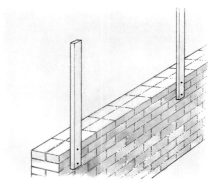

2 Drill one hole near the top and one near the bottom of each overlap section. Then, holding the supports up to the wall, mark at 1.8m (6ft) intervals the position of the corresponding fixing holes – in solid masonry, not mortar. Drill and plug holes. Fix supports to wall with rustproof screws or masonry bolts.

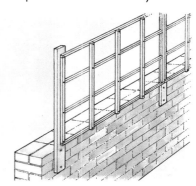

3 Secure each trellis panel to the supports with rustproof nails at 15cm (6in) intervals, hammering them in at an angle through the framework. Make sure it is nailed near the top and near the bottom of each support.

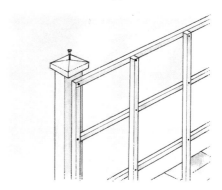

4 Nail a post cap to the top of each support. Then treat the timber supports and post caps with a wood preservative that is not harmful to plants. The preservative will have to be re-applied every few years to keep the wood in good condition.

◄ Old-world charm A terrace row of stone-built country cottages has retained the outward charm of a bygone age. Climbing roses scramble over walls and guttering, and identical trellis porches over the front doors are in perfect keeping with the rural scene. Lichen and golden-flowered houseleeks cluster on roof and porch tiles, and old-fashioned yellow corydalis spills over the footpath.

▼ Privacy screen Urban gardens are often short on privacy. Here, a heavy-duty, small-squared timber trellis is mounted on top of a low wall in a successful attempt at seclusion. It is decorative in its own right, and the natural finish blends well with the earthy colours of paving and plant containers.

▼ Town house elegance White, wall-mounted trellis brings an air of sophistication to a formal front door. It is particularly ornamental, without any floral attachments. Restrained colour comes from standard-trained bay trees on either side of the entrance.

ARBOURS AND PERGOLAS

**Ornamental structures add height to all
gardens. They can be clothed with climbers or stand as
decorative features on their own.**

Ornamental structures, such as arches, pergolas and arbours, help to give a feeling of permanence to a garden, however new they are. Such structures, especially when bought pre-assembled or in self-assembly kit form, are also the quickest way to add height to a garden. This is particularly important if the garden lacks mature trees or high walls, and young plants have not yet made an impact.

Arches, pergolas and arbours consist of hard geometric shapes and materials which contrast with the softer forms and textures of the surrounding foliage and flowers. They provide structural support for climbers and ramblers such as roses, clematis and honeysuckles. Large-scale pergolas and arbours can help conceal eyesores, though they should always be in scale with the garden, and all can frame a view – leading the eye to a distant vista or pretty garden feature.

Most manufactured arches, pergolas and arbours are reproductions of earlier styles, such as lacy Victorian metalwork, rustic timber or solid classical stone. Although matching the style of a garden structure to the style of the house is the traditional approach, 'mixing and matching' can be successful if done with restraint and consistency. An old-fashioned touch may be just what is needed in the garden of a new house. However, too many structures, in different styles and materials, tends to create a restless, confused effect.

In a small or medium-sized garden, a single, well-placed arch,

▼ **Rustic arch** A softwood arbour complements this cottage-style front garden. Made from untreated timber, it will support nothing stronger than climbing roses and has a comparatively short life-span.

◀ **Rose pergola** A framework of rustic poles gives welcome height to low formal flower beds. Softwood is inexpensive and readily available and will last for about ten years if stripped of bark and pressure-impregnated with a wood preservative.

Tall structures and those in exposed situations are better constructed from hardwood and set on concrete, brick or stone plinths.

▼ **Hidden retreat** A Victorian-style gazebo offers shade from the sun and a peaceful view of the garden. Made from white-painted timber trellis panels, it needs repainting every few years while the climbing roses and clematis are dormant. Strong, plastic-covered trelliswork requires less maintenance, but once the coating cracks, rust often sets in.

pergola or arbour is often more effective than having several structures that compete with each other. The structure should be large enough to command attention but not so large as to be overbearing.

Arches

Unlike pergolas and arbours, garden arches need no definition. If substantial, they can be free-standing, but are generally most effective as part of a garden wall or marking a way through a clipped hedge. Free-standing arches are available in wrought iron, in white or black plastic-coated steel, and in various designs of rustic wood. They can also be built of trellis panels or, more expensively, in brick.

Free-standing arches are sometimes wrongly sited – an arch in the middle of a lawn or bed looks abandoned rather than effective. It is better to place an arch where a path starts, or over an entrance gate. You can also use an arch to link different areas of the garden, such as the steps between a patio and lawn, or the transition from ornamental to kitchen garden.

Arches can frame a view, but only from one specific viewpoint. In modest-sized gardens it is usually better to think of them firstly as part of the view and, secondly, as a frame to a view.

Pergolas

Traditional pergolas are arching or flat-topped, plant-covered frameworks over paths or walks. Often linking the house to the garden, pergolas can also join the house to a garage, carport or shed, or link a group of small buildings together physically and visually. Always consider where a pergola starts and where it finishes – perhaps linking existing doors, paths and entrance ways. Pergolas can also be free-standing, dividing the garden into smaller areas.

It is generally better for a pergola to follow the geometry of a garden by running parallel to a boundary or building rather than at odd angles. Take into consideration, too, the spaces and proportions a pergola creates in a garden. A pergola off centre is usually more interesting than one in the middle of a lawn. Pergolas are usually built on level ground, although they can be successfully

combined with shallow steps leading to a paved area.

A pergola can provide privacy from adjacent houses. It is most effective in summer, once climbers are established. Avoid evergreens, which can have a dank, mournful effect in winter. Privacy can be reinforced with plant-covered trellis on one side of the pergola.

Because a traditional pergola acts as a tunnel, focusing the eye towards the light at the end, there should be something of importance there, whether it is the entrance to another building, a lovely view, a stone ornament or a large pot of colourful plants. A pool reflecting the sky can be a splendid end to a shaded walkway beneath a pergola.

▲ **Free-standing arch** Long-lasting hardwood, such as iroko, teak and oak, weathers to an attractive silver-grey. Sunk into 'metal shoes', such structures are durable and maintenance-free.

A pergola can incorporate a boundary wall as part of its structure. In a long, narrow garden, a pergola against the rear wall forms a loggia (semi-enclosed walkway) which will improve the proportions of the garden and make it seem wider.

Pergolas can be constructed as overhead beams above a patio adjoining a house. Fragrant climbers, such as summer jasmine, would be particularly welcome in south- or west-facing sites, and the heat retained in the walls and paving encourages flowering and fragrance. Honeysuckles are suitable for shady positions.

Pergolas range from simple, home-made structures of wooden posts, cross ties, and thick nautical rope looping from one set of posts to the next and ideal for training pillar roses, to quite elaborate classical stone columns, cross beams and copings. They can be constructed from metal, timber or brick – or a combination of these materials.

Arbours
Arbours are small shady retreats from which to view the garden. As well as being look-out points, arbours can also be decorative focal points with greenery trailing over the framework.

Arbours fit equally well at the end of a path or tucked away in a corner of the garden, set among shrubs and flowers. In a small garden, an arbour is almost inevitably the focal point, while in a large garden it may be a hidden treasure, to be discovered on turning a corner.

Domed arbours, circular in plan, are available in white plastic-coated, galvanized wire, with furniture to match. Larger and smaller arbours, plain or embellished, in wrought iron, have a longer life and are not unduly costly. DIY arbours, with a limited life, can be built from panels of sturdy trellis.

Materials
The choice of materials depends on personal budget and taste. A purpose-built feature is obviously more expensive than one in pre-assembled or kit form.

Arches, pergolas and arbours can be built of wood. Rustic softwood, such as larch and pine, with the bark left on, are inexpensive but short-lived. If they are stripped of bark and treated with a wood preservative, rustic fixtures have a longer life-span – about ten years – and require little maintenance.

Sawn softwood should ideally be pressure-treated or impregnated with preservative. Never use creosote, which is lethal to shrubby and climbing plants and remains toxic for several years. Unless you want a particular effect, such as matching the paintwork with that of the house, do not paint timber structures. The paint cracks with the movement

▼ **Modern arbour** A white-painted metal arch erected against a wall transforms a garden seat into an ornamental feature. Made from light steel to imitate wrought iron, it is inexpensive but needs regular repainting every few years.

▲ **Romantic arbour** Large intricate metal constructions were popular in Victorian times. They were smothered with heavily scented climbing roses and often contained garden statuary. Modern replicas in wrought iron are generally more modest in size.

▶ **Wrought-iron arches** Long-lasting and maintenance-free, wrought-iron structures can be decorative features in their own right. They do not have to support climbers, but can be used to frame an attractive garden view.

◀ **Flower pergola** A wooden pergola erected above a flower bed by the patio adds visual interest and complements the style of the house. Deciduous climbers are preferable to evergreens, which tend to make the area too dark in winter.

▼ **Timber pergola** Made from planed, stained timber, this modern hardwood structure has clean straight lines in keeping with the paved area. The sturdy uprights are sunk in concrete, and the bases are hidden in low square beds of summer-flowering annuals.

of the wood, and maintenance is costly and troublesome.

Hardwoods, such as teak, oak, iroko and Western red cedar, are the most durable and the most expensive. Untreated, they will weather to an attractive silvery grey. It is advisable to embed the uprights in concrete, brick or stone plinths, to prevent the wood from rotting. Metal 'shoes' are often used to fix wooden posts to such foundations.

Natural stone is expensive. Reconstituted stone and concrete can be attractive and are less expensive. Pergola columns, 'L' beams and copings are available in reconstituted limestone, which quickly weathers and becomes attractively encrusted with lichens and mosses. Both natural and reconstituted stone last indefinitely and need very little maintenance.

Brick is often used for the columns or piers of pergolas and arches. For a unifying effect use the same type and colour as the house bricks.

Brick is ideal for a large-scale structure. Piers should be at least one and a half bricks square. If the piers are tall and supporting the overhead beams directly, two or two and a half bricks square is better. Such weighty verticals can appear overly heavy, especially if they are spaced close together over a narrow path.

FANS AND ESPALIERS

**Trees and shrubs, grown as fans or espaliers
or over metal frames, create a range of architectural
effects to enhance any garden.**

In informal gardening, woody plants are allowed to grow naturally and pruning is kept to a minimum. The opposite approach is to shape suitable plants into geometric forms, with little or no allowance for their natural growth habit – formal hedges are the simplest example.

Another challenging alternative is to prune and train shrubs and trees into arches, tunnels and fans. With a little imagination, striking results can be produced.

Trained plants have formal overtones, especially if they are grown in pairs or rows. However, they fit easily into average-sized and even small gardens and occupy less space than conventionally grown examples.

Spacious gardens may have delightful large-scale features such as pleached avenues, laburnum tunnels and wall-trained fruit trees. A small or medium-sized garden is enhanced by pillar roses; and even a tiny garden has room for a clipped arch over the front door or gate.

Focal positions
Formally trained plants attract the eye, especially when seen in contrast to informal planting. Vertical effects in a garden are visually powerful, all the more so during the flowering season.

▼ **Metal frame** Small-leaved evergreen wall shrubs, such as pyracantha or, as here, *Rhaphiolepis x delacourii*, can be trained to sturdy frames fixed to a wall. The shoots should be tied in, and regular trimming is essential to retain the effect.

▲ **Feature frame** A wooden arch, with sturdy side panels of timber trellis, supports a leafy grape vine and frames the view of a garden statue. Pillar roses are trained against strong timber posts linked by chains of heavy rope.

▼ **Fan-trained cherry** North-facing sites can be difficult, but the morello cherry thrives in just such positions. Here, it is trained, fan-fashion, on a fence topped with trellis, brightening the shady site with delicate white blossom in spring.

Large-scale features, such as tunnels of formally trained trees, are traditionally linked to hard landscaping – perhaps spanning or lining a paved walkway. A single arch in a small garden has no such constraints though it should always direct the eye to a view further along.

Tunnels or arches of formally trained plants can frame a view or distant focal point, or emphasize the entrance to a garden or front door. Combined with a hedge or wall, an arch can also mark the end of one area of the garden and the beginning of another. Tunnels provide a sense of depth and mystery, and are pleasingly cool and shady in summer.

A row of two-dimensional trained plants such as fans, cordons or espaliers can enhance boundary fences and walls. Alternatively, train them against free-standing posts and wires along a path or surrounding a vegetable plot to provide decorative screening. This is especially effective for subdividing a small garden, where dense screens would further reduce the sense of space.

Plant material
Long-lived woody plants tolerant of close pruning and with a

moderate growth rate are best, since young flexible growth is important for training. Suitable trees and shrubs for formal training include hornbeam, lime, wisteria, laburnum, pyracantha, grape vine and ivies.

Fruit trees have long been trained artificially to produce good crops in a limited space. However, they are also decorative, and usually have attractive blossom. For fruit trees to be trained as fans, espaliers and cordons, buy maiden trees grafted on to dwarfing rootstocks. Trained trees are sold by specialist nurserymen, but they are more expensive than maiden trees.

Consider the ultimate size of the trained tree or shrub, and if you want flowers or fruit make sure that the style of training or

▲ **Bamboo frames** Apple trees trained in decorative festoons make a delightful feature in a kitchen garden. The side-branches are looped and tied over a framework of long bamboo canes – a method that is not only space-saving, but also encourages the production of fruiting spurs.

◄ **Wire shapes** Ivy is ideal for training into ornamental features and can be clipped like topiary. Elaborate wire frames, in animal and geometric shapes, are available; circular and conical frames are easier to manage.

▲ **Pyramid frames** Pressure-treated timber posts, in wigwam fashion, support a mass of climbing roses. Choose varieties of moderate vigour that can be untied and laid on the ground when the posts need staining.

▼ **Laburnum tunnel** Laburnums trained over a series of metal arches are a classical feature in large country gardens. They create a delightful walkway beneath the drooping yellow flower festoons in late spring and summer.

pruning is compatible with the plant's natural growth habit. Pruning a mature pyracantha espalier grown as a trained wall shrub usually means you will forgo both flowers and berries.

Pruning to shape

You can train and prune a suitable plant in a variety of ways. Pruning trained fruit trees can be a difficult task for the beginner. It varies according to fruit and variety, and must be done twice a year – in summer and winter. Pruning restricted fruit trees involves removing old, non-productive and misplaced shoots while maintaining a steady supply of young replacement growth for fruiting.

Fan-trained trees

These have branches radiating out, like a fan, from a central point. Trees and shrubs suitable for fan-training include plum, peach, nectarine, cherry, apricot, blackberry and loganberry. You could also try training ornamental *Prunus* or *Malus* species and varieties, fern-leafed blackberry and rambler roses.

Fan-training is usually done against a wall. South-facing walls or solid fences are ideal for peach, nectarine and apricot. Morello cherry and gooseberry will crop in north-facing sites, and plum, blackberry and loganberry are fine on all but north-facing walls and fences. There are rose varieties suitable for all aspects. The amount of space needed varies according to the spread of the individual plant.

Cordons

Cordons are the most compact form of tree, and fruit trees are often trained as cordons that produce a good crop in a limited space. Single cordons are restricted to one angled stem, double cordons to two vertical stems, and triple cordons have three vertical stems. Fruit is carried on short side-shoots or spurs on either side of the main stem or stems.

Suitable fruit trees and shrubs for cordoning include apple, pear, gooseberry, and red and black currants. Rows of cordons could attractively edge a path.

Espaliers

Espaliers consist of a central trunk with pairs of horizontal, opposite branches trained along

▲ **Brick arches** Massive, square-sectioned brick pillars support heavy timber beams hidden in high summer by a profusion of well-established climbers. The free-flowering, deep purple *Clematis* 'Etoile Violette' scrambles through sweet-scented honeysuckle, and the white-eyed, bright pink 'American Pillar' rose rambles over a second arch.

▶ **Apple espaliers** Decorative in flower and fruit, espalier-trained apples take up little space and crop well. The side-branches are trained horizontally and pruned to shape in summer.

wires fixed at 30-45cm (1-1½ft) intervals to a wall or free-standing posts. During training in the first few years, the new side-shoots are trained horizontally to higher wires.

Espaliers usually have three, four or five tiers of wires and side-branches, but can in theory have up to 20. Apple and pear trees are the most popular choices for espalier-training.

Pleaching

Pleached (or plashed) trees have their main side-branches trained horizontally, to interweave into a continuous line well above head height. All other branches are removed and new growth is cut back annually, usually in late autumn and winter, to the main horizontal framework. The trees are planted 1.8-3m (6-10ft) apart.

Lime is the traditional tree for pleaching, but beech, hornbeam and plane can all be pleached, and espaliered apple and pear trees are a form of pleaching on the flat.

As well as being trained in a straight line, pleached trees can be trained to grow in a Gothic arch, meeting overhead like a tunnel, or round a central area to form a dome.

Arches

Yew, holly and hornbeam hedges can be trained to form arches, giving a formal effect. Alternatively, climbers can be trained up an arch support of wood or metal – roses, honeysuckle, jasmine and clematis are traditional and popular subjects.

Pillars

Pillars are upright supports, most often used for training climbing and rambling roses. Other climbers, such as jasmine or clematis, look equally enchanting trained around a pillar.

Traditional pillars are 2.4m (8ft) high, and support one, two or three plants. The long, flexible shoots must be tied in, upright or spirally, while flowers are borne on the short side-shoots. Always match the vigour of the climber to the height of the pillar.

Pairs or series of pillars can be linked with looped metal chains or heavy ropes to connect them.

Pillars are not the most attractive sight during the dormant season and need careful siting – perhaps in a corner of the garden, in pairs either side of a path or in rows along a path, spaced at least 1.8m (6ft) apart. Closer spacing results in a tunnel effect. Alternatively, make the best of an unfruitful tree by training a vigorous climbing rose through it.

Tunnels

Traditional tunnels were trained over wooden frameworks, which would rot away once the trees had arched together. Today, it is more usual to train them over purpose-built frames of metal hoops and crossbars; a combination of wood posts and horizontal wires can also be used. Tunnels are paved underneath, being too shady in summer for a lawn.

Lime trees are a traditional choice for training to form a tunnel, but they cast dense shade. Robinia, with its light, feathery foliage, laburnum and wisteria, with their drooping flower cascades and delicate foliage, or fruit trees are better alternatives.

Ornamental shapes

Specimen plants trained into decorative shapes make attractive focal points. Tall plants with pendulous growth – such as the wil-

▲ **Metal hoops** More practical than a laburnum tunnel but just as attractive, this charming walkway of metal hoops supports climbing cucumbers and gourds, as well as a wealth of heavily scented sweet peas. Golden rudbeckias line the brick path.

low-leaved pear (*Pyrus salicifolia* 'Pendula'), *Cotoneaster frigidus* 'Hybridus Pendulus' or some standard roses – can be trained over special wire umbrellas.

Apples, pears, plums or similar trees can be festooned – that is, the young tree is trained so that the upper branches balloon out into a round shape. Tall stems at the top and bottom are tied into loops, encouraging fruiting side-shoots to develop.

ORNAMENTAL BUILDINGS

**A summerhouse, gazebo or other
outdoor sitting room is a valuable asset
to any garden, however small.**

Most people think of garden buildings as purely practical structures. Sheds, greenhouses and woodsheds are strictly functional structures and usually tucked away at the back of the garden. Yet purely ornamental garden buildings also exist, including summerhouses, gazebos, belvederes, pavilions and follies.

Although the main purpose of such structures is to look ornamental, they often have a practical purpose as well. They provide some protection from the sun and wind or from light showers and allow their occupants to sit in the garden instead of viewing it from the house.

Ornamental buildings are traditional in large country estates and parks, but more modest versions can be fitted into smaller gardens and often make them seem larger. Invariably such a building becomes the focal point of the garden, altering the perspective and making the boundaries appear to recede.

Ornamental buildings can be made of almost any material – timber, stone, brick, metal or plastic – or combinations of these. They should be sympathetic to other hard materials in the garden.

Summerhouses

Probably the most useful – and substantial – ornamental garden building is the summerhouse. While it can be open on one or more sides, it is usually enclosed, with glazed doors and windows. The doors are either wide, or double, so as to let in sun and air. It should ideally be south-facing.

Summerhouses were very popular in the 19th century, when people who had travelled extensively wanted a permanent reminder of their travels. Obliging manufacturers produced summerhouses resembling Chinese pagodas, Scottish crofts, Greek temples or whatever took the customer's fancy. Although some of the more exotic forms are no longer available, there is still a good variety of attractive and practical designs. Many come in kit form, or the DIY enthusiast can build a summerhouse to an individual design.

▼ **Chinese pagoda** An ornate summerhouse on a raised platform dominates the sunken garden area and determines the style of layout and planting schemes in this garden.

▶ **Romantic perspective** A stone urn takes on a wholly new importance as a result of the decorative metalwork arbour that enfolds it. Covered with leafy climbers and matched by a garden seat, the structure makes a highly ornamental focal point.

▼ **Wooden dovecote** Birds as well as people need privacy and shelter, and this charming dovecote in a secluded garden corner provides both. It tones well with the near-rural surroundings and is tall enough to be beyond the reach of predatory cats.

However, a summerhouse or any other ornamental structure should preferably fit into the overall garden and house picture and appear as a natural feature rather than a misplaced afterthought. It should be in proportion, both to the garden and the home, and be built from compatible materials.

Wooden summerhouses can be painted, especially if they are sited in dull corners. In a sunny position the paint will blister and flake and entail unnecessary maintenance; wood stain is usually preferable.

Alternatively, the building can be enhanced with plantings, at ground level in permanent beds, or with hanging baskets and containers of summer-flowering annuals. Golden hop or honeysuckles can tumble against the sides of the building.

One of the most effective places for a summerhouse in a small garden with no outside views is in the corner of two walls. All that is needed is a roof and one additional face, most of which will be taken up by the door and either a straight or bowed front.

Gazebos and follies

When there are good views across

▲ **Rustic gazebo** Wood is a natural element in the garden scene and blends perfectly with tree and shrub plantings. This open-sided gazebo affords uninterrupted views over the garden, shade from hot sun and shelter from the odd shower of rain.

▶ **Classical-style summerhouse** Ornamental buildings should be compatible with the size, layout and shape of the garden and main house. This neo-classical loggia-type summerhouse is suitable only for a relatively large formal garden.

and beyond the garden, the summerhouse may overlap with the function of a gazebo. The name is apt, for the purpose is to gaze out, and for this reason a gazebo is more open than a summerhouse. There are either open sides instead of windows, or the whole structure is open and lacy. Gazebos are often made entirely of fine metalwork crafted into ornate scrollwork patterns, rather like an enormous birdcage. They are rarely embellished with plants, which would obscure the view.

Where a gazebo is sited well away from the house, especially when set on a hill, it is known as a belvedere (from the Italian 'bel', beautiful and 'vedere', to see).

In the past, summerhouses or gazebos were often incorporated into follies, although true follies strictly have no useful purpose. The British countryside has many examples of such expensive whims, from purpose-built 'Gothic' ruins and classical temples to obelisks, towers, hermits' cells and bewildering mazes.

Modern pavilions

Summer retreats with clean and simple lines are more appropriate in modern-style gardens, with sparse planting to enhance the architectural effect. A canopy of tiles, slates, copper sheeting or bamboo slats can be attached to an A-frame or conical roof over an open structure. A few choice sculptural plants with dramatic leaves, such as hostas or yucca, or even a slender fountain of bamboo, will complete the picture better than a sprawling riot of flowers and shrubs.

With a four-sided roof that rises to a ball-capped apex, and four simple supporting pillars, the canopy can be converted to a pavilion by adding no more than curtains. Made of striped canvas that meets outside the corner pillars, curtains evoke a medieval atmosphere. And colourful floor cushions create an impression of the exotic East.

▲ **Thatched retreat** Restful in concept, this little summerhouse is tailor-made for meditation to the sound of softly running water. The deep thatch perfectly complements the earthy colours of wood and brick used in the other hard landscaping features.

▼ **Octagonal cedar** Constructed from sturdy, pressure-impregnated cedar, octagonal summerhouses are expensive though handsome and durable. They are large enough for comfortable sitting in summer and for winter storage of garden furniture.

FOCAL POINTS

**Plants form the background scenery in a garden,
but particularly decorative types, along with ornamental statuary,
are destined to be the focus of attention.**

Outstanding plants, or well-chosen garden ornaments, can be singled out to make focal points. This simple design device helps to structure a garden, and serves as a pivot around which other features can be built up, or towards which other features can lead.

A garden can be created to look like a painting when seen from various vantage points – landscape paintings frequently use the device of a focal point to draw the picture together.

Plants as focal points
Focal points never work in isolation – how successful a particular plant is in its impact will depend on its setting.

On a smooth, clipped lawn, for example, a small, gnarled statuesque pine stands out as a focal point. In a pine forest, with hundreds of similar trees, no individual tree holds special interest.

Contrast and harmony are the most important factors in creating effective focal points – the more a plant contrasts with, yet complements, its surroundings, the more powerful it becomes as a focal point. This is why plants in containers seem to stand out more on hard patio paving than they do in mixed planting in the open ground.

Contrast can be created through colour, form and size. An obvious example of colour contrast is the silver-grey foliage of *Senecio* 'Sunshine' set against a dark green background – or the flaming red autumnal foliage of stag's-horn sumach on a green lawn.

Pale colours, such as white, pink or light green, and 'hot' colours, such as scarlet, orange or yellow, attract the eye more than dark or blue-toned, cool coloured flowers and foliage. Pastel shades

are also ideal for visual deception – in distant corners they recede and appear to make a garden look larger. Bold colours have the opposite effect.

Contrast in form can be startling or subtle. A weeping tree, such as weeping beech, pear, cotoneaster or a grafted standard weeping rose, stands out because most woody plants grow upright, towards the sun.

A horizontal-growing plant, such as *Juniperus* x *media* 'Pfitzeriana', also catches the eye if it is

planted to contrast with upright-growing plants.

Topiary creates a more subtle type of contrast with controlled, dense and often geometric shapes seen against the natural, relaxed and usually looser growth habit of nearby plants.

A mass of miniature plants can also be a focal point – a sink or raised trough garden on a patio or balcony, for example, becomes a focal point in the absence of surrounding competition.

Flower and leaf size also con-

▶ **Floral frame** An arbour should lead to a distant vista or to a natural termination point. This rustic arch beautifully frames a stone statue, luminous against a dark background. A profusion of *Clematis montana* over the arch paints the picture in pink.

▲ **Dramatic focus** A magnificent view through a high brick wall pierced by an enormous circular opening focuses directly on a piece of statuary. Restful backgrounds are essential for a focal point to have impact and to give an impression of depth.

tribute to a plant's power as a focal point. The leaves of ailanthus or tree of heaven, for example, grow enormous if the tree is grown as a shrub and cut back to ground level (or stooled) annually. Such foliage adds a touch of tropical luxuriance to a garden, and captures the eye; many eucalyptus species, with their handsome blue-green juvenile leaves, are also grown as stooled shrubs.

The outrageously huge leaves of the moisture-loving *Gunnera manicata* are another example that has dramatic impact, particularly by a poolside. Mammoth sunflowers towering above all else in a garden also shows the effectiveness of flower size.

Massed planting can be an

▶ **Silver pear** Drooping above a white and silver garden, a willow-leaved pear (*Pyrus salicifolia* 'Pendula') becomes a simple but effective focal point. Its elegant grey-green foliage draws together the underplanting, and the statue beneath the canopy emphasizes its graceful lines.

room or upstairs windows also carries extra visual weight.

You can also choose a spot for a focal point and plan the garden around it. Curve a path or stepping stones towards it, or frame it between two herbaceous borders, a pair of shrubs or a break in a hedge or wall.

On the other hand, focal points can be created to reinforce other features or to obscure unavoidable obstacles. A garden seat at the end of a path becomes more inviting and eye-catching if placed

◄ **Simple statements** An imaginatively placed container can often be enough to arrest the eye. This warm-hued terracotta pot on a brick path lifts the view from the low edging and draws attention to the pot contents of sweet-scented nicotianas.

▼ **Bold colours** The vivid scarlet flowers of a rhododendron beckon a welcome through a covered archway and invite closer inspection of another part of the garden.

effective focal point, in spite of the small size of its components. A patch of bluebells in flower acts as a magnet to the eye, though the individual plants are quite modest. Naturalized swathes of crocuses or narcissi in flower on a lawn work in the same way.

The ultimate massed-planting focal point is the traditional carpet bedding favoured in municipal parks, where hundreds or even thousands of tiny plants spell out a single image – a clock, for example, or the name of a seaside town.

Rarity value is a different way of creating a focal point. In temperate though frost-free gardens, a palm tree, such as the windmill palm (*Trachycarpus fortunei*) or a huge spiny agave, will automatically catch the eye and excite the imagination with their unfamiliar and exotic appearance.

Simplicity is as important as contrast, especially in small gardens. The fewer focal-point plants there are to rival one another, the more effective each one will be.

Positioning focal points

Certain places in the garden tend to attract the eye more than others – either side of a garden gate, front door or steps by a patio, for example, or the centre of a lawn or the end of a path. Anything seen from the living

▲ **Autumn colour** The vivid autumn foliage of Japanese maples (*Acer palmatum*) is always impressive. The stunning effect is heightened by the surrounding trees which, apart from their supporting background role, also shelter the maple from drying winds. In spring, the tree is equally attractive, when the young leaves unfold to the palest green.

▶ **Stone pineapple** A humorous and eye-catching touch, a large stone pineapple seems to sprout from the centre of a glossy evergreen x *Fatshedera lizei*.

▶ **Summer scents** A sundial on a carved pedestal forms an exquisite focal point in a scented garden. It gives structural interest to the informal planting of modern pinks, feathery fennel and blue-flowered catmint.

in a bower of climbing and flowering plants. A handsome urn can hide the ugliness of a manhole cover, and a statue in one corner of a small square garden can alter the perspective by drawing the eye along a diagonal path.

Certain positions in flower beds and borders are natural spots for focal-point plants – the middle of a bed in a symmetrical formal scheme, for example, or planted at random in an informal scheme.

Specimen planting

In gardening terminology, a specimen plant can mean a perfect, mature example of its type, but it also refers to the isolated position of a plant.

On a broad expanse of lawn any tree or shrub becomes a specimen plant, but one with decorative leaves, flowers or fruit is doubly striking. Most specimen plants are large shrubs or trees and automatically become focal points because of their size.

Specimen plants can be associated with other plants as long as the latter serve a supportive role – low-growing ground cover around the base of a lawn-planted tree, for example, or trailing bedding plants round the base of a standard fuchsia in a pot.

Large, shrubby roses, such as the glorious cream-coloured 'Nevada', or a pillar rose, such as 'American Pillar', are ideal as lawn specimens as are standard and weeping standard roses, especially in formal schemes.

Ideally, a focal-point plant should be effective all year round, especially in a small garden. The evergreen *Fatsia japonica*, with its broad palmate leaves and handsome growth habit, is an excellent choice, and is quite happy in a shady site.

Consider also a plant's out-of-season appeal. Again, the smaller

▶ **Points to ponder** A crisp white bench beckons invitingly from the end of a path. It gives definition to beds of shrub roses edged with clumps of purple-leaved sage and feathery santolinas, and offers a pleasant sitting area to enjoy the view.

▲ **Solar eclipse** A sun-shaped pebble decoration set in crazy paving has dramatic visual impact. The circular shape is repeated in clumps of hebes beneath the climbing roses and the honeysuckles that frame the entrance porch in flowers and scent.

▶ **Movable feasts** A rustic wheelbarrow holds a massed display of mixed petunias and lobelias and adds cheerful colour to a paved area. It can be filled with plants to match the seasons and can be moved around to suit the vagaries of the weather.

the garden, the more important this is. The corkscrew hazel (*Corylus avellana* 'Contorta'), for example, is an attractive, crinkly-leaved shrub for a prominent position. However, its strangely contorted branches are more conspicuous in their winter nakedness and even more so when draped with long golden catkins in late winter.

Pampas grass is a traditional specimen plant for lawns. Although huge clumps can be most effective with their feathery plumes in late summer and autumn, they are relatively unattractive out of season.

Architectural plants

Sculptural or architectural plants make impressive focal points. Their growth habit separates them from more ordinary, run-of-the-mill species, and they tend to be bold in outline and foliage.

Architectural trees for an average-sized garden include stag's-horn sumach, certain magnolias, fig, weeping pear, amelanchier, Judas tree, corkscrew willows and mulberry.

Among the more architectural shrubs are the tall-growing bamboos, *Fatsia japonica*, the devil's walking stick (*Aralia*), Japanese maples, yuccas, and many species of *Viburnum*, *Cotoneaster* and *Mahonia*.

Large specimen perennials include acanthus, African lily, globe thistle, sea holly, New Zealand flax, euphorbias, hostas and irises, day lilies, red-hot poker, *Rheum palmatum* (ornamental rhubarb) and Solomon's seal.

To form an effective focal point, good-sized, well-established clumps are obviously essential. A few single or widely scattered plants have little impact.

Because climbing plants have no form of their own, but simply grow up and over whatever support is available, architectural climbers are primarily those with bold foliage, such as Boston ivy and the evergreen ivies which can be clipped and trained as topiary against a flat surface.

Tropical touches

Exotic-looking plants are fascinating, especially in temperate climates, where outlandish foliage and flamboyant flowers can provide an exciting tropical scene in summer.

For exotic drama, combine spiky plants such as yuccas, phormiums and cordylines. Yuccas are fairly hardy and have rosettes of tough, sword-like leaves and spectacular spikes of large creamy-white, drooping flowers in mid to late summer. The half-hardy New Zealand flaxes, mostly colourful varieties of *Phormium tenax*, are clumpy evergreen perennials with tough and leathery, strap-shaped leaves. They can grow as much as 3m (10ft) tall under ideal conditions, and the foliage is greyish-green, or variegated in creamy-yellow, white, purple or red.

Spikes and rosettes complement low-growing succulents such as echeverias, aloes and crassulas. Chiefly grown as house plants, these succulents benefit from a spell outdoors in summer. For stunning contrast, use the castor-oil plant (*Ricinus communis*). A half-hardy foliage annual up to 1.5m (5ft) tall, it has magnificent lobed magenta or bronze-green leaves up to 30cm (12in) across.

The bronze-purple leaves and showy, gladiolus-like red, pink, orange, yellow and white flowers of Indian shot plants (*Canna* x *hybrida*) provide splendid tropical colour, and tiger flower (*Tigridia pavonia*), a rather tender bulb with spotted blooms of many colours, is another highly exotic plant. Alternatively, simulate jungle lushness with the large-leaved evergreen false castor-oil plant (*Fatsia japonica*). Up to 1.8m (6ft) tall and wide, it contrasts handsomely with *Arundinaria murielae*, a non-invasive bamboo with arching green-yellow canes and dark green foliage.

Container plants
It is a good idea to grow tender plants – fuchsias, marguerites and oleanders – in large pots. They can be placed in focal positions in summer and moved under cover for the winter. Pots of sweetly scented orange and lemon trees, and loquats with their outsized leaves, can add tropical luxuriance to the tiniest patio or balcony.

▶ **Tropical splendour** The pure white flower spathes of arum lilies (*Zantedeschia aethiopica* 'Crowborough') provide an exotic touch. The 90cm (3ft) tall stems provide a splendid backcloth in early summer for the creamy yellow flower spikes and iris-like foliage of *Sisyrinchium striatum*.

The gorgeous, fluffy-flowered silk tree (*Albizia julibrissin*) can be grown in a large pot in a sunny sheltered courtyard. It may not survive the winter outdoors and will eventually outgrow its pot, but meanwhile it is a graceful specimen shrub, with elegant foliage and clusters of bright pink flowers in late summer.

Tender bulbs
Many bulbs from South Africa and Mediterranean regions are

▲ Plant architecture In southern frost-free and sheltered gardens, the succulent *Agave americana* 'Marginata' from Mexico has dramatic impact. The long, spine-tipped leaves arch in a perfect rosette shape and may reach a height of 1.2m (4ft). Smaller specimens can be used in bedding schemes.

▼ Mediterranean summer Treated with tender care and strictly for frost-free regions, the little evergreen *Convolvulus cneorum* flowers through summer and early autumn. It bears large white funnel-shaped blooms that open from pink buds amid small narrow leaves covered with silky and silvery hairs.

borderline cases of frost-hardiness. They need hot summers, perfect drainage and usually poor soil. Narrow borders between a sunny wall and a paved path make ideal sites.

For maximum impact, large swathes, clumps or pots of one type of large-flowered bulb – agapanthus, amaryllis, nerine or crinum – in a clear, single colour are more effective than scattered planting. The tender South African pineapple lily (*Eucomis*) makes an impressive focal point in a sunny sheltered border. It has wide rosettes of handsome, bright green, gently undulating leaves and sturdy stems topped with spikes of star-shaped flowers surmounted with a pineapple-like tuft of leafy bracts. Except in frost-free regions, lift the bulbs in autumn and store them frost-free.

Specialist collections of diminutive flowers, such as the yellow-green snake's-head iris (*Hermodactylus tuberosus*) or the white and blue peacock iris (*Moraea tricuspis*), look lovely in raised beds, sink gardens or shallow troughs.

A raised spot is also ideal for flowering plants with a strong scent, such as freesias. And some plants have flowers with subtle or exquisite markings – baboon flower (*Babiana stricta*), harlequin flower (*Sparaxis tricolor*), peacock orchid (*Acidanthera bicolor*), tiger flower (*Tigridia pavonia*) and tritonias, for example – which can all be best appreciated in a raised site.

Caring for tender plants
□ Take care of newly planted and young plants. Use fine netting to protect wall-trained shrubs from late spring frosts. Fix a batten across the top of the wall and attach netting to it, which can be lowered when necessary.
□ From autumn until late spring, once the top growth dies down, protect dormant bulbs and perennials outdoors with a thick layer of leaf-mould or fern fronds.
□ Protect free-standing trees and shrubs with bracken, straw or leaf-mould heaped around the base and over the roots.
□ To protect the roots of plants grown in pots, wrap the container with hessian sacking or old blankets. Alternatively, move the pots to a frost-free garage, greenhouse or conservatory.

▶ **Summer focus** A raised stone container makes a suitable focal point in a low bed of pink, red and white wax begonias. It adds welcome height to a corner site, and the trailing stems of silvery helichrysums, dark blue lobelias and ivy-leaved pelargoniums break the severity of a formal layout.

▶▼ **Specimen plant** A standard-trained fuchsia, laden with drooping bells during several summer months, lifts the view from the flat expanse of lawn and patio. Nothing detracts from its splendour, and a clump of blue-grey carnation foliage only serves to intensify the fuchsia-red flower colour.

▼ **Classical urn** An ornate stone urn framed in soft greenery immediately draws attention to itself. The addition of a single, spiny-leaved agave adds bold contrast and creates an instant focal point.

▲ **Foliage garden** A large pot of trailing fuchsia draws attention to tall clumps of green and purple-leaved New Zealand flax (*Phormium*) and adds spots of colour to a garden of foliage plants. The stylish layout suits a small town garden, with wide brick paths and infills of gravel.

◄▲ **Trompe l'oeil effect** White-painted trellis gives illusionary depth to a narrow border and frames the focal point. Centrepiece in the composition is a huge, blue-glazed pot holding magnificent lilies in pale pink, a colour repeated in the climbing rose above the trellis. Purple-leaved New Zealand flax adds complementary footnotes in the foreground.

◄ **Pure formality** A mature windmill palm (*Trachycarpus fortunei*) forms the centrepiece in this formal garden. It is surrounded by a close-clipped octagonal box hedge and rises from a sea of white-flowered osteospermums.

GARDEN CENTREPIECES

**Small gardens planned around a stylish
centrepiece or prominent focal point have
both charm and individual character.**

Small and tiny gardens sometimes
lack character and focal points may
be difficult to place to advantage in
a limited space. In order to have
any impact, focal points, whether
they are statuary, ornamental
structures or specimen plants,
should be comparatively large.
However, by their very size they
can appear out of proportion to the
rest of the garden's elements.

In such situations, it is worth
considering a garden layout
designed around a central feature.
Many gardens already possess a
centrepiece – which does not necessarily have to be in the middle
of the garden – such as a handsome tree, a statue or other large
garden ornament, a pool or rock
garden or a beautifully planted
herbaceous bed.

Centrepieces

A prominent feature should ideally be effective throughout the
year, especially in small gardens,
and living plants are preferable
to inanimate objects. For many
gardeners at least one specimen
tree is desirable, and the choice
can be difficult because as a
centrepiece it has to serve several
purposes.

Shape is important – even more
so at maturity – and types such as
copper beeches, weeping willows
and cedars have no place in small
gardens. As lawn specimen trees
and centrepieces, fastigiate or
upright trees, such as the
flowering cherry (*Prunus*
'Amanogawa') or the familiar
rowan (*Sorbus* 'Joseph Rock'),
take up little ground space with

their slender narrow shapes. They
are handsome in spring with
cheerful flower clusters and again
in autumn with vivid leaf colours
and bunches of berries.

Upright trees strike a note of
formality that ties the other garden features to it. Rounded trees,
like ornamental crab apples
(*Malus*), varieties of our native
hawthorn (*Crataegus*) or the
charming willow-leaved pear
(*Pyrus salicifolia*), have much

▼ **Shade tree** An old apple tree,
retained for its ornamental rather than
its culinary value, is the centrepiece in a
small town garden. In spring, it is a
frothy delight of blossom, in summer it
casts light shade over the hexagonal
seating, and in autumn it yields crops
of cooking apples.

▲ **Woodland pond** Water is always fascinating, and pools should ideally be sited in open sunny positions. In a small shady garden, a simulated woodland pond can become the dominant feature and turn a difficult site into a positive asset. Duckweed covers the water surface, and where it meets a beach of water-washed stones, shade-tolerant *Helxine soleirolii* or mind-your-own-business continues the green carpet.

◀ **Pond plants** Clumps of woodland ferns, flag irises and variegated gardener's garters (*Phalaris arundinacea* 'Picta') grow at the water's edge, with spots of colour from pansies, French marigolds and campanulas.

looser growth habits that suggest more informal planting schemes.

Many ornamental trees are of slow growth, and a young sapling can take several years to have much impact as a centrepiece. Specialist tree and shrub nurseries offer semi-mature trees suitable for small gardens, such as ornamental almonds, cherries and rowans. They are obviously more expensive than young trees and need careful attention until properly established, but they create an instantly mature effect.

Evergreens
There are few evergreen trees suitable for specimen planting in small gardens, though standard-

► **Change of perspective** Although this apple tree is on the centreline of the garden, the curving asymmetrical lines of the lawn and meandering path help to avoid a feeling of rigid geometry within a square plot.

trained hollies can make stunning focal points, particularly in winter with their cheerful bunches of berries. Columnar or spire-shaped conifers are other possibilities, although these, too, suggest formal layouts with underplantings of heathers.

The strawberry tree (*Arbutus unedo*) is usually grown as a multi-stemmed shrub. With its glossy green leaves, clusters of white winter flowers and bright red strawberry fruits it makes a fine specimen plant in most southern gardens. Just as suitable and much tougher are the mahonias; their shiny, holly-like leaves are brilliantly decorated with scented yellow flower clusters from late autumn to spring, bringing colour and life to dreary winter scenes.

A prostrate juniper would look charming as a centrepiece, its branches perhaps creeping over a well-placed rock.

Climbing plants

All climbers require support and in tiny gardens they are best relegated to walls and fences, where they take up little ground space. Free-standing arbours, arches and pergolas, which have most visual impact when they lead the eye towards a distant view, are usually out of keeping with a restricted space.

However, an arbour can be erected against a wall and partially enclose a sitting area. Covered with climbing roses, clematis or honeysuckles, such a structure then becomes the centrepiece of the garden, and flower beds and specimen planting can radiate from this vantage point.

Water features

Highly ornamental and individual gardens can be designed around

► **Eyesore transformed** An old tree stump has become a delightful focal point. It is hidden by the magnificent blooms of *Clematis* 'Comtesse de Bouchaud', which flowers freely from early to late summer. Total, year-round cover could also be provided by any of the ivies, green or variegated.

water. A pool makes an admirable centrepiece, reflecting the sky above, inducing a sense of tranquillity, and attracting a rich and varied wildlife.

The shape of pool usually determines the layout of surrounding features: a formal concrete pool, stocked with water lilies and fish, calls for orderly beds and borders, while an informal pool allows for a more relaxed and free-flowing design. Preformed pools are available in a range of shapes and sizes; alternatively, it is not too difficult to excavate a suitable site and line it with heavy-duty butyl rubber.

Flowering water plants need plenty of sun and free air flow, often lacking in small town gardens. However, a shady site can be converted into a replica of a woodland pond, with shade-loving ferns and hostas, primulas and marsh marigolds growing densely among the margins. Such centrepieces almost invariably suggest a semi-wild setting, with rough grass and plantings predominantly of native flowers.

In tiny gardens, an enchanting water feature can consist of something as simple as a waterproof half-barrel. Such a container is deep enough to hold fish, a clump of water iris or variegated grass and a miniature water lily, such as the yellow-flowered *Nymphaea odorata* 'Sulphurea'.

Moving water is as attractive as a still pool surface, and the sound of water playing softly into a basin has a soothing effect. Fountains can be free-standing, and the more elaborate – and expensive – types come with pumps that can be preset to alter the force of the water or the direction of the sprays at regular intervals.

On a smaller scale, there are water features which can be built into wall niches, with a lion's head or stone mask splashing water into shallow stone basins.

Specimen planting

A meticulous eye for detail is important in planning small gardens where everything is immediately visible. Centrepieces, around which the garden is designed and planted, can turn out to be costly mistakes; sometimes it is a good idea to settle for a temporary feature until a more permanent solution suggests itself.

Statuary, in inexpensive reconstituted stone, can easily qualify for a prominent focal point, and objects such as a pedestal birdbath, a sundial or a small statue can be accommodated in garden corners at a later stage.

Many shrubs and perennials are of sculptural outline and suited to central positions. Camellia, for example, is stunning in spring with its exquisite flowers, and the glossy foliage never loses its appeal. *Fatsia japonica* is another evergreen shrub for a central position, with handsome palmate

▲ **Whimsical focal point** A reproduction stone mask contrives to lose its air of mystery with a crowning glory of trailing ivies. Statuary and other ornaments are invaluable for bringing life and interest to dark areas where few plants will thrive.

leaves and white autumn flowers.

Pampas grass (*Cortaderia*) is too massive for a small garden, but yuccas, with their sword-shaped foliage and impressive, creamy white flower spikes, make centrepieces of tropical splendour.

FILLING GARDEN CORNERS

**Odd nooks and corners can be rescued
from obscurity and turned into perfect settings
for garden ornaments and specimen plants.**

Every garden has a few corners, perhaps near the house or in out-of-the-way spots, and these areas can make a valuable contribution to the overall design. Whether formed by boundary walls and fences, house or shed walls, corners can effectively be made into attractive focal points or seating areas. Because they tend to be out of the main line of vision, the potential of corners can often be overlooked.

Corners at the far end of a garden are frequently neglected and left to accumulate leaves and litter – a waste of both space and opportunity.

Even a dark, dank corner can be given a focal point or become a haven for a plant that needs a sheltered spot and will do well in a shady site. And screening a corner with attractive fencing or a line of conifers creates a perfect hiding place for sheds, compost heaps and dustbins.

Corners noticeably greater or lesser than 90° may seem awkward, but they can be put to good use. Wide-angle corners can become mini-landmarks – they can be given their own distinct character with a planting scheme different from the rest of the garden. Alternatively, they can be furnished with a set of crisp, white garden furniture. And striking specimen plants make ideal features for smaller, narrower angles of less than 90°.

Putting corners to use

A corner makes a well-defined area with a sense of depth, and it can often be more interesting than a stretch of wall, fence or hedge. It draws the eye – making it the perfect place for positioning a focal point. If the corner has a plain background, such as green foliage, and provides a strong contrast to the object or plant being displayed, a sense of drama can be created.

The two walls which converge to make a sunny corner provide shelter on the inside corner. Slightly tender plants that would not survive in the open often thrive in these conditions.

Shady corners present a challenge, but they are easily enlivened by white or pale sculpture, furniture and certain flower-

▼ **Corner retreat** Ornate white furniture on a raised paved platform brightens a shady corner. Ivies decorate the trellis-covered walls with evergreen foliage, and in the front beds rhododendrons revel in the shelter and dappled shade of this secluded spot.

ing plants. At night a spotlit corner plant or sculpture can take on a theatrical air.

Specimen planting

Container-grown plants can help to make a corner into a feature, especially if the containers are made of attractive materials, such as terracotta, stone or reconstituted stone, wood or cast iron.

In exhausted urban soil, plants are more likely to thrive in large pots filled with loam-based potting compost. In paved corners, plants in containers are the most sensible option. You can choose between filling a corner with one enormous pot, perhaps containing a specimen plant, or creating a display with a multitude of containers at different heights,

including wall-hung pots. However, there should be a unifying theme to the pots and plants, and at least one should be dominant and eye-catching.

Tall, colourful or boldly shaped specimen plants are ideal for planting in containers for a corner display. Eye-catching plants for sunny corners include New Zealand flax, cabbage palm and yucca, while aucubas, fatsias, camellias, mahonias, Mexican orange and snowberry bush thrive in shady corners.

To add height to a paved corner with small plants, use tiered, corner plant stands made of wood or white plastic-coated wire. A single tall topiary plant (perhaps a pyramid or a spiral shape) set in a corner can also be stunning, espe-

▲ **Purple focus** An unpromising corner becomes a splendid focal point for a *Cotinus coggygria*, whose intensely coloured foliage instantly draws the eye from across the garden. Hostas and lady's mantle (*Alchemilla mollis*) flourish in the light moist shade beneath the tree canopy.

cially if seen in contrast to more informal planting nearby.

Where two open borders meet at a corner, the junction can culminate in a larger bed – perhaps a formal semicircle, or a more flowing curve. Border planting can also emphasize a corner, with the largest or showiest specimens making a feature.

Trees and climbers

Corners and trees are natural

partners, especially in small gardens where a corner tree creates a pleasant sense of asymmetry and will leave some of the garden in full sun. Small trees with strong shapes are usually best for planting in corners – fig and stag's-horn sumach are excellent. They can be underplanted to great effect with ground-cover plants – for example, hellebores for winter interest, small bulbs for spring-flowering, and blue or pink forget-me-nots for early summer.

Corners and climbers also go very well together – the walls providing the necessary support. Corners formed by low walls or fences can be made higher by fixing trellis panels above them.

Stunningly decorative effects can be created with climbers – for example, a strong-growing species, such as *Clematis montana*, trained from a corner outwards in both directions, makes a sweeping

▼ **Rustic setting** A quiet sitting area is enclosed by stout wooden trellis, its warm hues complemented by a rustic bench and table. Hanging baskets and pots of bedding plants add colour to the summery scene.

▲ **Raised beds** Corner sites are perfect for sculptural plants, such as the bold-spreading evergreen *Fatsia japonica*. A white-painted raised bed is the finishing touch that unites the trellis surround with the paving.

feature, softening the geometry of the corner.

For sunny corners, rambling and climbing roses, wisteria and jasmine are attractive and grow well, while ivy, honeysuckle, parthenocissus and *Hydrangea petiolaris* thrive in shady corners of the garden.

Sitting areas

A high-backed corner can create the pleasantly enveloping feeling of an armchair. Two benches placed at right angles can emphasize the tucked-in feeling, but angled seating across a corner often gives a more interesting, diagonal view of the garden and leaves room for a tree or shrubs behind. For a tiny garden there are triangular wooden armchairs especially manufactured to fit into corners.

If space allows, seats can be combined with a table or flanked by plant-filled tubs, so that the

seating area becomes a focal point. And trellis can add a dramatic touch if the seating area is enclosed by an arbour covered in fragrant climbers.

Ornamental features

A statue, birdbath, fountain, well-head or millstone, either placed on hard paving or rising out of massed flowers and foliage, can effectively punctuate a corner. In a tiny garden, a wall niche, nesting box, plaque or corner fountain and basin can add small-scale interest while leaving the space beneath free.

A wall-hung, trompe l'oeil mirror angled across a corner adds a sense of space and mystery. It is especially effective in small urban gardens if the mirror is surrounded by climber-covered three-dimensional trelliswork.

For the corners of a large garden, ornamental features can be more architectural – a gazebo, summerhouse or classical temple, for example.

▲ **Secret hide-out** In large gardens, a summerhouse can be tucked away in a far corner. Partly hidden by dense planting and surrounding trees, it becomes a delightful and secret retreat, invisible from the main body of the garden and the house.

▼ **Roof angle** An awkward corner in a roof garden has been transformed into a major feature. The shallow, sunken gravel-filled bed below the wooden decking provides drainage and wind shelter for a collection of half-hardy foliage plants, open to sun and air.

Concealing utility areas

Concealed corners are ideal for garden structures of no decorative merit – sheds or log piles for example. Clothes-lines and compost heaps – and on a smaller scale,

▲ **Corner fountain** The sight and sound of splashing water can be enjoyed from the house as well as the garden. A small water feature has become a major focal point embellished with moisture-loving marginals.

▶ **Colour emphasis** An eye-catching terracotta pot filled with bright petunias, pelargoniums and lobelias punctuates a dark green corner in a small garden. It is particularly effective in being raised on an old chimney pot.

dustbins – can be sited in corners provided there is paved access.

Corners are often naturally concealed – for example, in the short leg of an L-shaped garden. In an ordinary rectangular garden, a screen may be necessary to hide unsightly features.

Where space is limited, a fence, narrow hedge or woven rustic hurdle work well as a screen. In a larger garden, a generously deep shrubbery or a row of golden conifers could screen off a utility area from the rest of the garden. For camouflaging a greenhouse, choose trellis or loose-weave chestnut paling to allow light to filter through.

Secret corners
A spacious corner, out of the general view, can take on an entirely different character or style from

▲ **Sun trap** A stone container fits neatly into a corner of a tiny cobblestoned courtyard. Filled with a colourful mixture of zonal pelargoniums, petunias and trailing blue lobelias, it makes an arresting focal point.

the rest of the garden – a knot garden, Japanese garden or herb garden, for example, could be entered romantically through an arch or pergola.

On a smaller scale, out-of-view corners are perfect for growing plants that are too fussy, exotic or brilliantly coloured to fit comfortably within the general garden scene, or have a stunning but brief period of display.

Watchpoints

☐ Corners are liable to be either very dry or very damp. Water and fertilize plants in dry soil regularly and grow moisture-loving ferns, primulas and hostas in continually damp soil.

☐ Hedges compete with nearby plants for nutrients and moisture, so plants in a corner formed by hedges will need extra feeding and watering.

☐ Cats may use secluded, sheltered corners as lavatories, killing plants and leaving an unpleasant odour. Use proprietary cat repel-

lents, or stick rose prunings or holly leaves in the soil.

☐ Lack of air circulation in a corner can encourage the build-up of pests and fungal infections. Choose disease-resistant plants and check regularly for signs of a problem. Mildew is particularly troublesome in stagnant air.

☐ Direct access to deep corners can be difficult – where a border widens in a corner include a stepping stone path.

☐ Corners collect wind-blown debris, which looks unattractive and can smother plants. Sweep or rake corners regularly.

☐ Avoid growing large dense trees in corners, as their roots can damage nearby walls and they may cast excessive shade.

▼ **Trumpeting defiance** The elegant angel's trumpet (*Datura x candida*) is hardy only in mild areas like the Isles of Scilly. In southern gardens, sheltered in a sunny corner against solid walls, it looks magnificent in summer with its huge drooping trumpets. Container-grown, it can be moved to a frost-free conservatory for the winter.

Herb gardens

Few gardens today are modelled in the style of medieval herb gardens, yet most contain the occasional clump of herbs for culinary use. They are often relegated to the kitchen garden, but herbs deserve a more prominent position, where their scents, flowers and contrasting leaf textures, shapes and colours can be appreciated. Most gardens have room for a proper herb bed, and this can often be the centrepiece around which the rest of the garden is planned.

A herb garden of annual, perennial and evergreen plants is a place of tranquillity and induces a sense of calm and contemplation. It can consist of formal beds of geometric, equal-sized shapes, divided by paths of bricks, beaten earth or gravel, with the traditional centrepiece of a sundial, bird-bath or rustic garden seat. More informally, groups of different herbs can drift into each other, mingling their shapes and scents. Usually, a herb garden is contained within a low hedge of clipped box, santolina, lavender or rosemary.

Ambitious herb gardens can be modelled on medieval knot gardens of interlaced ribbons of different herbs woven around infills of gravel or old-fashioned flowers such as pinks, marigolds, violets, pansies or miniature roses. Elizabethan herb gardens were created within walled enclosures, with roses and fruit espaliers against the walls, walkways of pleached trees and cloistered seats or statuary in shady arbours. There would be water channels and fountains, chamomile lawns and banks of scented thyme.

The great majority of herbs need full sun and shelter from cold winds. They thrive in all types of well-drained soil, often preferring poor, sandy or stony ground. The leaves should be harvested young, and the more they are picked, the more they produce.

Herb bed A circular bed of aromatic plants has at its hub a clump of purple-flowered perennial chives.

GROWING HERBS

Decorative and culinary herbs can be grown in beds of their own, among vegetables and ornamental plants or in paving and pots.

A herb garden has an old-fashioned, orderly charm and is a source of pride to the self-sufficient gardener, especially if space doesn't allow for a fruit or vegetable garden. Most herbs are easy to grow and fascinating to harvest and to experiment with in the kitchen. Many fragrant herbs are also handsome in flower or leaf and worthy of space in an ornamental garden.

Herbs are cheaper to grow at home than to buy from shops, and a herb garden provides a steady, fresh supply close at hand. You can also grow a wider range of herbs, including exotic types.

The definition of 'herb' in its broadest sense includes any cultivated or wild plant that has culinary, medicinal, cosmetic, magical or domestic value. To most people, though, 'herb' means a cultivated plant grown largely for its flavour.

The size of a herb garden can vary from a flower pot or window-box to an entire garden, though a plot 2m (7ft) square is more than ample for a good selection of culinary herbs.

Most herbs need well-drained, not-too-rich soil and full sun, away from overhanging trees. Some herbs, such as mint, angelica, chives, balm and chervil, will grow in semi-shade. Herb gardens are usually on level ground, although raised beds and gentle slopes, with their excellent drainage, are also suitable.

Although most herbs are annuals or herbaceous perennials, evergreen shrubby types such as rosemary, sage and thyme also belong in a traditional herb garden. Low evergreen hedging or edging gives structure to a herb garden, even in winter, and fresh, evergreen kitchen herbs are particularly welcome then.

Types of layout

Some people grow herbs in rows or clumps in the vegetable patch. An ornamental herb garden, though, can reflect the general style and layout of the garden as a whole, or it can have an entirely separate identity.

Formal herb gardens are based on geometric shapes. The smaller the area, the simpler the geometry should be. Try various patterns on paper, using a compass, straight edge and set square. Base a circular design on concentric circles, with herbs arranged according to height; alternatively cut a circular bed into wedges.

▼ **Herb bed** Annual and perennial herbs mingle happily in a sunny bed centred around an ornamental fountain. Crisp curly parsley, feathery fennel and pungent tarragon are grown for kitchen use, while chives have been allowed to flower and set seed.

▲ **Container-grown herbs** Pots of herbs are both decorative and useful. They can be sited in any sunny spot, including patios and kitchen window-sills. Annual and perennial types are easily raised from seed, shrubby herbs from cuttings.

◄ **Herb pot** Strawberry pots are ideal for growing a variety of herbs where space is at a premium. Large, deep containers are less susceptible to waterlogging and freezing temperatures.

▼ **Kitchen herbs** Easy access to herbs is important. Grow clumps of herbs as edging to a vegetable plot or in an open sunny site by the kitchen door. Pots of young herbs are easy to move around.

Divide a square into four equal squares, with a circular or diamond shape in the centre. For a chequerboard effect, lay paving slabs or brick squares, with alternate spaces for herbs. Or place large-mesh plastic-coated trellis on the soil surface, and plant each separate square or diamond with a different herb.

Larger, more intricate layouts can be based on old-fashioned formal knot gardens, including scroll-shaped patterns as well as geometric ones. Brick edging or a dwarf hedge help to emphasize the formal layout, especially as herbs sprawl or straggle and grow at different rates, confusing the overall design. A tall central feature, such as a bay tree, bird-bath or statue, adds formality and serves as a focal point. In a large herb garden, you can place an ornamental feature in each of the corners, with perhaps a garden seat in the centre.

In symmetrical herb gardens, one half exactly mirrors the other in layout and plants. If space is limited and you want a wide range of herbs, you can maintain a rough symmetry by pairing herbs according to form and expected height. Creeping thyme and creeping pennyroyal can be partners, as can rounded clumps of sage and lavender, or tall-growing dill and fennel.

A herb garden can also be modelled on the physic beds of medieval monasteries. Here, monks tended large plots of herbs for drying and use in a variety of potions, ointments, oils and tisanes. Herbs have been used since the earliest times to combat disease, and their healing properties are still acknowledged in present-day pharmacology. A small physic herb garden could be planted for its historical interest, for use in home remedies or simply for the pleasure of its scents; many medicinal herbs are especially fragrant – chamomile, fennel, pot marigold, evening primrose and rosemary among others.

Informal herb gardens are based on drifts of contrasting or complementary colour and form, like an old-fashioned cottage garden. Planting clumps of three, five or seven of a single herb is more natural looking than dotting them about, although large herbs, such as rosemary or bay, are effective by themselves. Try

to balance rounded shapes with upright and sprawling ones, and cool strongly contrasting colours, such as purple-leaved basil and golden marjoram, with greys and greens.

Whatever the layout, easy access to the herbs for care and harvesting is essential. A path within 75cm (2½ft) of the herb garden is sensible.

Herbs as companion plants

Herbs can be grown almost anywhere in a garden. Variegated mints, lemon balm and sage; purple basil, sage and fennel; moss-curled parsley, strongly scented lavender and rosemary are all highly ornamental plants for a herbaceous or mixed border. (Such herbs, like cut flowers, should be harvested little and often so that the appearance of the border doesn't suffer.)

Herbs are sometimes grown as companion plants in vegetable gardens, to keep nearby plants healthy and pest-free. Chives and garlic, for example, can help to deter carrot fly; mint and artemisia are useful near brassi-

cas. Try growing herbs as companion plants in ornamental gardens, where they have the same beneficial effect.

Old-fashioned herb lawns, paths, benches or seats set among hardy herbs and sunny banks are delightful, though they do need regular hand weeding as chemical weedkillers are unsuitable. For lawns and seats, the compact, non-flowering chamomile (*Anthemis nobilis* 'Treneague') is the most suitable as it does not need regular clipping. A carpet of creeping thyme, either a single type or a mixture of differently coloured and scented varieties, is another possibility.

A herb path of chamomile, pennyroyal (*Mentha pulegium*), creeping thyme or Corsican mint (*M. requienii*) is equally attractive, and wonderfully fragrant when walked on. Again, regular hand weeding is essential and, since many herbs are prolific at self-seeding, herb paths need constant attention. Herbs are unsuitable for much used paths. Growing herbs between paving stones cuts down weeding and allows

▲ **Chequerboard herb garden** In this traditional pattern, paving slabs alternate with planting squares for different types of herbs. It creates a pleasing and fragrant scene of contrasting shapes and colours, and the individual herbs are easy to pick.

light crushing of the leaves to release their fragrance.

Plant herbs such as lavender, hyssop, thyme or rosemary where they can tumble over the top of a sunny retaining wall, softening its appearance and making use of the retained heat.

Dry-stone walls, with soil between the joints, are an ideal home for thyme, hyssop and dwarf artemisia. Plant them as the wall is being built, or pack large joints in existing walls with moist soil into which seeds or tiny rooted cuttings are placed.

Large herbs, such as rosemary or lavender, can be used for low hedging. Smaller herbs, such as dwarf cotton lavender, or a dense row of golden feverfew, chives or parsley, make a delightful edging to an ornamental bed or herb garden.

flavour, colour and aroma can enhance the simplest dish. Annual and herbaceous perennial herbs can also be harvested and dried or frozen for winter use.

Popular herbs for the kitchen garden include basil, bay, chives, dill, fennel, garlic, marjoram, mint, parsley, rosemary, sage, salad burnet, winter and summer savory, tarragon and thyme. Anise, caraway, chervil, coriander and lovage are also grown for their distinctive flavours.

Kitchen herbs usually have modest flowers, but some have showy blooms, ideal for adding colour to a garden and for garnishing dishes. The bright blue flowers of borage, heartsease and violets are pretty in summer drinks, and can be crystallized or frozen in ice cubes. Pink or purple hyssop flowers, orange, yellow or scarlet nasturtium flowers and scarlet, blue or pink bergamot blooms add colour to a vegetable or fruit salad.

Medicinal herbs have been grown for thousands of years and many of these herbs play a role in modern homoeopathy. Herbal

▼ **Box edging** Low-growing evergreen box (*Buxus sempervirens* 'Suffruticosa') is traditionally used to edge individual herb beds. It responds well to clipping and is effective in outlining the shape of the small beds.

▲ **Traditional herb garden** Since medieval times, square or geometric designs have proved the most popular. Typically, a herb garden is planned around an ornamental feature, such as a bird-bath, sundial or statue, with beds of equal size and shape separated by gravel or brick paths.

Any free-draining container – flower pots, sinks and troughs, window-boxes, tubs, urns, wheelbarrows, hanging baskets, half-barrels – can house herbs. Strawberry pots are as ideal for herbs as they are for strawberries. The larger the container, the less it is prone to waterlogged, bone-dry or freezing growing conditions.

Types of herb

Most herbs are used for culinary purposes; others go into medicinal and cosmetic preparations, or pot-pourris, while a few are used for natural dyes.

Kitchen herbs are universal favourites, because their fresh

teas, or tisanes, are popular for soothing a wide range of minor ailments.

Chamomile tea is a relaxant and helps to induce sleep, and mint, fennel or dill tea can aid digestion. Horehound tea soothes sore throats, and bergamot tea is a digestive as well as a tonic. Lemon balm and lemon verbena also make relaxing teas. Medicinal herbs are commercially distilled in water, made into essential oils, smoked or worked into ointments, to be applied externally or taken internally.

Scented and cosmetic herbs have an equally long history. Lavender has been added to bath water since Roman times; its name is derived from the Latin word 'to wash'. Sage water is said to restore colour to greying hair, and to cure dandruff. Rosemary enhances the gloss of brunette hair, while chamomile makes fair hair even lighter. Lovage water is used to clean oily skins. Many other herbs

▲ **Soil and site** Many herbs are of Mediterranean origin and grow well in poor, stony soil – over-rich soil will encourage lax growth. They need an open site and most thrive in full sun, though chives tolerate light shade, and mint prefers it.

◀ **Herb beds** Keep herbs with different growth habits separate. Tall-growing lovage and feathery fennel would soon overshadow and obliterate ground-hugging thyme, and mint, unless it is restricted, is highly invasive, spreading rapidly from underground runners.

are used in cleansing and astringent lotions, in aromatherapy oils and in soothing creams.

Dye herbs have been largely replaced by commercial aniline dyes, but some herbs are still used in natural colours, especially for dyeing home-spun wool. Weld (*Reseda luteola*) and woad (*Isatis tinctoria*), the main traditional dye plants, can also be grown as decorative plants.

Decorative herbs

Many herbs are particularly noteworthy for their showy leaves. There are golden and silver-variegated forms, many grey-leaved types and several purple or bronze-leaved varieties.

The value of such herbs is twofold – their flavour is invariably as good as their green counterparts and, at the same time, they make ideal foils for flowering plants in mixed borders.

Of the plants with yellow and white markings, golden marjoram (*Origanum vulgare* 'Aureum') is among the richest coloured of all golden-leaved plants; it makes an eye-catching splash of colour in a lightly shaded spot.

The variegated lemon balms (*Melissa officinalis* 'Aurea' and 'All Gold') have larger, mint-like leaves, splashed with rich yellow, and are ideal for bringing light to a semi-shaded border. For a more subtle effect, choose variegated ginger mint (*Mentha* x *gentilis* 'Variegata') with bright green foliage veined with gold.

Cream or pale yellow leaf markings provide additional contrast of colour in a border. The variegated pineapple mint (*Mentha* x *rotundifolia* 'Variegata') is a particularly decorative example, having broad, irregularly shaped, creamy white leaf margins. The variegated rue (*Ruta graveolens* 'Variegata') has delicately lobed blue-green foliage marbled with rich cream.

Grey and blue foliage can be used on its own as a decorative feature, or it can be mixed with blue, mauve, yellow or white flowers for gentle contrast. Though there is a good range of garden plants with grey or bluish foliage, a selection of decorative scented herbs widens the choice.

Most members of the genus *Artemisia*, including southernwood and wormwood, bear grey or silvery leaves, usually deeply cut or lacy in shape. Curry plant (*Helichrysum angustifolium*) is often grown purely for its powerful spicy curry scent, but it is also worth growing for its needle-like silvery grey leaves. Clusters of mustard-yellow flowers top the plants in late summer.

The grey-green, needle-like leaves of rosemary (*Rosmarinus officinalis*) are coated with a white felt on the undersides – most noticeable in a gentle breeze. Sprays of pale mauve-blue flowers adorn the branches in late spring.

▼ **Informal herb garden** Clumps of herbs – culinary, medicinal and ornamental – grow unrestricted, mingling their scents and their foliage. Yet each retains its individuality in leaf, flower and seed heads.

The sub-shrubby rue (*Ruta graveolens* 'Jackman's Blue') is especially dramatic. It has deeply divided leaves with an acridly aromatic scent. Rarely used as a culinary herb, it makes a decorative foliage plant in a border or it can be grown as a low informal hedge.

One of the most familiar of all decorative herbs, purple-leaved sage (*Salvia officinalis* 'Purpurascens'), thrives in warm, dry positions. The leaves are rich red-

---

▶ **Paving pockets** Small pockets of soil between paving slabs are ideal for low-growing herbs. They are clean and easy to harvest and soften hard paving with pools of colour. Golden marjoram contrasts well with the greens of mint, chives and parsley.

▼ **Flowering herbs** Unless dead-headed in bud, chives flower profusely in early summer, and production of the onion-flavoured, grassy stems slows down. But flowering is so prolific and long-lasting that chives are often grown as a decorative edge to herbaceous beds and borders.

purple in colour and have a distinctive wrinkled texture.

For a dark, rather metallic red-purple choose *Ocimum basilicum* 'Dark Opal' – a decorative form of sweet basil. It looks stunning alongside silver-leaved plants.

Bronze fennel, a coloured-leaved form of *Foeniculum vulgare*, has the most delicate and feathery foliage of all garden plants. Though not as vigorous as the green form, bronze fennel can reach shoulder height and makes a spectacular focal point in a garden border.

Green foliage is not difficult to come by, but the richness and mossy texture of parsley

▶ **Gravel beds** A small formal garden of culinary and medicinal herbs has as its focal point an aromatic bay shrub. The individual beds, contained within brick walls, are edged with feverfew clipped to prevent self-seeding.

▼ **Herb wheel** A semicircular herb garden, with rosemary at its hub, is divided into wedge-shaped beds. Vigorous herbs, such as chives and lemon balm and salad burnet, are kept well apart from creeping thyme.

(*Petroselinum crispum*) is exceptional. Parsley's traditional role as a flavoursome and culinary garnish can be greatly extended. Grow it as a lush edging around a bed of bright summer annuals, or among softer green and golden foliage plants.

Sweet Cicely (*Myrrhis odorata*), with mid green, deeply divided leaves, has a fern-like appearance, and for a really bold centrepiece plant the towering angelica (*Angelica archangelica*), whose rounded heads of yellow-green flowers tower above huge bright green leaves.

Flowering herbs

For culinary purposes, most leafy herbs should not be allowed to flower, and the leaves should be harvested while they are still young. However, left to their own devices, many herbs bear handsome flowers that attract bees. A couple of plants can be allowed to flower for decoration.

Chives (*Allium schoenoprasum*) are very free-flowering, bearing a profusion of globular, rose-purple flower heads on upright stems in early summer among tufts of lush green, grass-like leaves.

English lavender (*Lavandula spica*) and French lavender (*L. stoechas*) have become such familiar flowering plants that their traditional uses – for fragrant sachets or pot-pourris, and for herbal medicine – tend to take second place. There are varieties with purple, mauve and white flower spikes.

Borage (*Borago officinalis*) and rosemary are also attractive when in bloom. Though not eye-catching, their shapely blue-mauve flowers deserve close inspection and are a constant lure for bees.

Sweet Cicely (*Myrrhis odorata*) – 'that herbe of very good and pleasant smell' according to the 16th-century herbalist, Gerard – bears airy clouds of white flowers in late spring, followed by clusters of shiny black seeds.

Herbs for scent

Herbs are unique among garden plants in that nearly all of them have aromatic foliage. Rub the

▶ **Herb parterre** Based on a traditional design, this newly planted herb garden is laid out in geometric shapes formed by concrete kerb stones. Each section is allotted a different herb.

leaves gently between your fingers to release the maximum scent from the volatile oils.

Among the strongest scents are the lavenders, mints and thymes, as well as lemon verbena. Thyme tolerates being crushed underfoot, so plant it in cracks between paving where it can waft its spicy perfume.

Picked and dried before the flowers develop fully, strong-scented herbs are popular in pot-pourri and sachet mixtures – they were formerly used as 'strewing' herbs and were included in nosegays to ward off pestilence.

Initial cost

Establishing a herb garden from scratch is no more expensive than starting a mixed or herbaceous border, and there are many ways to economize. Obviously, the larger the herb garden, the more plants will be needed, and the higher the cost.

Long-lived shrubby herbs, such as rosemary, lavender and especially bay, are more expensive than perennial herbs, such as fennel and chives, and annuals, such as sweet basil and chervil.

Lavender, rosemary, rue and box grow easily from cuttings taken in early summer and rooted in an outdoor nursery bed.

The slow-growing bay is propagated from heel cuttings taken in late summer and rooted in a cold frame. They are sometimes difficult to strike, and rooted cuttings take a couple of years to make sizeable plants.

Site and soil

Herbs vary in their demands for soil type and sun or shade – they include members of many families and come from dozens of different countries and climates. In general, they need ordinary well-drained soil and full sun.

Pale-leaved and variegated forms prefer dappled shade, or the leaves may scorch in summer. Mints do well in shade.

Lavender, marjoram and rosemary thrive on chalky soil, and borage, chamomile and thyme do well on sandy soil. Moist loamy soil is ideal for angelica, comfrey, lemon balm, parsley, chervil and sweet Cicely.

Sowing and planting

Most herbs can be grown easily from seed, generally sown in spring, and all annual herbs can only be raised in this manner. Buy seeds and carefully follow the instructions on the packet – sowing times and required temperatures for germination vary from herb to herb. Chives are increased by division.

Perennial and shrubby herbs, including variegated varieties, are raised commercially from cuttings. To ensure the best quality, buy young plants from a reputable nursery. They are usually container-grown and can be planted at any time of year, though the best results come from spring or autumn plantings.

Aftercare

Herbs benefit from a mulch of bark chippings or other organic materials to retain soil moisture and smother weeds.

On culinary, leafy herbs, all flower buds should be pinched out as they appear. A herb which flowers and sets seed will lose the flavour of its leaves as well as its compact habit. Trim shrubby herbs, such as lavender, after flowering to maintain compact growth. Straggly plants can be cut back in early spring.

▼ **Decorative herbs** Bronze-coloured fennel makes a feathery foil for the bold, silver-felted leaves and flower stems of verbascum. Silvery helichrysum and bluish-green, pungent rue add to the colour contrasts, and yellow irises punctuate the scene.

A-Z OF HERBS

**Culinary herbs are easy to grow, strong on flavour
and rich in vitamins and essential minerals.
They deserve a place in every garden.**

ANGELICA

Angelica makes a majestic display at the back of a herb garden or flower bed, especially as it can reach a height of 2-3m (7-10ft). It is a short-lived perennial or biennial that dies after it has produced seeds. However, if the flower stalks are cut off every year before the flowers develop, it can be kept alive for four or five years.

An ultra-hardy herb, thriving in damp meadows and on river banks, angelica is easy to grow, though it needs plenty of space.

The young, slightly bitter leaves can be boiled like spinach or added fresh to salads; the roots can be cooked like a vegetable, and the seeds used as a substitute for juniper berries and to flavour liqueurs. Most commonly, the young stems and leaf stalks are harvested before flowering and candied for decorating cakes and sweets.

Cultivation

Angelica does best in deep, rich, moist soil in a sunny or lightly shaded position. Dig the soil thoroughly during the winter before sowing.

Sow bought seeds in the prepared ground in early spring, or home-saved seed as soon as ripe, in late summer. Sow the seeds 1cm (½in) deep in groups of three or four and about 1m (3ft) apart, in their growing position, with a cloche over the drill in cold areas. As the seedlings develop, remove all but the strongest in each group.

Alternatively, sow the seeds in a seed bed and transplant the seedlings to their final site in late autumn or the following spring.

In the first year, angelica produces leaves but no stems. In the second or third year, it shoots up a tall flower stem bearing clusters of greenish-white flowers in early summer. If the flowers are allowed to go to seed, the plant dies, though self-sown seedlings appear freely.

Few pests trouble angelica.

▲ **Angelica** Young stems are candied for cake decoration and to sweeten acidic fruit desserts. Chopped leaves are added to salads, and the seeds are used in liqueur manufacture.

BASIL

Basil is grown for its pale green, highly aromatic leaves. It is a tender annual which cannot withstand frost and is therefore sown annually. There are two species: sweet basil (*Ocimum basilicum*), which reaches about 60cm (2ft) in height, and the coarser bush basil (*O. minimum*), which grows 15-30cm (6-12in) tall and is inferior in flavour.

The young leaves of sweet basil have a pleasant clove-like scent; they should be harvested at frequent intervals and used fresh, torn into pieces rather than chopped. They do not dry well and are better preserved packed, with a little salt, in jars of olive oil.

The purple-leaved cultivar 'Dark Opal' is highly decorative and equally suitable as a culinary herb.

◄ **Sweet basil** Popular as a flavouring for tomato dishes, basil is the chief ingredient in *pesto*, a green sauce for salads, vegetables, fish and pasta.

Cultivation

Basil needs a warm, sheltered site with well-drained, fertile soil. For early plants, sow seeds of sweet basil in early spring under glass. When the seedlings are large enough to handle, prick them out into trays of potting compost.

Harden off the plants in late spring, then plant them out into their final site, setting them 30cm (12in) apart. Water well until the plants are established. Basil seedlings can also be potted up and grown on a sunny windowsill. Give a liquid fertilizer once a month.

Alternatively, sow basil seeds outside in late spring in their growing position. Thin the seedlings to 30cm (12in) apart. Water well during dry weather and pinch out flower buds to encourage bushy growth. For a continuous supply of fresh leaves, make sowings at fortnightly intervals.

Slugs can be troublesome in wet summers.

BAY

▲ **Bay leaves** Strongly aromatic, bay leaves are used fresh or dried to flavour savoury and sweet dishes.

Sweet bay, or bay laurel (*Laurus nobilis*), is an evergreen shrub or small tree grown for its aromatic leaves. Although native to the Mediterranean, it is generally hardy in southern England and will normally survive most winters outdoors. It flourishes in coastal areas if protected from cold north and east winds.

Bay can reach 6m (20ft) or more if left to itself, but it is often grown in a tub or pot and kept to the desired shape and size by annual pruning.

Bay trees are highly ornamental as well as functional – clipped and trained cone-shaped or mop-headed specimens are often available from nurseries and garden centres. They are expensive, but long-lived as decorative specimen plants. As a free-growing shrub,

bay is suitable for a sheltered mixed border.

Bay leaves can be used fresh or dried. They flavour fish dishes, stews and casseroles, milk puddings and custards, and are essential in a traditional bouquet garni.

Cultivation

Bay grows in ordinary garden soil in a sunny, sheltered position. Use a loam-based potting compost for pot-grown specimens. In cold districts move them indoors or to a cold but frost-free greenhouse for the winter.

Plant in early or mid spring and water well until the shrub is established. Prune in summer to maintain shape. The leaves can be picked at any time of year.

To propagate, take heel cuttings in late summer or early autumn. Root the cuttings in pots of compost and keep over winter and the following summer in a cold frame; they are often slow to root. Water them just enough to prevent them from drying out. Grow the rooted cuttings on in a sheltered nursery bed for a couple of years.

Bay is generally disease free.

◄ **Bay tree** Often trained as standards and grown as specimen tub plants, bays can be clipped into topiary shapes. Trim to shape during summer.

BORAGE

Borage (*Borago officinalis*) is a hardy annual herb grown for its leaves – which have the cool taste of cucumber when crushed or bruised – and for its bright blue star-like flowers which are added to salads and summer drinks. Borne in drooping clusters, they are attractive to bees and ideal in raised positions. The plant grows 45-90cm (1½-3ft) tall.

Cultivation

Although borage grows in almost any soil, it does best in well-drained ground in a sunny position. Sow the seeds in mid spring and thin the seedlings to 30cm (12in) apart.

The seeds germinate readily and the seedlings grow rapidly; the leaves are ready for use about eight weeks after sowing. They become covered with fine woolly hairs as they age and should be harvested while still young. Use

them fresh, roughly chopped, as an addition to salads or iced drinks. Borage seeds itself freely, and once it is introduced to the garden it perpetuates itself from self-sown seedlings.

Borage is disease free; aphids may sometimes attack.

◄ **Borage** The young leaves are used to flavour salads and drinks.

▼ **Borage flowers** The bright blue starry flowers can be candied and used for cake decoration. They can also be floated fresh on chilled wine cups.

CARAWAY

Caraway is a hardy biennial that grows wild throughout Europe. In its first year it produces feathery leaves and grows about 20cm (8in) high. In its second year it sends up slender, branched stems 60-90cm (2-3ft) high.

Airy clusters of white or pink flowers are produced in late spring and early summer of the second year, followed by seed heads. The plants die after flowering.

Caraway is grown for its seeds – their strong, distinctive and liquorice-like flavour is used in breads, Victorian seedcakes and gingerbreads. They have digestive properties and are popular in German and Austrian cheeses and in cabbage and coleslaw.

The young green leaves can also be eaten – fresh in salads or cooked in soups – they have a less pungent flavour than the seeds.

The young taproots, too, are edible and much used in East European cookery.

Cultivation

Caraway likes fertile, well-drained soil in a sunny position. Seeds can be sown in early autumn, when germination is quick, or in early to mid spring. When the seedlings are about 5cm (2in) high, thin them to stand at least 20cm (8in) apart; they do not transplant easily. Autumn-sown seedlings will flower and set seed by the following summer.

The seeds begin to ripen in early to mid summer. Harvest the seed heads before the seeds have turned brown and begun to burst open – the plants seed themselves freely and self-sown seedlings could soon be all over the herb garden.

Cut the seed heads and hang them upside down enclosed in paper bags to dry in a cool place. When the seeds are thoroughly dry, clean them of chaff and stalks and store them in an airtight container until needed. They are used whole or ground.

▶ **Caraway seeds** Popular in East European and Scandinavian cookery, the pungent dried seeds are used whole or ground to flavour bread, cakes and cheeses.

CHERVIL

▲ **Chervil**
Small white flowers appear from early to late summer. The leaves have a delicate anise flavour and are used in *fines herbes* mixtures.

Chervil is an annual grown for its bright green feathery leaves which should be harvested while young. The plant grows 30-45cm (12-18in) high and bears clusters of white flowers.

Cultivation

Chervil grows in most well-drained soils in a sunny or partially shaded site.

Make successional sowings in the open between early spring and late summer. Sow the seeds 6mm (¼in) deep and thin the seedlings to 30cm (12in) apart.

Remove flowering stems as soon as they appear. Pick the leaves six to eight weeks after sowing and use fresh in soups, salads and egg dishes, and for garnishing.

CHIVES

Chives are hardy perennial plants grown for their bright green grass-like leaves which have a delicate onion flavour.

Cultivation

Chives grow in most good garden soils in a sunny or semi-shaded position.

It is quicker to buy young plants and set them 30cm (12in) apart, although chives can also be raised from seed sown in spring and transplanted a year later. They spread rapidly and established clumps should be divided and replanted every three years in early spring. Remove the flower heads as they appear to maintain a supply of leaves.

For fresh chives in winter, lift a clump in early autumn, set it in a 10cm (4in) pot of potting compost and place on a sunny window-sill.

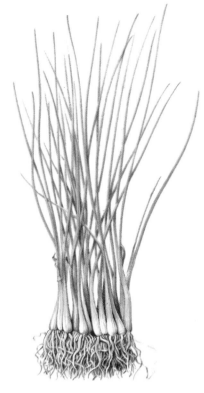

▲ **Chives** Cut the leaves close to the ground and scissor them over egg dishes, salads and dressings.

◀ **Flowering chives** The bright and cheerful flowers should be removed in favour of a long harvest of leaves.

CORIANDER

Coriander is a hardy annual grown for its parsley-like leaves and for its seeds, which have a bitter-sweet flavour and are used in curries, pickles, cakes, puddings and cheeses. The leaves are used fresh in the same way as parsley: chopped over vegetables and salads, added as flavouring to lamb and pork dishes and also used for garnishing. The leaves do not dry well, but are suitable for freezing.

Coriander seeds are sweetly aromatic; they are commonly used to flavour Eastern dishes and are essential in curry spices. Store the harvested seeds whole and grind them as required.

Coriander grows 45-60cm (18-24in) high as a slender, sparsely branched plant. It bears clusters of white or pale mauve flowers from early to late summer followed by small brown seeds.

◀ **Coriander** One of the ancient herbs and popular in Eastern cookery, coriander is grown for its pleasantly aromatic leaves. Its flowers are followed by seeds, which are used dried in savoury dishes and pickles.

Cultivation

Coriander grows in any good well-drained soil and needs a sunny sheltered position.

Sow seeds outdoors 6mm (¼in) deep in late spring. When large enough to handle, thin the seedlings to 10-15cm (4-6in) apart. About a dozen plants will provide enough leaves and seeds for the average household.

Begin to pick the leaves when the plants are 15cm (6in) high. The seeds are ready for harvesting in late summer when they become pale in colour and smell pleasantly spicy.

Cut the plants at ground level and hang them upside down to dry in a cool and airy place. Shake out the dry seeds and store them in an airtight container. The seeds can also be used for sowing the following spring; they remain viable and can be used for propagation for up to five years.

Coriander is easily grown in pots – indoors or out. They are best supported with thin canes as they become top-heavy with the ripening seed heads.

DILL

Dill is a hardy annual, up to 1m (3ft) high, and grown for its delicate leaves and its seeds.

It thrives in any well-drained but moist soil in an open, sunny site. Sow seeds at monthly intervals from early spring to mid summer for a constant supply throughout the summer and autumn, thinning the seedlings to 23cm (9in) apart.

Harvest the leaves fresh and use in sauces, with cucumber, beetroot and tomatoes, and for garnishing. They can also be frozen or dried though they lose much of their aniseed flavour in drying.

The seed heads ripen in late summer and are used fresh or dry to flavour pickled cucumbers.

Avoid growing dill near fennel; the two cross-pollinate easily, and the resulting seedlings are neither one thing nor the other.

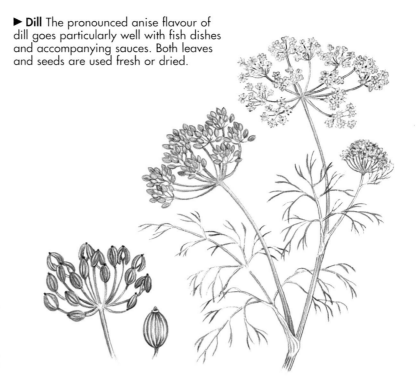

► **Dill** The pronounced anise flavour of dill goes particularly well with fish dishes and accompanying sauces. Both leaves and seeds are used fresh or dried.

FENNEL

▲ **Fennel** The feathery leaves are best used fresh – in fish and cheese dishes. Fennel seeds, with a much stronger flavour, are used in pickles.

► **Decorative fennel** Bronze and green-leaved fennel are highly ornamental and suitable for growing as foliage plants in borders. Both can be used for culinary purposes and grow 1.5-2.4m (5-8ft) high.

Fennel is a tall, graceful perennial grown for the aniseed flavour of its leaves and seeds.

Cultivation
Fennel likes any well-drained soil in a sunny position.

Sow seeds thinly in early spring for seeds to ripen in early to mid autumn, and in mid to late spring if grown for leaves only. Thin the seedlings to 30cm (12in) apart.

Harvest the leaves from early summer onwards and dead-head unless seeds are wanted. Gather the seed heads in early autumn when they are pale brown and hang them upside down to dry in a cool and airy place. Store the seeds in airtight containers.

Cut the tall stems back to ground level in late autumn.

GARLIC

The onion-like garlic is indispensable in Mediterranean cookery and grows well in temperate climates. It grows to a height of about 30-90cm (1-3ft).

Garlic likes light, fertile soil and full sun. At the end of late winter or in early spring, plant cloves 15cm (6in) apart, pointed end upwards and just covered by soil. Remove any flower stalks as they appear.

Lift garlic at the end of summer when the foliage has begun to die down. Ease the bulbs out with a fork and leave them to dry thoroughly in a dry and shady site for two or three weeks before storing them.

Garlic is sometimes affected by onion eelworm and white rot.

▲ **Garlic bulbs** Each bulb contains a dozen or so cloves with a papery covering. Fresh or cooked, they are used to flavour innumerable savoury dishes.

▶ **Harvesting garlic** Lift the bulbs carefully as the foliage dies down. Dry the bulbs for several weeks before storing them.

HORSERADISH

Horseradish grows wild in many places and it is easy to grow a few plants in a corner of the garden; site it carefully as the taproots and long branching side-roots sucker freely and are almost impossible to eradicate.

The fleshy roots are long, white and sharp-tasting and grow to a length of about 30cm (1ft). The basal leaves grow 60-90cm (2-3ft) high and die down in winter.

Cultivation

Horseradish prefers rich, moist soil in a sunny or partially shaded position. The winter before planting, dig the plot deeply, working in plenty of compost.

Plant young root cuttings, known as thongs, in early spring, spacing them 60cm (2ft) apart and with the thick upper part of each cutting 7.5-10cm (3-4in) below ground level. Leave the young plants in the ground for at least two years before harvesting, but each year, in early summer, dig around the plants and rub out any side-roots so as to ensure a single, well-formed taproot.

Dig up the roots in late summer when they have the best flavour, or as and when required. The roots can be stored over winter in damp sand. If necessary, spare roots can be cut into 15cm (6in) pieces and planted out in spring.

Horseradish may be affected by leaf spot and white blister.

◀ **Horseradish** Traditional as an accompaniment to roast beef, horseradish has the best flavour when freshly peeled and grated – to floods of tears by the cook.

HYSSOP

Hyssop is a hardy, evergreen sub-shrub which grows 60cm (2ft) high and wide. From mid summer to autumn it bears spikes of blue, pink or white flowers which are attractive to bees. The foliage releases a pungent scent when bruised. Hyssop is frequently grown as a low hedge around herb beds and vegetable plots; it is said to discourage cabbage-white butterflies.

Cultivation

Hyssop grows best in well-drained soil in a sunny position.

Plant in autumn or spring or sow seeds outdoors in late spring. When the seedlings are large enough to handle, thin them to 7.5cm (3in) apart. Transplant them to their permanent positions between autumn and spring, spaced 30cm (12in) apart.

Encourage bushy growth by removing the tips of main shoots. When well established, trim the plants to shape in spring.

Pick hyssop leaves for use in salads in early summer.

▶ **Hyssop** Once used as a strewing herb, fragrant hyssop is now mainly grown for decorative purposes. Its minty young leaves can be used in salads.

LEMON BALM

Lemon balm (*Melissa officinalis*) is a strongly aromatic perennial. It has a bushy habit with hairy, upright stems reaching a height of 90cm (3ft). The lemon-scented leaves measure 7.5cm (3in) long and are pale green. Small flowers – usually white – appear in mid summer. The golden-leaved variety 'Aurea' is particularly decorative.

Cultivation

Lemon balm is slow to germinate and should be grown from seeds sown under glass in early spring.

Alternatively, grow from stem cuttings or from divisions in spring or autumn.

Set the plants 30cm (12in) apart in ordinary, even poor soil in a sunny position. Keep well watered during the first summer. In subsequent years, cut the stems back to 15cm (6in) in early summer to encourage new growth. In severe winters cover with straw or bracken. Harvest throughout summer for immediate use; leaves for drying should be picked before the plants begin to flower.

▲ **Lemon balm** Traditionally used as a mild substitute for lemon, the leaves of lemon balm can also be floated on chilled drinks and used to flavour egg and chicken dishes.

▶ **Variegated lemon balm** Of limited culinary value, lemon balms are decorative foliage plants. Dried leaves can be added to pot-pourris.

LEMON VERBENA

▲ **Lemon verbena** A half-hardy shrub, lemon verbena has a strong flavour and, used sparingly, adds a pleasant flavour to fruit salads, jellies and drinks. Use the young leaves only – older ones tend to be tough.

Lemon verbena (*Aloysia triphylla*, syn. *Lippia citriodora*) is an aromatic, half-hardy shrub, which can grow to a height of 3m (10ft) in ideal conditions, but is rarely more than 1.5m (5ft) tall in temperate climates.

It has woody, branching stems with narrow pointed leaves that have a strong, persistent smell and flavour of lemon. Small white or pale mauve flowers appear from mid to late summer, but are insignificant.

Cultivation

Plant in ordinary to poor, well-drained soil in late spring, in a warm and sheltered site, ideally against a sunny wall.

Lemon verbena needs protection from strong winds and during winter if grown outdoors. Cover the root area with a thick layer of straw to reduce the effects of frost. Alternatively, lemon verbena can be grown in containers and pots and brought indoors for the winter.

Pot-grown plants need regular watering in summer, very little in winter. Prune in late winter to within 30cm (1ft) of the base and

pinch out the shoots during the growing season to prevent the shrub from becoming straggly.

Harvest the leaves as the flowers come into bloom and store in an airtight jar after drying. They keep their aroma for several years.

Increase the plants from stem cuttings taken in early summer. They can also be grown from seeds sown under glass during early spring.

Lemon verbena has several uses. It can flavour salads, jellies and iced drinks, but should be used sparingly because of its strong flavour.

Dry the leaves quickly in a warm dark place so that the aroma is retained. They can be used in cushions and sachets to scent clothes and bed linen; a mixture of lemon verbena, lemon balm and lemon-scented geranium imparts a fresh fragrance. Or use the dried leaves in herbal bath infusions. The essential oil extracted from lemon verbena is used in the manufacture of soaps, perfumes and cosmetics.

Lemon verbena is prone to attacks by red spider mites.

LOVAGE

◄ **Lovage** A tall aromatic herb, lovage is used to flavour soups, salads and casseroles. Young leaves can be cooked as a vegetable or to add celery flavour to a dish, and the dried seeds can flavour soft cheeses, cakes and biscuits.

Lovage (*Levisticum officinale*) is a hardy giant perennial reaching a height of up to 2m (7ft). It has an erect stem with large, dark green, deeply divided leaves. Small, pale, green-yellow flowers are produced between early and mid summer. Lovage seeds are oblong and brown. All parts of the herb are edible and have a strong aroma and flavour reminiscent of celery.

One plant will provide ample fresh and dried leaves as well as seeds for culinary purposes. The stems can be candied and used like angelica.

Cultivation
Sow lovage seeds in late summer or early spring in a seed bed or where the plants are to grow – preferably at the back of a herb border. Lovage can also be grown by dividing the fleshy roots – each piece should have a strong growth bud. Plants die down to the ground in winter.

Sow ripe seeds in rich, moist soil in sun or partial shade. When the seedlings are large enough to handle, thin them to 30cm (1ft) apart, or transplant them to their permanent positions, leaving a similar space between the young plants. In good soil lovage will last for many years. It is, however, invasive and will self-seed unless dead-headed.

During summer remove the early flowers to encourage the growth of young leaves. Use the leaves fresh or lightly blanched. They are excellent in vegetable soups, mixed salads and as flavouring for vinegars. Finely chopped, they can be sprinkled over young carrots and beans and added to herb butters.

The dried leaves are used in pot-pourris, the dried seeds in cake and biscuit making.

Lovage is generally pest and disease free but may occasionally be attacked by leaf mining fly and celery fly.

MARJORAM

There are two main types of marjoram. Sweet or knotted marjoram (*Origanum majorana*) is a tender perennial, reaching up to 45cm (1½ft) high with sweetly scented, grey-green leaves and tiny pink or white flowers in summer. Pot marjoram (*Origanum onites*) is a hardy sub-shrub with mauve to pink flowers; it grows 30cm (1ft) or more in height. Its leaves are less sweet, often bitter.

Wild marjoram or oreganum (*Origanum vulgare*) grows wild on chalk downs in Britain, but when grown in cold northern climates, the leaves lack the pungent flavour of Italian oregano.

Cultivation
Marjoram needs full sun and well-drained, fertile soil. Sweet marjoram is treated as a half-hardy annual and sown under glass during early spring; prick out the seedlings when they are large enough to handle into pots of potting compost. Harden off before planting out in late spring and space 30cm (1ft) apart.

Pot marjoram, which is fully

▲ **Marjoram** Pinch out the flowers as soon as they develop to encourage the growth of fresh shoots and leaves.

hardy, can be sown outdoors in mid to late spring; thin to 60cm (2ft) apart. Pot marjoram can also be grown from cuttings of basal shoots in early spring.

Begin harvesting leaves and stem tips when the plants are 10cm (4in) high. New stems and shoots will continue to grow. The leaves can be used fresh; they are also suitable for drying and freezing.

▲ **Culinary marjoram** Sweet marjoram (left) and pot marjoram (right) are used in cooking. Both are aromatic and flavour meat, fish, egg, pasta and cheese dishes. Marjoram is also excellent with tomatoes, potatoes and in salad dressings.

MINT

Mints are hardy perennial plants, with a wide range of flavours and scents. Although mint has been known and used as a flavouring since antiquity and was introduced to Britain by the Romans, it is now little used in European cookery. It remains the favourite herb in Britain and also features strongly in Middle Eastern dishes.

Spearmint or garden mint (*Mentha spicata*) is probably the most commonly grown and is used to flavour young vegetables, chilled drinks, cold sauces, jellies and chutneys. It grows up to 60cm (2ft) high, with bright green leaves with serrated edges; mauve flowers are borne from late summer to early autumn.

Peppermint (*Mentha x piperita*) grows to the same height, but has green or black-green, oval, deeply indented leaves, on green or reddish-purple stems. The small mauve or white flowers are sterile. It is used commercially to flavour sweets and liqueurs.

Apple mint or round-leaved mint (*Mentha rotundifolia*) is considered the best mint, with a refreshing scent and flavour of apples and mint. Growing up to 45cm (1½ft) high, it has reddish, erect stems and oblong or round, toothed leaves, green above and white and velvety beneath. The flowers are white or pale mauve.

Bergamot mint (*Mentha x piperita* 'Citrata') smells like eau-

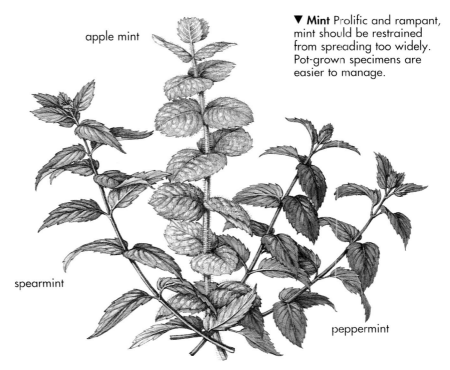

apple mint

spearmint

peppermint

▼ **Mint** Prolific and rampant, mint should be restrained from spreading too widely. Pot-grown specimens are easier to manage.

de-Cologne. It grows up to 60cm (2ft) tall with dark green leaves, tinged with purple; the flowers are mauve.

Among the many other species are decorative pineapple mint, with long stems, long downy leaves, variegated cream and apple green; and spicy ginger mint, which has oval, pointed shiny leaves, variegated with yellow and green.

Cultivation

Mint is only too easy to grow – the problem is keeping it from spreading all over the garden. The creep-

ing rhizomes can be contained by tiles sunk in the ground or by growing the plants in bottomless containers in the soil.

A deep moist soil in a semi-shaded area is suitable, but mint will grow almost anywhere, including damp, dark corners where few other plants survive.

Dig over the ground in late winter, incorporating a spadeful or two of well-rotted garden compost or manure.

Plant mint in early spring, 5cm (2in) deep and 15cm (6in) apart. Three or four shoots should produce an ample supply for cooking and drying.

Water the soil thoroughly after planting. After this, mint should need little attention. If necessary, the plants can be divided and replanted in late autumn. Mints die back each winter and reappear from early to mid spring, producing leaves for picking any time from late spring until early autumn. They can be dried but quickly lose their flavour.

For fresh supplies of mint throughout the winter, put young plants or pieces of root in pots of potting compost in mid autumn and keep them on a window-sill.

Mint is hardly ever troubled by pests, but may suffer from rust and powdery mildew.

◄ **Ginger mint** (*Mentha x gentilis*) One of the more decorative forms, ginger mint bears pointed leaves, variegated yellow and green. Quick-spreading, it makes unusual ground cover.

PARSLEY

▲ **Parsley** The most commonly grown herb, parsley is an essential ingredient in *fines herbes* and bouquet garni and is used to flavour a wide range of savoury dishes.

Parsley (*Petroselinum crispum*) is a hardy biennial herb usually grown as an annual. Rich in vitamins A and C, and with a distinctive, mildly spicy flavour, it is widely used for garnishing and for flavouring stocks, soups, sauces, dressings and stuffings.

The leaves are triangular and deeply incised and most varieties are curled. Plain-leaved parsley has a more intense flavour.

Cultivation

Parsley thrives in well-drained, fertile soil in a sunny or partly shaded position. Sow in drills 6mm (¼in) deep, where the plants are to grow. The seed is slow to germinate in spring, sometimes taking up to five weeks; germination can be speeded by soaking the seeds for 24 hours in lukewarm water or by watering the drills with warm water. Keep the soil moist by watering through a fine rose.

Thin the seedlings to 7.5cm (3in) apart, later to 23cm (9in). Provide partial shade for seeds and seedlings sown in mid summer. In cold districts, cover late-sown parsley with cloches so as to

▲ **Parsley varieties** Curled and flat-leaved varieties are available. They thrive in well-drained, fertile soil in a sunny or partly shaded position.

encourage winter growth. Parsley is easily grown indoors on a sunny sill, in ordinary pots or purpose-made, lipped containers.

The leaves can be dried though they lose much of their flavour in the process. They are better frozen, coarsely chopped, in ice-cube trays and added to soups and sauces.

Parsley is occasionally attacked by aphids and carrot fly. It is also susceptible to leaf spot.

ROSEMARY

An evergreen, strongly aromatic shrub, rosemary (*Rosmarinus officinalis*) grows to a maximum height of 2m (7ft), though rarely more than 1.2m (4ft) in Britain. Fresh or dried, rosemary leaves are used to season roast meat and game, and strongly flavoured fish.

Rosemary leaves are narrow and tough, dark green above and white and downy underneath. Pale mauve-blue flowers, sometimes white, are borne in small clusters in the leaf axils from mid spring to early summer.

Cultivation

Rosemary thrives in any well-drained soil, in a sunny position and sheltered from cold winds. Set out young plants in mid or late spring.

Old shrubs tend to grow leggy; prune them hard back – by up to half – in mid spring.

Increase rosemary from 15-20cm (6-8in) long cuttings of half-ripe, non-flowering shoots between early summer and early autumn. Root them in a cold frame. Transfer the rooted cut-

▲ **Rosemary** One of the oldest herbs – the herb of remembrance – rosemary is a handsome evergreen shrub for sunny and sheltered borders.

tings to 7.5cm (3in) pots of potting compost and plant out the following late spring.

Hardwood cuttings, 15-20cm (6-8in) long, taken in early or mid autumn, can be rooted in a sheltered outdoor nursery bed.

Rosemary sprigs can be dried, but as the plant is evergreen, fresh supplies are always available.

▶ **Flowering rosemary** The pale mauve-blue flowers of rosemary open from mid to late spring, but mature plants may produce a few flowers at almost any time of year. The narrow, dark green leaves are heavily scented, most strongly just before flowering.

SAGE

An attractive evergreen shrub, sage (*Salvia officinalis*) grows 60cm (2ft) or more tall. It has wrinkled, slightly hairy grey-green leaves with a strong, rather bitter taste and aroma. It is excellent for flavouring rich, fatty meats and stuffings.

There are hundreds of varieties of *Salvia*, but the most useful for cooking is common sage which has lilac, purple or blue flowers in summer. Purple sage (*Salvia officinalis* 'Purpurascens'), with deep purple leaves, is a highly decorative foliage plant and also suitable as a culinary herb.

The wonderfully aromatic pineapple sage (*Salvia rutilans*), with bright scarlet flowers, is half-hardy to tender and will not survive the winter outdoors. It can be grown as a pot plant under glass. Use the leaves in pot-pourris.

Harvest the leaves as required – flavour is at its best in mid summer, just before the flowers appear. They can also be dried, though this is hardly necessary.

Clary (*Salvia sclarea*) is a biennial, usually grown as an annual. Like common sage it can be used as a culinary herb, fresh, dried or frozen, to flavour soups and stews, but it is decorative enough to be grown in flower borders. It bears hairy, triangular and pungently aromatic leaves and, in late summer, tubular blue-white flowers with striking purple-blue bracts.

▼ **Decorative sage** Culinary salvias are evergreen and retain their leaves through most winters. Even when top growth is killed by severe frosts, the plants often shoot again from the base.

Cultivation

Sage does best in a sunny, sheltered position and needs a rich, well-drained, slightly alkaline soil. Dig over the ground in late winter, incorporating well-rotted garden compost or manure.

Small pot-grown sage plants are widely available, or seeds can be sown in a greenhouse or cold frame in early spring. Prick out the seedlings into trays, later potting on into 7.5cm (3in) pots. Plant out the seedlings when the roots fill the pots and all danger of frost is past, setting the plants 30cm (12in) apart.

Alternatively, sow seeds directly in open ground in mid to late spring. Transplant the seedlings to a nursery bed; move to the final site in autumn.

Keep the growing plants well watered during dry spells, and weed carefully to avoid damaging the roots. On established plants, cut the previous year's growth back in mid summer to keep the plants from becoming straggly. In cold areas mulch the plants with straw before the first frost.

Propagation

Sage becomes woody with age and should be renewed every four or five years. Take semi-hardwood cuttings in summer and root them in a cold frame. Pot the rooted cuttings on into individual pots and overwinter them in the cold frame. In early spring pinch out the growing tips to encourage bushiness. Plant out in mid spring.

Alternatively, take 15-20cm (6-8in) long hardwood cuttings in late summer or early autumn and root them in an outdoor nursery bed.

Pests and diseases

Capsid bugs sometimes attack leaves and shoots. Grey mould fungus may also occur.

▼ **Sage** The distinctive pungent flavour of sage blends well with rich, strong-flavoured meat. Finely chopped leaves can be added sparingly to cream cheese, omelettes and casseroles.

common sage

purple sage

golden sage

SALAD BURNET

Salad burnet (*Sanguisorba minor*), a hardy perennial, is one of the lesser well-known culinary herbs, though it is regaining popularity. Its young leaves have a fresh cucumber taste, pleasant in salads, soups and sauces and as a garnish. They are also used to flavour iced drinks. Use only young leaves – old ones are bitter.

This is a native herb of Britain's chalk downlands, but in cultivation it grows much larger – up to 60cm (2ft) – than in the wild. It is almost evergreen, the leaves staying green throughout winter if the weather is not too harsh.

Salad burnet thrives on light, well-drained soil in a sunny position. A dressing of lime is beneficial on all but chalky soils.

Set out pot-grown plants in spring, or sow seeds outdoors in a seed bed in early or mid spring. When the seedlings are large enough to handle, transplant them to their permanent positions.

Keep the soil moist until the plants are established, and hoe often until the salad burnet is large enough to smother weeds.

Pick and use the leaves while they are young and tender, before the plants have a chance to flower. They are suitable for freezing. Cut back the flowering stems with greenish and purpled-red flowers as they develop to encourage more young leaves. If allowed to flower and set seed, salad burnet will spread widely through self-sown seedlings.

To increase stock, lift and divide established plants in early or mid spring, replanting the divisions immediately.

Salad burnet is generally free of pests and diseases.

▲ **Salad burnet** Finely chopped fresh leaves can be added to soups, sauces, dressings and salads. The fresh, cucumber-like taste goes particularly well with egg, fish and vegetable dishes.

SORREL

There are several varieties of sorrel, including the wild dock. Common or garden sorrel (*Rumex acetosa*) grows wild in Britain and has sharp-tasting leaves with a high oxalic acid content which can be poisonous in large amounts.

Less acid and altogether more delicate in flavour is French or buckler-leaved sorrel (*Rumex scutatus*), traditionally used in sorrel soup and in the green sauces served with roast pork and goose.

Herb patience (*Rumex patientia*) is a close relation. Growing up to 1.5m (5ft) tall, it is used as a green spring vegetable.

Nurserymen offer seeds of both types, but young plants at garden centres are not always clearly labelled. The different types of sorrel can be identified as follows:
☐ Common sorrel: long, narrowly arrow-head shaped leaves with lobes that point downwards; branched stems with small green and red flowers in erect spikes. Height in flower 30-60cm (1-2ft).
☐ French, shield or buckler-leaved sorrel: smaller, broader and bright green arrow-head shaped leaves. Tiny green flowers with red tints are borne in loose spikes. Height in flower 45cm (1½ft).

Sorrel is a perennial and can be left to grow in the same spot for several years. It does well in any well-drained soil, particularly if it

common sorrel

French, shield or buckler-leaved sorrel

▲ **Sorrel** The pointed and narrow leaves of common sorrel look like those of a small dock; they are one of the first green growths of spring.

▲ **French sorrel** Used in traditional sorrel soup, the chopped leaves are also used in stuffings for fish. As a purée, they can be eaten like spinach or added to omelettes.

is acid, and likes to be kept moist. Common sorrel tolerates partial shade; French sorrel is better in sun and prefers dryish soil.

Prepare a bed by thorough digging in late winter, adding well-rotted compost. Sow seeds in mid spring and thin the seedlings to 3-5cm (1-2in) apart.

Set the plants out in permanent positions in mid to late spring, 30-45cm (1-1½ft) apart.

Pick sorrel leaves when young – old leaves are tough and acidic. Common sorrel leaves picked when they are no more than 7.5-10cm (3-4in) have a pleasant lemony taste. French sorrel can be picked at any time. Cut flowering stems down to base before they have developed, to encourage the growth of leaves.

To increase stock, divide and replant mature plants in spring or autumn; both kinds will self-seed if allowed to flower.

SUMMER AND WINTER SAVORY

Two types of savory are grown for their small, peppery, aromatic leaves which are used in stuffings or with legumes such as peas and beans. Summer savory (*Satureia hortensis*) is a bushy annual and has the sweeter flavour, reminiscent of thyme, but more bitter. Winter savory (*Satureia montana*) is a hardy perennial or evergreen sub-shrub. The leaves of winter savory can be picked all year round, and, like summer savory, are suitable for drying.

Cultivation

Both types grow well in a sunny position in ordinary well-drained garden soil.

Sow summer savory seeds in mid spring. When the seedlings are about 5cm (2in) high, thin to approximately 15-23cm (6-9in) apart. It is important to keep the plants watered in dry weather.

Make successive sowings at fortnightly intervals for a ready supply of young leaves.

Winter savory is slow to germinate and is usually started from rooted cuttings planted 30cm (12in) apart in early spring. It becomes woody with age and should be replaced every few years with new stock.

Old leaves often have a slightly bitter flavour, so pick fresh young leaves and shoots as needed – use them to flavour peas and beans, in the same way as mint. Chopped, they can also season sauces, meat stuffings and bouquets garnis.

Savory is pungent and should be used sparingly. The leaves dry well, losing little of their sharp flavour. Pick the shoots of summer savory for drying in summer before the pink flowers appear.

Savory is generally free of pests and diseases.

winter savory

summer savory

SWEET CICELY

Pleasantly scented and decorative, sweet Cicely (*Myrrhis odorata*) is not a herb for the window-box or small herb garden – it is a large long-lived perennial which will, in time, reach 90cm-1.5m (3-5ft) in height and spread.

Also known as giant chervil or anise fern, sweet Cicely has a sweet anise-like fragrance and taste in all its parts. In the past the long taproot was boiled and

▲ **Sweet Cicely** Once known as sweet fern, the delicate fern-like leaves of sweet Cicely are used to temper the acidity of tart fruit. Ripe seeds can be included in fruit chutneys.

served sliced, dressed with vinegar, and the green seeds were used in salad dressings. Today, sweet Cicely is more often grown as an ornamental border plant although the leaves are good for adding a sweet flavour to stewed fruit. Add a chopped frond or two to stewed rhubarb, gooseberries, tart plums or apples, and the amount of sugar can be reduced.

The seeds of sweet Cicely share the aniseed flavour of the leaves. Unlike most other herbs, flowering does not impair the flavour of the leaves, and the seeds ripen to a glossy black colour.

Cultivation

Sweet Cicely grows well in most conditions but does best in moist acid soil. Set pot-grown plants out in spring, 60cm (2ft) apart.

Alternatively, sow seeds in the permanent site between winter and late spring or from late summer to mid autumn. To germinate successfully, the seeds should be exposed to cold. Leave them in the refrigerator for about a month before sowing.

Keep the plants well watered in hot weather and pick leaves often to encourage more to appear.

The plant dies down in autumn, but starts into growth again early in spring.

sweet Cicely

Sweet Cicely self-seeds freely and seedlings can be used to increase the stock. Alternatively, take root cuttings in autumn or winter and leave in a cold frame; or divide and replant the roots in spring or autumn.

Sweet Cicely is usually trouble free; remove any leaves that turn brown at the tips.

TARRAGON

A hardy perennial, tarragon is one of the classic herbs, essential in *fines herbes* mixtures. The sweetly aromatic leaves are also used to flavour fish, veal and chicken dishes, sauces, salad dressings and vinegars.

Tarragon is easy to grow and needs little attention, but for culinary use it is important to choose the right type.

French tarragon (*Artemisia dracunculus sativa*) has smooth dark green leaves and a superior flavour to Russian tarragon (*Artemisia dracunculus inodora*), which is a fresher green with rougher leaves. Not all garden centres distinguish between the two, so take care when buying. French tarragon has a strong, sweet smell; test by crushing a leaf between your fingers. Packaged seeds are invariably Russian tarragon.

Cultivation

Tarragon thrives in a sunny position in any well-drained soil. Dig strawy manure into heavy soil at the rate of one bucket to the square m/yd in the autumn before planting.

Tarragon reaches 60cm (2ft) or more in height, and quickly spreads to clumps from underground runners. It flowers in late summer, with clusters of tiny green-white flowers that rarely open fully.

Buy pot-grown plants and set out in permanent sites in mid autumn or early spring. Keep them well watered during dry spells.

Once established, tarragon survives for years. However, the plants retain their flavour best if lifted and divided every three years. Lift in early or mid spring and pull the underground runners apart. Replant the divisions immediately, setting them 38cm (15in) apart.

Pick fresh leaves from summer until autumn. Sprigs can be dried or frozen, but they have less flavour than fresh tarragon.

THYME

Although wild thyme grows profusely on the chalk downs of southern England, the common thyme used in cooking comes from the Mediterranean. It is a hardy evergreen shrub with tiny leaves that have a distinctive, slightly sweet, spicy flavour. There are many varieties, including the sweetly scented orange and lemon thyme.

Both common thyme (*Thymus vulgaris*) and lemon thyme (*T. x citriodorus*) reach a height of 20cm (8in), with a spread of 30cm (12in) or more. The tiny flowers are lilac or purple in colour. Lemon thyme has larger, more rounded leaves and comes into flower as ordinary thyme finishes. Bees love them both.

Thyme is an essential ingredient in bouquets garnis, and its highly aromatic leaves are used to flavour salads, soups, stews, sauces and all types of baked, grilled and roast meats and fish. Commercially, thyme is used in antiseptic preparations, in soaps and in the manufacture of liqueurs. Lemon thyme is also used in custards and stewed fruit; dried it goes into potpourri mixtures.

Cultivation

Thyme thrives in full sun in a

lemon thyme

common thyme

well-drained soil. Plants can be grown from seed, though germination is slow.

Sow seeds in a cold frame in spring. When the seedlings are large enough to handle, prick them out into 5cm (2in) pots and grow on for one or two years before planting out.

It is quicker to raise plants from cuttings of side-shoots with a heel taken in mid summer. Root the cuttings in a cold frame. Pot up the rooted cuttings and plant out in early autumn.

Alternatively, divide and replant the roots of established plants in spring. Thyme roots naturally from layers where they touch the soil.

Pick sprigs of leaves as needed. Because thyme is evergreen, there is little point in drying or freezing the leaves.

▲ **Aromatic thyme** One of the main herbs in a bouquet garni and much used in cookery, thyme makes a delightful carpeting and paving plant.

Decorative features

Plants are the mainstay of the garden, but their visual impact can be greatly enhanced with a range of ornaments. Pots and containers, in a wide choice of sizes, shapes, colours and materials, from inexpensive plastic to costly natural stone, are widely available. They are ideal for window and patio displays, for miniature pools and alpine landscapes and can be moved around to fill empty spaces, bring colour to dark backgrounds, create charming focal points and hide eyesores.

Sculptures and statuary have been used for garden ornaments since ancient times. Properly sited, they add individual touches and serve as focal points, half-hidden surprises or humorous afterthoughts. They range from modern abstract shapes to reproductions of classical statues, mythical beasts and animal representations, sundials, wall fountains and colourful garden gnomes.

Stone, metal and wood have natural affinities with the garden and are used for both decorative and functional purposes. Timber features – rustic seating and fencing, front gates and wooden bridges – suit almost all types of gardens, while ornate metal gates and wrought-iron furniture often look more appropriate in formal settings. The choice of garden furniture is largely a matter of personal taste and budget, and while expensive materials such as teak will last a lifetime, there is much to be said for less costly and maintenance-free plastic furniture and lightweight sun loungers.

The ultimate finishing touch for the garden scene is outdoor lighting. It is important for safety and security by front entrances and paths, and well-placed spotlights can create dramatic effects among foliage plants and fountains and illuminate barbecues and patios for outdoor entertaining.

Pot assembly Ornate glazed urns, terracotta pots and old coal scuttles make suitable plant containers.

POTS AND CONTAINERS

Convenient to plant and easy to move around, containers of all shapes, sizes and colours create instant focal points and are indispensable in small gardens.

Containers are essential for housing plants on a patio or other hard surface. They are the mainstay of small and tiny gardens, and in a conventional garden, composed of lawn and flower beds, containers make ideal finishing touches.

The range of shapes, sizes, colours, materials and costs is vast. Before buying, consider such practical points as size and strength. Containers should be large enough and deep enough for the plants; they should also be sturdy so they are not blown over. Restrict the use of heavy materials such as stone and concrete to permanent sites.

Cost relates partly to size, partly to material. Plastic, terracotta and wood are all inexpensive, although the price of terracotta rises dramatically for large, ornate pots. Stone and concrete are more expensive, while cement-based reconstituted stone is cheaper than natural stone.

Unusual containers

Apart from the standard, specially designed garden pots, many household items can also be used to hold plants. Buckets and saucepans, chimney pots and chamber pots are all suitable. Make drainage holes and cover with crocks or small stones for extra drainage.

Chimney pots look especially attractive in a group arrangement. Scrub them clean, position them, and fill the bottom third with crocks or gravel before planting. As chimney pots are hollow, without a base, they cannot be moved once filled.

Tree stumps or thick branches can be hollowed out to house several plants. They can also be used like strawberry pots, with holes drilled at intervals down the length of the trunk.

▼ **Summer bedding** A multi-level display brims with cheerful colour. When the annuals have withered, and the pelargoniums have moved indoors at the end of summer, miniature bulbs, winter pansies, primulas and dwarf conifers can take their places.

◄ **Standard bay** Containers for trees and shrubs should be large enough to give the roots space to develop, with enough good compost to nourish them. Tubs and pots should also be sufficiently sturdy to cope with their weight and not topple over in strong winds. It is essential that they are frost-proof.

Bay trees trained and clipped as round-headed standards are ideal in traditional containers, such as large terracotta pots or plain urns. Here a bay tree, underplanted with anemones, makes a striking focal point by a bed of white-flowered bush roses.

▲ **Stone urn** A container of classical design and massive proportions demands a prominent position. The planting scheme of pelargoniums, petunias and trailing lobelias is repeated in two raised containers flanking an ornate seat. Natural stone urns are expensive, but reproductions in reconstituted stone or plastic are readily available.

▼ **Pools of gold** A group arrangement of pot plants often has greater impact than if they are dotted about individually. Pots of French marigolds form a carpet of golden-yellow that hides the bases of a pot-grown climbing rose and a jasmine.

All pots and containers must have drainage holes so that excess moisture can run off.

▲ **Miniature pool** Wooden half-barrels, treated with a timber preservative, make excellent containers and are compatible with all styles of gardens. As plant containers they should have drainage holes; and lined with heavy-duty plastic they become ideal small pools for miniature water lilies.

▼ **Water butt** An old slate butt is the centrepiece of this container garden. It is planted to resemble a miniature alpine landscape, and its natural colour blends well with the warm hues of terracotta pots and quarry tiles. A pale-coloured chimney pot with purple goat's rue adds vertical interest.

CHOOSING POTS AND CONTAINERS

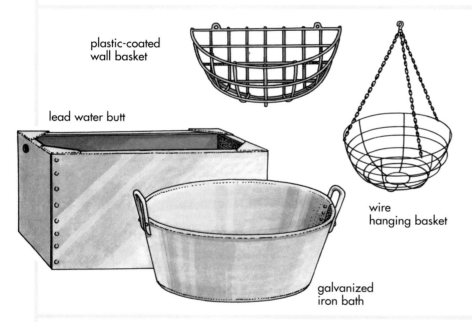

chimney pots

vase-type pot

standard pot

strawberry pot

ornate tub

square fluted planter

bulb planter

standard pots

Terracotta

The warm colour and rough texture of terracotta pots – moulded from clay – give a mature, mellow appearance to most gardens. In addition, terracotta is excellent for bridging the gap between natural and man-made materials – linking a group of pots of different materials or a paved area with grass.

Since it is a natural material, terracotta should be used with some care. Frost can damage glazes, and unglazed pots are preferable – but in any case don't put terracotta pots where they will be exposed to severe frost. Clay is porous and absorbs water; in frosty weather the water expands and the pot cracks. The porous quality means that plants in terracotta pots must be watered frequently. Heat is also lost quickly. As it is brittle, terracotta breaks if dropped or knocked.

The price is low for pots with a diameter of up to 25cm (10in) but rises with size, and for ornate containers.

plastic-coated wall basket

lead water butt

wire hanging basket

galvanized iron bath

Metal

Old metal tanks, troughs and baths make extremely decorative containers, and add character to every garden, although they can be hard to come by.

The traditional material, lead, is expensive. Copper and cast-iron containers are sometimes available, at a price, but there is a risk of the metal reacting with any fertilizer added to the soil and/or with the plant itself. The problem can be solved by using a smaller plastic pot inside the decorative copper or iron one.

To stop rust forming, galvanize metal containers or paint them with bitumen or a rubber-based product.

At the inexpensive end of the scale are light wire hanging baskets, often coated with plastic, and available in different colours, shapes and sizes.

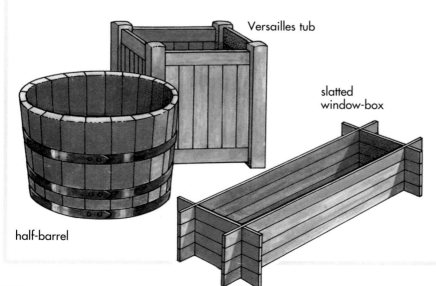

Versailles tub

slatted window-box

half-barrel

Wood

Wood looks good in nearly all situations. Unpainted, it gives a natural 'cottage garden' feel; painted black or white it looks more formal.

It is also an easy material to use if you want to make your own window-boxes or tubs. Choose a hardwood such as oak, teak or mahogany.

Wood lasts well when properly looked after – treat it with a wood preservative and raise containers on bricks to help to prevent rot. Wood also retains heat, and is relatively inexpensive. Half-barrels are easily obtainable from garden centres. Make sure they don't dry out, though, or the metal support bands will fall off.

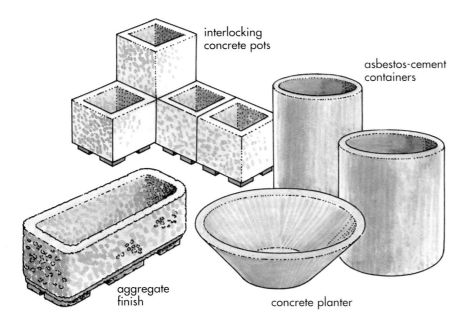

interlocking
concrete pots

asbestos-cement
containers

aggregate
finish

concrete planter

Concrete

Since concrete is fluid, it can be poured into a huge range of shapes; it also comes in a variety of different textures.

Although extremely heavy (which pushes up transport costs), it is strong enough to last a lifetime and needs no maintenance. However, its weight restricts it to ground-level use – it is best not to put concrete containers on balconies or roof gardens. Concrete retains heat but becomes cold in winter; it is an excellent choice for large, permanent shrubs.

Asbestos-cement is light but long-lasting and suitable for a modern setting. However, its manufacture has been restricted for safety reasons – inhaling the dust can be dangerous – and few containers are now offered in this material.

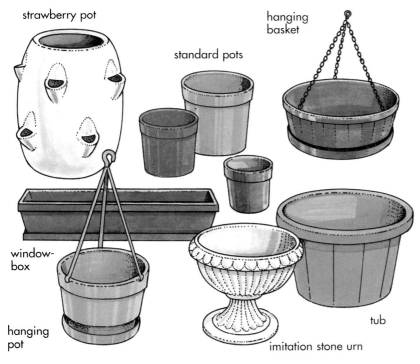

strawberry pot

standard pots

hanging
basket

window-
box

hanging
pot

imitation stone urn

tub

Plastic

Plastic comes in the widest range of shapes, sizes and colours. Heavy-duty engineering plastic is often moulded and finished to resemble ornate stone urns, simple terracotta pots or wooden window-boxes.

Heavy-duty plastic is the kind generally used for large pots such as shrub tubs. It is strong but light, making it suitable for balconies and roof patios (though any container becomes heavy once filled with soil). It is also fairly inexpensive.

Inexpensive lightweight polythene pots, hanging baskets and seed trays are readily available. They are non-porous and come in many colours. One disadvantage is that they break easily as they age. Plastic hanging baskets are particularly convenient since they don't need watering too frequently; they often have built-in drip trays and don't have to be lined with moss. On the other hand, they hold fewer plants than wire baskets

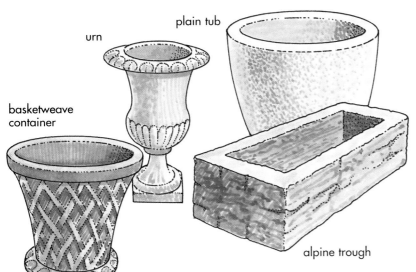

urn

plain tub

basketweave
container

alpine trough

Stone

Natural stone is expensive, with high transport costs. Local stone is always cheaper, and the available range includes granite, slate, red or yellow sandstone or limestone. All enhance their settings in a way that few other materials do. Stone also lasts a lifetime, and quickly takes on a weathered appearance that suits a traditional garden.

However, natural stone is extremely heavy, even without compost and plants, and sometimes difficult to find.

Cement-based reconstituted stone is a cheaper alternative and more easily available. It reproduces the qualities of natural stone and weathers attractively.

▲ Houseleeks Old country cottages with tiled roofs are often home to self-sown seedlings of houseleeks or sempervivums which flourish in the minimum of soil. This terracotta tile makes an original container for a collection of these small, enchanting succulents.

◄ Plastic dustbins Cheerful and tough, ordinary plastic dustbins make suitably large containers for tall-growing plants such as lilies and mallows. They may be less durable than stone or timber, but they are cheap enough to be replaced every few years.

▼ Wheelbarrow load A freshly painted wheelbarrow holds trailing, ivy-leaved pelargoniums and distracts from a manhole cover. Holes in the bottom and a layer of crocks or pebbles beneath the compost ensure good drainage.

Container gardening

Many houses – especially in towns – have little or no garden and would seem to present few possibilities for growing outdoor plants. In fact, nearly all houses have some feature – a roof terrace, basement area, balcony, porch, window-box, wall or narrow front border – which can be used to grow a wealth of flowers and foliage.

When choosing plants for pots and other containers, consider how much sun and shelter the site gets. Some climbers, such as ivy, will tolerate any aspect, while wisteria does best in a sunny spot.

Half-hardy plants, such as passion flower, thrive against sheltered courtyard walls at ground level. However, they are not likely to succeed on balconies and roof terraces which are subject to drying winds and temperature extremes. Grey- and silver-leaved plants and those with thick, glossy leaves are the most tolerant of exposure and drought.

House plants, such as oleanders, begonias, fatsias, azaleas, palms, ferns, Cape primroses and cacti, can be moved out in their pots for the summer. This benefits the plants and makes for much greater variety in the outdoor display.

▶ **Container colour** Pots and urns are especially effective when they are filled with plants whose shapes and colours harmonize with the containers. Here, a classical stone urn overflows with pink-flowered *Begonia semperflorens* and trailing blue lobelias; upright silvery *Pyrethrum ptarmaciflorum* complements the urn's scrollwork. The companion terracotta pot of bronze-leaved, white begonias is equally elegant.

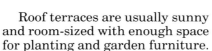

Containers can be planted with evergreen foliage plants or with seasonal displays. Tulips and hyacinths associate well with low-growing spring bedding plants. Forget-me-nots (*Myosotis alpestris*) are classic partners for tulips, while double daisies (*Bellis perennis*), with their white, pink or red mop-like blooms, look stunning with hyacinths.

In summer, dwarf snapdragons, pink ageratums, verbenas and scarlet salvias, planted with red, pink or white pelargoniums, make a sizzling display. Visual relief can be introduced with foliage plants such as hostas, hellebores and pulmonarias.

Upright fuchsias, stylish in themselves, look even better with an underplanting of silver-leaved *Helichrysum petiolatum* or senecio. Dwarf conifers are excellent in a winter window-box. They come in all shapes and sizes with foliage shaded green, blue or gold. Complement the conifers with ivies (*Hedera helix*) or periwinkle (*Vinca major*) to cascade over the edge, and a winter-flowering heather (*Erica carnea*) for its white, pink or red blooms.

Balconies and roofs

Balconies vary from an extended window-sill, on which a row of pot plants can be tended from indoors, to larger areas with room for some furniture. Some balconies are open and sunny, others shaded by a roof or nearby buildings.

Roof terraces are usually sunny and room-sized with enough space for planting and garden furniture.

As many roof terraces and some balconies are windy, reinforced glass panels, trellis or cane screens can be fixed to parapets or railings to give shelter; opaque screens provide privacy.

Most roof terraces and balconies have an asphalt or similar waterproofing surface. It's a good idea to protect this from the sun with chippings, lightweight tiles, decking or paving, which also give a more finished, stylish look.

Large tubs can be planted with shrubs and small trees, or flowering and foliage perennials. However, they may be too heavy for a balcony or roof terrace. Glassfibre containers and soil-less compost are lightweight, but check loading tolerances with a surveyor.

Small containers of flowering annuals give continental-style bursts of seasonal colour when fixed to balcony walls or railings.

Tall shrubs and trees which grow above the height of the para-pet in a roof garden or windy balcony should be hardy. Suitable choices for an exposed site include rowan, whitebeam, sea buckthorn, weeping silver pear, stag's-horn sumach and buddleia.

Climbers can be trained up trellis fixed to house walls, railings or parapets and entwined around balcony columns. If there is enough space on a balcony or roof terrace, make a tall bower by training climbers up and over a free-standing trellis support.

Porches and verandahs

Warmer and more sheltered than balconies and roof gardens, open porches and verandahs can take heavy loads. They can be adorned with hanging baskets, attached at regular intervals to the roof and supporting columns.

To create an idyllic, cottage-style mood, train climbers – perhaps honeysuckle or roses – over the pillars and roof of a front porch. In the shade of an airy porch, display foliage plants such as ivies, ferns and spider plants.

Shelves or tables in an open porch are ideal for displaying bulbs – for example, winter-flowering iris and forced hyacinths – or alpines, such as lewisias and echeverias.

House and boundary walls

Dull walls can be brightened with climbers – Virginia creeper, clematis, roses or honeysuckles. Winter jasmine can be tied to trellis, and shrubs, such as pyracantha, camellia, ceanothus, chaenomeles, laburnum, evergreen magnolia, fig and other fruit trees are excellent as wall plants, even on those of a north-facing aspect.

Hanging baskets, half-baskets, mangers and flowering pot plants can also add interest to a wall. The tops of low walls can be fitted with plant troughs for trailing or upright plants. Trellis fixed above a low wall creates a large area over which to train climbers and gives extra privacy – often welcome in urban areas.

Window-boxes

A window-box can make a colourful foreground to the view out of a window, as well as creating a cheerful display for passers-by.

Window-boxes come into their own in summer when filled with traditional bedding plants. Alternatively, create a silver, yellow and white scheme from dwarf marguerites, *Helichrysum petiolatum*, silver-leaved cineraria and yellow-leaved creeping Jenny or coleus. Herbs are ideal for sunny window-boxes, too, and some compact vegetables – such as bush tomatoes – are another possibility.

For year-round foliage in green, yellow, white, grey or blue, plant a window-box with ivy, dwarf conifers and euonymus, with small pockets for seasonal colour.

For winter colour, choose winter-flowering pansies, snowdrops or dwarf iris. In mild areas, winter cherry, cyclamen, calceolaria or cineraria could be included in a winter scheme.

In spring, enchanting displays can be created by filling window-boxes with bulbs – perhaps hyacinths, daffodils, tulips, crocuses, scillas or chionodoxas – and other flowering plants, such as biennial wallflowers and forget-

▼ **Window-boxes** A charming summer display of scarlet pelargoniums and white petunias spills from a window-box safely anchored to the sill. The colour combination perfectly matches the background of weathered brick and green woodwork.

► **Colour coordinates** A tiny balcony can take on an air of cheerfulness on the dullest day. A red parasol and striped red and white director's chairs are matched by deep planting beds filled with red and white petunias.

me-nots. And adding small-potted azaleas, hydrangeas or camellias to the scheme gives a garden-in-miniature feel. For an autumn display, pot chrysanthemums, ornamental capsicums and heather can create a range of delightful effects.

Courtyards and basements

These areas are normally hard-surfaced and can be improved enormously with a selection of plant-filled containers. Small pots look best in rows, tiers or groups. Large tubs can be planted with permanent shrubs and climbers.

Basement areas are shady but sheltered, and ideal for camellias, aucubas, ferns, clematis, fatsias

and ivies. Annuals, such as wax begonia, coleus, busy Lizzie, tobacco plant, godetia and mignonette also thrive in shade.

Aftercare

The compost in small containers dries out faster than in large ones. And the soil next to walls also tends to be dry. In summer, container-grown plants may need daily watering, perhaps twice a day during a heatwave. They also need a weekly feed, and regular dead-heading. In cold weather, protect plants in containers from frost by lagging, mulching or moving them indoors.

Self-clinging climbers can damage old brickwork – especially if the stems send out aerial roots. For house maintenance, such as repointing or painting stucco, climbers and wall-trained shrubs may need to be removed.

Window-boxes, wall pots and containers on balconies should be secure so that there is no danger of them falling. It may be a good idea to chain large containers to the wall to prevent theft.

◄ **Warm welcome** The open entrance porch of a small cottage bursts with glorious colours. Lacking a garden proper, the house still achieves a floral setting: roses scramble up the end wall, and hanging baskets overflow with fuchsias, petunias, large-flowered begonias and trailing pelargoniums.

▲ **Flights of fancy** In shade for most of the day, a long narrow ledge holds a collection of pot-grown ferns and other shade-loving foliage plants. Wooden cut-outs of pink flamingos are an amusing and eye-catching addition.

▼ **Roof planters** Wooden troughs filled with wind-tolerant spurges, sage, begonias and dwarf rhododendrons line the edges of a roof garden. A bamboo screen gives shelter to the seating area dominated by an oriental statue.

STATUES AND ORNAMENTS

Architectural ornaments and classical statuary can act as focal points or centrepieces and give a garden its crowning, finishing touch.

For almost as long as there have been gardens, there have been garden ornaments and statues. The earliest ones often had a religious purpose, such as outdoor shrines dedicated to deities. Statues of gods and famous athletes were an important feature of Greek gymnasiums and ancient Roman public places.

In Renaissance gardens, newly rediscovered classical statues were given pride of place. In baroque and rococo gardens, statues emphasized the classical style of the buildings, and the Victorians put statues in their gardens as status symbols.

Today, most garden statuary is purely ornamental and used to create pleasing focal points in a setting of foliage and flowers.

Statuary

Garden statues come in every conceivable historical and geographical style – Egyptian, Roman, Greek, Georgian, Gothic, Victorian, Regency, Renaissance, Baroque, Elizabethan, Tudor, Oriental, Moorish, Mediterranean – far more than any one garden can accommodate. Choose statues that match or complement not only the style of the house but also one another. A pair of stone lions may be acceptable at the gate of a suburban garden, but if this also sports gnomes, windmills, griffins and sphinxes, the effect is confused and incongruous.

The word statue usually refers to an artistic, three-dimensional figure of a person or animal. Statues can be original works of art, such as priceless antiques or modern abstract sculptures. Most garden statues sold today, however, are mass manufactured and reasonably priced, though top-quality reproductions of original works of art are expensive. Mass reproductions try, with varying degrees of success, to achieve the spirit of a particular historical style.

Contemporary garden statues range from realistic, inoffensive figures to colourful garden gnomes, which have their devoted supporters and equally committed opponents.

Representations of the human figure range from purely classical or Oriental statues to simple but elegant busts on pedestals.

Animal statues can be realistic representations of birds, puppies, rabbits and squirrels or semi-abstract sculptures. There are also stately mythological beasts, such as the unicorn or the half-man, half-goat satyr.

Garden ornaments

Traditionally, garden ornaments were made of natural stone, iron, lead or terracotta. Today, concrete, plastic, steel and glassfibre have all but replaced the original materials, and garden ornaments are widely available at prices that most people can afford.

◄ **Trompe l'oeil effect** A cleverly placed mirror, its edges half-hidden by ivy, reflects a Grecian-style statue in a grove of foliage. Mirrors give depth and light to a small shady garden and make it appear larger. White Madonna lilies and double peonies add cool tones to the peaceful setting.

The choice of ornaments is wide. While statues chiefly serve as decoration, other ornaments, such as sundials, weathervanes and bird houses, also have practical purposes.

Garden ornaments do not have to be highly ornate to be attractive. Plain objects, such as old-fashioned terracotta chimney pots or stone wellheads, can be very effective if they are used imaginatively and positioned with care.

Ornamental plant containers come in all shapes, sizes and materials – urns, vases, pots, barrels, window-boxes and sinks. Wheelbarrows, old tubs, hollowed-out tree trunks and old water butts are other possibilities. Empty containers, such as huge terracotta Ali Baba jars, can also be ornamental.

Finials, including stone balls, pineapples, acorns and covered urns, are used to top roofs and piers, especially on either side of an ornate gate. They can also be placed on tall pedestals.

Sundials can be horizontal or vertical, for display on pedestals or on south-, west- or east-facing walls. As well as wall-fixed sundials, there are decorative wall plaques, featuring coats of arms, classical figures, cherubs, gargoyles and animals. Small decorative wall tiles can be used singly or in panels.

Although a garden pool is a decorative feature in its own right, other ornaments are often used to enhance the setting. Free-standing or wall-fixed fountains are functional as well as decorative since they oxygenate the

water and add a soothing background sound to the garden. Popular fountain designs include single or double shallow bowls, spouting dolphins, lions, frogs and gargoyles. Herons and cranes are traditional poolside ornaments.

Small, still-water ornaments, such as bird-baths or troughs, are also attractive. They need regular topping up in hot weather, and cleaning to prevent algae.

Architectural ornaments for the garden include classical columns, in Corinthian, Doric and simple Tuscan style, complete with capitals and pedestals. Obelisks are square or rectangular columns, ending in a pyramid-shaped point, and sometimes topped with a stone ball. They give a garden a formal classical feel. For an Oriental-style garden,

◀ **Dramatic focus** Appearing to rise from the ground and melting into the fluted trunk of a willow-leaved pear (*Pyrus salicifolia* 'Pendula'), an enigmatic statue creates a dramatic focal point. A deliberately understated planting of green and silvery foliage plants heightens the effect.

▶ **Focal point** A bust placed on an ivy-covered tree stump serves to pull together the various elements in an informal garden. As a focal point it draws the eye, to itself and to the background of large-flowered clematis.

▼ **Modern sculpture** A bold partnership of wood and greenery centres around the fluid curves of a female nude as she emerges from clumps of lady's mantle. Glossy-leaved pieris and honey-coloured brickwork make a perfect backdrop.

there are stone replicas of Japanese lanterns and hand basins, on cantilevered or pillar bases.

Plenty of humorous garden ornaments are available and include brightly coloured gnomes engaged in various activities, baby animals with glass eyes, miniature windmills with revolving sails, and wishing wells.

Bird houses and dovecotes range from cottage-style huts with reed-thatched roofs on rustic supports to wooden houses on stone columns, and plastic bird houses. For keen naturalists, some bird houses are designed for particular species.

Materials
Garden ornaments come in a variety of different materials, and choice depends on taste, budget,

---

▶ **Fox covert** Shady settings, where little but foliage plants will grow, are ideal for statuary. A fox peers stony-eyed from its hiding place among deadnettles (*Lamium*) and adds a touch of humour and surprise.

▼ **Mythical griffin** Wall niches are tailor-made for garden ornaments. A splendid griffin, the fabulous beast of Greek mythology, stands watchful guard in its sentry box covered in Boston ivy.

and the immediate setting and style of the garden.

Marble is beautiful but costly, and vulnerable to damage from frost and dissolved carbonic acid in rainwater. White marble statues can also contrast too sharply with greenery.

Natural stone is an attractive and long-lasting garden material and maintenance-free, but carved natural stone statues and ornaments are costly. Reproductions in reconstituted stone – made with sand and aggregate of a particular natural rock – vary in colour and quality, but are less expensive and equally long-lived.

Both natural and reconstituted stone ornaments are heavy, and larger pieces may need special foundations, and machinery to position them.

Concrete is as long-lasting as natural and reconstituted stone; concrete is less expensive, varying in price according to the design and size of the ornament. Some types of concrete have a specially soft composition that encourages weathering and the growth of lichens and mosses; once weathered, they can look convincingly natural.

The kind of aggregate, sand and dye (if any) used in concrete ornaments affects the quality and colour. Simulated Portland stone, Cotswold stone, creamy Doulting stone, yellow-buff Ham Hill and red Devon sandstone are some of the types available.

Concrete can be a harsh white or fiercely coloured, although the passage of time eventually softens this. Some manufacturers offer 'antiqued' concrete ornaments, with darker staining worked into crevices. This can be successful, but sometimes the contrast

◄ **Japanese-style garden** Statuary and stones are essential features in Oriental gardens, symbolizing nature's enduring elements. Stone lanterns and wash basins would be placed by the entrance to a tea-house.

▼ **Bronze geese** Life-like and highly ornamental, a pair of bronze geese are far less threatening than their live counterparts as they graze in a small copse of birches.

between the staining and the main colour is so great that it merely emphasizes the artificiality.

Wood, like stone, is a natural material, sympathetic to most garden settings. Carved wooden hardwood statues are expensive; driftwood can be had for free. Untreated softwood and rustic-work are short-lived and unsuitable for carving.

Wooden ornaments come in rustic softwood (with the bark left on) of sawn pine or larch, or in a more durable wood, such as oak, teak or iroko. Softwoods rot quickly unless they are treated with a timber preservative, and painted wood needs regular maintenance if it is not to rot or look shabby. Hardwoods are far more durable, but tend to be more expensive.

▶ **Geometric designs** Large formal gardens are frequently decorated with statuary. Geometric or architectural shapes, like these imposing stone obelisks, accentuate and flatter the symmetry of formal beds.

▼ **Oriental flavour** A stone Buddha gazes across a miniature Oriental village, complete with temples and pagodas. The rocky landscape above smoothly flowing water is planted with bonsai conifers.

Bronze, lead and copper statues are beyond most people's budgets, and one of any size would be very heavy, but they are long-lasting and impressive. Bronze and copper can be regularly polished, or left to assume a soft patina. Lead is not suitable for polishing, but its natural appearance is always attractive.

Ferrous metal, such as painted cast iron, is also expensive and heavy. Stainless steel is sometimes used for modern sculptures; though stainless, it still needs regular polishing to retain its high gleam.

Metal ornaments, made of lead or cast or wrought iron, are expensive but long-lasting. Mild steel is less expensive, but not as suitable, as it rusts fairly quickly. Bronze and brass, used primarily in sundials, are expensive but hard-wearing. Brass, if not polished regularly, loses its brightness and turns bronze.

Terracotta, like stone and wood, has a natural affinity with garden settings. Terracotta statues range from moderate to expensive.

The most familiar forms of terracotta – unglazed, brownish-red pottery – are old-fashioned flower pots. Terracotta ornaments are not cheap, but relatively long-lasting and, except for those in a rather harsh orange colour, give a well-established appearance. Some cheaper types splinter or chip in cold weather if they get wet and then freeze. Check with the supplier that you buy frost-proof terracotta, unless you are prepared to bring the ornaments indoors every winter.

Plastic is cheap and usually looks it. It is lightweight, and some types are easily damaged, short-lived and tend to crack or turn yellow after prolonged exposure to weather. New, brightly coloured plastic can stand out glaringly in a garden – it may be safer to settle for plain white or dark green.

Glassfibre is longer lasting and more attractive than plastic; glassfibre can be manufactured to look convincingly like other materials, such as lead. It is relatively expensive but lightweight.

Using ornaments

Care should be taken not to overdo the use of ornaments – it is

▼ **Ornamental bird-bath** Garden ornaments should serve a purpose, practical or visual. In a small garden, this charming little statue combines both, lending an air of tranquillity and intimacy to a corner and supplying a watering hole for visiting birds.

tempting to think that because one looks attractive, two will look twice as good. The keys to success are restraint and consistency.

Always decide where you intend to place a statue or other ornament before buying it – not the other way round.

A small garden may only have room for a single ornament, or perhaps one large and a smaller one, such as an ornate bird-bath and a small wall plaque. The lay-out could culminate in one statue or eye-catching ornament which attracts the eye and towards which all other garden elements lead. The larger the garden, the more ornaments it can contain, especially if the garden is split up into separate areas.

Every ornament should have a purpose, whether practical or visual. Inanimate objects bought on impulse tend to appear more obviously pointless than plants bought on a whim.

A large ornament in the middle of a circular bed, a statue at the end of a path or under an arbour acts as a focal point, drawing the eye towards it. A wall fountain or a bust in a niche in a brick wall has a similar effect.

A pair of columns can frame a fine vista or another garden ornament in the distance; a pair of finials can mark the entrance to a

▲ Ornamental container Elaborate stone urns should not be overwhelmed with massive plantings. A simple spring arrangement of tulips, forget-me-nots and primulas is beautifully contained within the scrolled edges of this stone urn and serves to enhance its ornate style.

► Glazed container The rich warm colours and graceful shape of this modern urn are ornamental in their own right. Like a piece of sculpture or statuary, it makes a fine focal point without the distraction of flowers or foliage.

▶ **Bird house** Safe feeding and resting places attract a varied birdlife. They can range from simple raised platforms to rustic structures with thatched or tiled roofs, and elaborate stone-built dovecotes. Whatever the style and size, bird houses should be sited well away from the reach of cats.

garden or a terrace. Placed with no apparent purpose, they look forlorn and lose their impact.

Each ornament needs its own stage setting, and the larger the ornament the more space it commands. However, ornaments can also be grouped so as to present a unified effect – a bench flanked by two huge urns, for example, or a group of different sized terracotta pots at the base of an obelisk. Avoid using several ornaments of equal visual impact but of dissimilar appearance.

Sometimes an ornament dictates its own position – a bird-table should be well out of reach of cats but in full view of the window of a much used room, and a weathervane needs full exposure to wind. In the wrong positions, ornaments look odd as well as being ineffective.

Ornaments positioned within a framework, such as a wall niche, a clipped topiary arch or between wall piers, gain emphasis from the setting. Those placed at random on a lawn often look lost or trivial.

In large gardens, an avenue of columns or statues placed at regular intervals along a wide path or in topiary niches often leads to a distant vista. Such grandiose schemes are out of keeping with the average garden, though the device can be adapted to a smaller scale – where a straight path terminates at a boundary wall, a statue or large ornament placed at that point will give the path a visual reason for its existence.

Statuary can also be used to establish a mood or garden style. A Buddha in a Japanese garden or surrounded by Japanese plants creates a sense of calm. A statue of Pan playing his pipes enhances the wilderness quality of a woodland garden, and a Roman bust would emphasize the formality in a formal garden.

▶ **Pool ornament** A life-size ornamental heron makes an elegant addition to a poolside. It may also deter real birds from swooping down and snatching fish from the pool.

background carefully. Simple brickwork, paving, rendering, ground cover and hedging is usually more successful than a jumbled setting, such as intricately perforated concrete block walling and mixed borders. Certain types of foliage – fig, ivy, and bamboo, for example – go well with ornamental objects, because they have character and uniform colour without being overpowering.

Choosing and siting garden ornaments are matters of personal taste, but it is sensible to err on the side of restraint.

Classical statues can appear pompous, or even silly, in a small garden. They can, however, look magnificently at home in a completely enclosed setting, such as a courtyard garden.

It is sound advice to take a good look at the space you wish to fill with an ornament of some kind, then consider what would be most appropriate. Think carefully about the options; a mistake could be very expensive.

◄ **Wall fountain** Wall-fixed water features, such as a spouting dolphin or lion's head, bring charm to a garden and take up little space. The gently trickling water makes a soothing background noise.

▼ **Counting sunny hours** Traditional sundials are popular as focal points in herb gardens. They should be placed in open sunny sites so that the time of day can be fixed from the shadows cast.

Backgrounds and surrounds

Ornaments are most effective if they contrast in colour and texture with their surroundings. The shapes, textures and colours of foliage, flowers and stems complement solid, man-made ornaments. Pale statues look good against dark backgrounds, and vice versa. Heavily ornate objects show up best against a plain backdrop, while simple ones are set off well by fussier backgrounds.

In grand buildings, statues are often set in niches or shallow recesses in walls, but there are other, more modest ways to set off statues and large ornaments to advantage. The centre of a lawn, pool or ornamental shrubbery is a popular spot. A statue placed in a corner of a garden helps to give it a *raison d'être*, anchoring it to the landscape.

Consider the foreground and

RUSTIC FINISHES

Rustic garden furniture, arbours and other structures add old-fashioned charm and informality to a garden, whatever its setting.

Rustic work is roughly finished wooden garden furniture, fences, and structures such as pergolas, gazebos and arbours. The woods most often used are larch, chestnut, hazel or pine. Willow rustic work usually takes the form of flat woven panels, wattle hurdles and wicker furniture.

Various lengths of branch or trunk are used for rustic work – either cross-sawn or in rounded sections. Items can be made of both curved and straight wood, and can have simple, clean geometric lines or graceful curves.

The bark can be left intact on rustic work, but is likely to flake after a time. It is therefore generally stripped off and treated with a timber preservative to help prevent rot and insect infestation.

Rustic work has old, modest origins and became popular in Victorian times because it symbolized a picturesque way of life.

The rustic style has become popular again because it is appealingly old-fashioned, environmentally friendly and exploits the natural shape and surface of wood – a material sympathetic to the garden scene. The natural variation in wood and the handiwork involved also make each piece of rustic work unique.

Softwood rustic work is one of the quickest and cheapest ways of providing screening or support for plants but is not particularly durable. In contrast, hardwood – oak and beech – can last a lifetime if well looked after.

Rustic supports make an excellent framework for foliage and flowers. The appearance of rustic

props or planks used in this way is more modest than when they are used as focal points.

Suitable settings
Rustic work can complement a wide range of house styles, including genuine and mock Tudor, Georgian and Victorian, especially Victorian Gothic. It also fits easily into suburban and rural settings.

Ideal for leafy, overgrown gardens, and for woodland and cottage gardens, rustic work usually looks out of place in urban and

▼ **Garden seat** The natural colour of wood is sympathetic to most garden styles. Made from stripped hardwood, such as oak or beech, and treated with a timber preservative, a rustic seat is weather-resistant and durable.

◀ **Rustic bench** Rustic poles are inexpensive and readily available. They can be used for a number of DIY features, from fencing and arbours to seats and tables in attractive designs. Use brass nails and screws in the assembly, to prevent rust.

Rustic arbours can direct the eye to a focal point in the garden and provide a shady, fragrant, walkway. In a new garden on the flat, an arbour adds instant height and a feeling of depth. Once clothed with climbers, it can conceal an unsightly area, although it has a limited life-span. An arbour can also be erected against a tall boundary wall, which will provide some support.

In large gardens, rustic gazebos make charming focal points or centrepieces, as well as providing sheltered and shady seating in summer, and storage space for garden furniture in winter.

Rustic furniture, such as tables, chairs, seats and benches, can be arranged in groups or individually, depending on the space available. A rustic table and

highly formal gardens, or those with grand classical aspirations. The exception is woven willow panels, which are neutral enough to complement a modern garden.

Rustic furniture looks especially charming in the dappled shade of trees and climbers. There, it appears to be a part of the natural landscape and creates a nostalgic cottage-style quality.

Rustic features

In a small garden a single rustic-work bench or arch can create a focal point. Larger gardens can present a unified rustic theme with groups of furniture, pergolas, gazebos and boundary fences.

Rustic pergolas create a smooth transition between house and garden and add character to a featureless façade. The sitting area beneath a large sturdy pergola makes a shady, partly enclosed space for outdoor living in summer, especially attractive if the pergola is covered with scented climbers.

▶ **Rustic gazebo** A sturdy construction of straight poles and planed timber logs makes a charming rustic feature in a woodland garden. The thatched roof complements both the design and the setting.

chairs in a woodland setting are especially charming.

Genuine rustic seats can be made from old tree stumps, sawn level where they stand. The bole of a good-sized, sound tree can also be used as a rustic seat provided it is firm and cannot tip over.

Rustic arches can make a feature of certain aspects in the garden. For example, they can span the entrance to a garden, the front or back door of a house or the gap between two walls.

More commonly, arches span a garden path at particular junctions – perhaps where a path runs between two parallel borders or where the ornamental garden finishes and a vegetable area or woodland glade begin.

In large gardens, a line of two or three arches can enhance perspective and multiply the picture-frame effect of a distant view or a fine garden ornament.

Rustic screens are inexpensive, and ideal for creating privacy and

▶ **Bower of roses** A simple structure of rustic poles provides support for a magnificent climbing rose. It creates an enchanting and fragrant arch over a small seating area.

▼ **Woven fences** Split poles in a diamond pattern give a natural appearance to a country garden. Stripped of bark, the wood weathers attractively.

◀ **Log seat** A plain wooden seat fits perfectly into a woodland setting. Simply made from a hardwood log cut in half lengthways and sawn to shape, the seat rests on large logs sunk in rammed hardcore in holes 45cm (1½ft) deep. It is secured to the uprights with long brass nails, the heads sunk well below the surface.

ual unattractive plant pots, or contain a mixed display of plants.

Bird tables and nesting boxes attract wildlife and serve as focal points as well as providing food and homes for birds. Some rustic bird table designs have conical thatched roofs, perhaps more reminiscent of African huts than thatched cottages.

Nesting boxes, dovecotes and bird feeders come in various sizes

marking out boundaries between different sections in a garden. They can be used on their own or fixed above solid walls and fences.

Inside the garden, rustic screens can conceal unattractive features such as rubbish bins, or they can be positioned to separate a garden into 'rooms'.

Woven screens make efficient windbreaks and are ideal for protecting newly planted shrubs, especially conifers and broadleaved evergreens, from drying spring winds. On a decorative level, weathered woven screens make a pleasing backdrop for flowering plants and foliage; they are not strong enough to support vigorous climbers.

Plant and nesting boxes

Plant containers of rough wood are perfect for ferns, mossy plants such as saxifrages, and woodland wild plants. On a larger scale, hollowed-out tree stumps can be filled with a variety of colourful summer annuals or more permanent plants – stonecrop, ivy or slow-growing hedgehog holly (*Ilex aquifolium* 'Ferox').

Flat-sided, woven wall baskets filled with flowering plants can decorate an otherwise dull-looking wall. A large, woven willow butt or basket can conceal individ-

▶ **Rustic gate** Straight and sturdy poles are used for the framework of this gate. Narrow curving branches are nailed to the frame in an irregularly woven pattern typical of rustic work. The gate takes on a pleasing patina as the bark peels off with age.

▲ **Wattle hurdle** Tightly woven willow hurdles have a true rustic look and are ideal for filtering the wind without causing turbulence. Wattle hurdles are fairly expensive and available in panels, usually 1.8m (6ft) wide, and in various heights.

◄ **Log bridge** In keeping with the natural scene, a wooden bridge spans a woodland lake. Made from whole, stripped logs, butted together edge to edge, the bridge has a handrail on one side for safety, and appearance.

and shapes; nesting boxes can have a hole entrance or an open front.

The rustic garden

Cottage-garden and woodland plants match the mood of rustic features. Old-fashioned species usually create a more effective scene than large-flowered and flamboyant hybrids.

To enhance a rustic theme, plant fruit trees, old shrub roses, foxgloves, hollyhocks, delphiniums, peonies, columbines and poppies; love-in-a-mist and pot marigolds are also good choices for a rustic garden.

Climbing plants are natural partners for rustic work – clematis, honeysuckle, jasmine, climb-

ing and rambling roses. Vigorous climbers, such as ornamental and fruiting vines, and those with thick woody trunks, such as wisteria, are less suitable.

Watchpoints

☐ Rustic work has a strong character and too much in a small garden can make it look like a children's adventure playground. Every piece should serve a purpose, and generally rustic work is better in a group arrangement than scattered about.

☐ Rustic structures should be erected on strong, sturdy foundations, and designs should include diagonal members in both directions to withstand the force of wind and the weight of plants.

☐ Trellis crossbars should ideally be notched as well as nailed in place. The joints are inherently weak and leaning or collapsed features are far from attractive.

☐ Softwood rustic work, such as larch, is short-lived. However, its life-span can be extended by treating it annually with a timber preservative. Never use creosote, which is poisonous to plants.

☐ Rustic furniture may be uncomfortable and require cushions – it is also difficult to keep clean. Rustic bridges may need handrails and possibly non-slip rubber strips as wood is slippery when wet or moss-covered.

▲ **Miniature rustic hurdle** A small-scale hurdle made from stripped and sawn poles makes an intriguing focal point in a semi-wild herbaceous planting. It supports a clump of lady's mantle and prevents the stems from sprawling.

▼ **Plant container** The hollowed-out stump of an old elm tree is filled with golden Siberian wallflowers (*Cheiranthus* x *allionii*). Such old-fashioned cottage-garden flowers are well suited to rustic containers.

GARDEN EDGINGS

**Small but important, edgings to beds and borders
enhance a garden's appearance, provide a decorative
finish and cut down on maintenance.**

Although edgings take up little space, they are a major garden feature. For a garden path especially, they can carry as much visual weight as the main surfacing material, and can make the difference between a dull and an attractive finished effect.

There is a wide choice of edging materials ranging from inexpensive to costly. Some, such as precast concrete strips, are easy to lay and can be bedded on sand; others, such as cobbles, are difficult to obtain and slow to lay, requiring skill and patience. Choose an edging that complements both the existing hard materials and style of the garden, and one that does the job it is meant to do.

Useful edges

Edging can be purely decorative, and those made of small, individual units – cobbles, setts and bricks, for example – provide contrast and relief to bland, extensive surfaces. Old-fashioned, decorative edgings, whether original or reproduction, can give a garden a well-established period feel, especially if the edging matches the style and colour of the house.

The most practical function for edging is keeping one surface material, whether soil, gravel or plants, from spilling over into neighbouring areas. Edging establishes boundaries, and can also act as a buffer zone, allowing plants to overhang a path, softening its appearance without encroaching too much on foot space.

Tidiness is a higher priority with some gardeners than others, but edging does give borders and lawns a tidy, finished appearance, and makes tying or pruning errant plants back into place much easier.

Sites for edging

Wherever one garden surface, hard or soft, meets another, there is a potential site for edging. The boundary of a lawn is a prime site, and a mowing strip at the base of a wall or edge of a border can do away with the need for hand trimming. Mowing strips should be set slightly lower than the lawn, for looks and ease of mowing. They should also have a smooth, flat surface, such as brick or concrete, to prevent damage to the mower.

Lawn edges tend to erode or crumble into adjacent borders – often assisted by gardeners themselves, when weeding beds – and lawn grasses quickly become invasive weeds. Hard edging can reduce the need for weeding and eliminate the use of an edging iron, or having to repair or returf the lawn edge. At the same time, hard edging helps to keep the soil in a flower bed where it belongs.

Paths and patios are often edged to give a decorative finish. Hard surfacing materials, such as concrete and tarmacadam, which are poured wet, need a definite 'rim' to set the levels and contain

▶ **Granite setts** A neat and tidy edge of square granite setts complements a wide path and prevents the gravel from spilling into the flower beds. Granite setts are expensive and difficult to find; sandstone concrete setts make suitable alternatives.

▲ Pool surround Bricks, gravel and cobbles laid in an attractive pattern make a perfect edging for a circular pool sunk in crazy paving. The bricks match the shallow steps and the curved wall around the upper garden level.

▼ Mowing strip A path of paving stones is decorative as well as practical. Set slightly below the level of the lawn, it allows the mower to cut fully over the grass line and keeps flowering plants away from the grass.

them, and also to prevent them from crumbling. Thin strips of wood, flush with the surface, are sometimes used for economy, but more decorative edgings are available, such as pebbles or brick pavers, which should be set in place while the concrete is still wet.

Loose, small-scale surfacing materials, such as gravel or wood bark, also benefit from an edging, to prevent the boundary between them and the adjacent surface from gradually disappearing.

Although precast concrete paving slabs do not need edging for structural reasons, edging is an ideal way to fill in small spaces. Where, for example, the dimensions of a patio do not quite equal multiples of paving slabs, and you do not want to cut slabs to fit, a complementary edging of bricks, pebbles or even gravel gives an attractive finish.

Similarly, you may find that a single width of paving slab is too narrow for a path, and a double width is too wide. Edgings allow you to build up exactly the required width. Brick edgings are often used to finish garden steps made of precast concrete paving.

Many potentially good-looking prefabricated pools are ruined by poor edging detail. Generally, edging that protrudes over the rim and slightly overhangs the water is the most effective; it also protects the plastic liner from exposure to sunlight. For swimming pools, special, non-slip pool copings are available.

Edging materials
The choice of material depends on cost (including transport and foundations), availability, the skill required in laying, and the setting in which the edgings are seen.
Concrete This can be used for edging, but itself needs edging, usually with wooden shuttering, against which it sets. Concrete is inexpensive if you mix your own, slightly more expensive if you buy it ready mixed and bagged.

A path of a single row of plain precast concrete slabs can be made more interesting with decorative inserts and edging of dark-dyed concrete or one given a textured aggregate finish.
Stone setts Old-fashioned natural stone edgings of granite and whinstone are beautiful and extremely long-lasting, but expensive; second-hand ones can

sometimes be bought. They are available in long lengths, or in square setts. The latter are ideal for edging a curving path of gravel or concrete.

Precast concrete Among the simplest and cheapest are 25 x 5cm (10 x 2in) sections of various lengths, with flat or rounded tops. Such edgings are used on end and are easily bedded on a concrete base. They are more suitable for straight runs than for curves. A heavier-looking alternative is the 25 x 12.5cm (10 x 5in) pre-cast concrete kerb, laid flat as edging. Pre-cast concrete edgings add little character to a garden, but are a quick and efficient way of edging a concrete or tarmacadam path.

More expensive, but with more character, are reconstructed stone edgings, including reconstituted

▲ **Ivy hedge** A neatly clipped low hedge of green-leaved ivy makes an unusual, highly decorative and evergreen edging to a rose bed. Types with small leaves are the most suitable.

▼ **Edging strips** No less than three different materials are used here to edge a formal shrub bed. Terracotta, roll-top kerb tiles, gravel and brick form a carefully chosen, successful mixture.

bricks

railway sleepers

concrete kerbs

stone setts. Reconstructed limestone edging sections are available with twisted rope tops or a classical scroll motif, with special edging posts for corners.

Bricks and pavers These can be expensive, but make excellent, long-lasting edgings, if a suitable frost-proof brick is chosen. The bricks can be laid on end to form a raised kerb, for edging a gravel or pulverized wood bark path; flat and level with the adjacent paving, for a continuous surface; set on a slant, at an angle of about 45° and raised above the level of the path; or slightly recessed below the path, for a channel or mowing edge. A striking edging for a pre-cast concrete paving path can be made with two or three rows of brick laid flat, with a brick on edge to form a kerb.

Brick and York stone paving are a classic pair; brick and a good-quality reconstructed York stone paving would do equally well. Brick edging is particularly attractive matched as closely as possible to an adjacent brick house or garden wall, so that vertical and horizontal surfaces appear to flow into one.

Pavers – hard, thin bricks – are usually laid on the flat, and have all the advantages (and disadvantages) of bricks. Particularly attractive are old, dark stable pavers, with incised square or diamond-patterned surfaces.

Concrete paving slabs Some manufacturers offer small or half slabs, measuring 23 x 23cm (9 x 9in) or 48 x 23cm (19 x 9in), which can be used to edge a path or terrace made of larger slabs from the same range, or of an entirely different

surface material, such as gravel. The advantages are low cost, ease of laying and a tidy finish. The disadvantages are anonymity and the often harsh colours.

Terracotta Glazed quarry tiles and French-style pantiles can be used horizontally for edging, but are slippery when wet. Victorian terracotta edging tiles are upright, often with a decorative trim or scroll. They are hard to come by, but are ideal for retaining soil in a slightly raised planting bed adjacent to a gravel path.

Metal/plastic Decorative rail edgings are low and meant to discourage trespass, such as on to a flower bed, by presenting a visual rather than a physical barrier. White, black or green metal interlocking hoop edgings are inexpensive but are easily bent or knocked askew. Low wooden or concrete posts and chain link fencing, either of steel or plastic, and white, polyethylene mini-picket fencing are alternatives. Hand clipping is necessary around rails used in lawns, and they are more sensibly sited in gravel or flower beds.

Wooden planks Suitable timber includes long-lasting hardwoods such as oak and elm. Softwoods are less expensive, but should always be pressure impregnated. A timber board, measuring 15 x 5 or 3.25cm (6 x 2 or 1¼in), attached to wooden pegs sunk in the ground provides ideal informal raised edging between a gravel path and rough grass.

Tree trunks Short lengths of tree trunks can be wired together and inserted vertically into the ground to form a mini-palisade log edging. Removing the bark and treating the timber with a wood preservative helps to extend its life. Oak is excellent, but beech

log palisade

metal hoops

is usually short lived when used outdoors. Palisades look best as edgings to gravel or forest bark.

Railway sleepers These are very difficult to come by and comparatively expensive. They make an excellent, long-lasting edging, especially in an informal setting. Sleepers are rarely used flush with the ground, but can be half sunk, or rested on the ground, to give the effect of a modest retaining wall. Treat any newly cut surfaces with a wood preservative. Railway sleepers, gravel paths and ground cover make a natural trio.

Cobbles These are uncomfortable to walk on but make an attractive edging to concrete or precast concrete slabs. They are best laid shoulder to shoulder on wet concrete. Cobbles themselves need an edging, such as an unobtrusive strip of wood or precast concrete.

Corrugated plastic lawn edges Strips, 8.5cm (3¼in) high, come in various lengths. They are usually green and set flush with a lawn, and so have little visual presence. They do, however, give a precise finish to a lawn, and help to prevent weeds from encroaching into flower beds.

Dwarf hedges Box, lavender and cotton lavender are traditional edgings to paths, and their modest height adds interest and definition. The old-fashioned English lavender is a great sprawler, and compact forms, such as 'Hidcote' or 'Munstead', are more suitable. Cotton lavender also sprawls, but 'Nana' is a suitable compact variety. Edging box grows upright, but needs trimming once or twice during the growing season to keep it low and in shape. *Buxus sempervirens* 'Suffruticosa', is the type usually grown.

Annuals Ribbon bedding is a traditional soft edging to beds and lawns, and consists of narrow bands of brightly coloured annuals

decorative shells

corrugated lawn edging

clipped box hedging

cobblestones

145

and bedding plants. For informal edging, try a mass of busy Lizzies along the edges of a shady path; or dwarf sweet peas or dwarf nasturtiums along a sunny one.

Aesthetic considerations

Generally, the fewer types of edging material used, the better. Using a single edging material in a garden with several types of hard surfacing can have a strong, unifying effect. However, a mixture of materials may be preferable if the main surfaces are dull. Brick and setts can be interspersed, for example; stone edging can be combined with single rows of cobbles; and dull precast concrete slabs can alternate with warmer-hued quarry tiles.

Unusual and decorative, if time-consuming, edging can be made from narrow-width plastic or plastic-coated trellis. Rest or half sink it into the ground, horizontally, then fill each square or diamond shape with a different annual or bedding plant.

▼ **Timber edging** A front edging of low, white-painted wooden planks separates flower beds from the path. It matches the fence and white-painted woodwork of the house.

▲ **Floral edges** Low-growing summer annuals are popular as edgings for bedding schemes. Alyssum, lobelias and French and African marigolds weave a bold ribbon of colour along the lawn.

▼ **Pot line-up** Warm-hued terracotta pots make an informal edging to a mixed border. The gravel path serves a practical purpose in providing good drainage, essential for pot plants.

DECORATIVE METALWORK

Wrought iron, stainless steel and other metals lend themselves to practical uses as well as ornate scrollwork and classical statuary.

Metalwork is often underrated for garden decoration, although metal furniture and other structures – from modest to highly ornate designs – can be reasonably priced.

Ornate cast-iron garden furniture, painted either black or white, looks traditional in both town and country gardens. Alternatively, metal furniture in modern, streamlined designs can be painted in eye-catching colours – such as red or racing green – to add cheerful bursts of colour to a paved urban or shady garden.

Metal sculptures, in bronze, lead or stainless steel, can make stunning focal points. And many metalwork objects are suitable for plant displays and supports.

Metal in the garden

Metalwork comes in a surprising range of colours and finishes, from traditional black- or white-painted iron, to highly reflective, polished stainless steel, the soft warm reflections of polished bronze and the mellow green of weathered copper.

Cast and wrought iron are usually painted. Cast iron is often beautifully worked but heavy and costly. Wrought iron is moulded into similar designs but is less

---

▼ **Custom-built wellhead** A hand-crafted dome of black-painted metal bars turns an old stone well into an impressive focal point. Cemented into the stonework, the bars make a strong and long-lasting support for heavy climbers such as wisteria. In late spring and early summer the dome is festooned with drooping clusters of lilac flowers.

▲ Modern furniture The striking curves of modern garden furniture illustrate the versatility of metal. It can be crafted into simple or ornate shapes and despite its light and graceful appearance it is extremely sturdy. Table and chairs, with wooden slatted seats, are painted bright scarlet and add welcome colour to a leafy corner; they must be stored under cover in winter.

▼ Iron gates A splendid gate and fence in wrought iron mark the entrance from the ornamental to a woodland garden. Though expensive, wrought-iron fencing is long-lasting and open enough to allow views into and out of the garden while keeping animals out. The intricate pattern is painted royal blue, with flowers and scrolls picked out in gold; it needs regular repainting.

heavy. Both need regular coatings of protective paint to prevent rust.

Steel, like iron, is a strong metal that can be moulded in a variety of ways. Stainless steel will not rust; it is extremely expensive, but popular for abstract sculptures in municipal parks.

Aluminium is now more commonly used than iron for garden furniture. It is cheap, lightweight, maintenance-free, and usually coated in coloured plastic or baked polyester powder, which comes in various colours, including bronze.

Copper is attractive, rust-free, heavy and expensive. It can be polished to a high gloss, but in outdoor settings looks more natural with its green patina.

Metalwork designs

Metals such as iron, steel and aluminium are strong enough to be cast or wrought into finely detailed and elaborate styles, which have an elegance often lacking in other materials.

Metal wire can be made into delicate, lacy patterns or pulled taut to create perfectly straight lines. In the garden, fences, pergolas and furniture made with metal wire can create a pleasing contrast with the soft, natural forms of plants and the solidity of brick and stone.

Sheet metal is used to make planters and garden structures, especially roofs. Tubular metal is used in furniture manufacture

Bronze is another extremely decorative and expensive metal, chiefly used for classical statues. It, too, is rust-free and heavy. Bronze can be either polished or left to weather to a soft green.

Brass is sometimes used to make handsome sundials, door knockers and house numbers. It is rust-free but expensive and needs regular polishing.

Lead is an attractive but expensive metal traditionally used for ornate plant containers. It is the heaviest metal of all but very soft, and is easily bent and damaged. Old lead water cisterns can occasionally be found; they make attractive containers for landscapes in miniature.

▲ **Wrought-iron furniture** Traditional garden furniture is embellished with scrolls and graceful swirls. Usually painted white it stands out against all backgrounds, including stone walls. With age it becomes fragile and is more suitable for decorative than functional purposes.

which – depending on the design – can look modestly functional or outlandishly modern.

Beaten or cast metal statues and garden ornaments have the same three-dimensional look as stone but in warmer colours.

Metal furniture ranges in style from ornate iron or aluminium chairs and tables based on Victorian, Gothic, Regency or Georgian

Reproductions of Victorian tiered plant stands are usually made of plastic-coated wirework and are available in upright, circular or half-circular styles. There are even wheelbarrow and old-fashioned pram designs with wirework wheels and filigree canopies. Such wirework stands can look charming when filled with pots of trailing ivy or seasonal displays – spring-flowering bulbs, and fuchsias and pelargoniums in summer.

Plant supports and fences
Metal supports can be attached to walls or form the sides and roof of a pergola. Arches, arbours and pergolas are often made of plastic-coated galvanized wire and mild steel. Climbers, such as clematis or wisteria, look enchanting growing over such features. However, once the plastic covering cracks, the metal is prone to rust.

Metal fencing such as galvanized chain link fencing is cheap, and matching gates are some-

---

◄ **Poolside ornament** Frozen into permanent immobility, a bronze heron by a wild-garden pond makes an enchanting focal point. It is equally suitable for an ornamental garden pool.

▼ **Copper urn** With age, copper exposed to the air acquires an attractive green patina that blends perfectly into the garden scene. As a plant container it should be lined with heavy-duty plastic as the metal can react adversely with plants and compost. This urn is filled with white marguerites and blue and white petunias sunk in their pots into moist compost.

originals, to crisp, unfussy modern styles. Metal furniture can be painted in bold, bright colours as well as black or white.

Ornaments and sculptures
These may be made from bronze, iron, copper, lead or stainless steel. There are abstract types as well as life-sized or scaled-down realistic and imaginary figures, animals, busts and bas-relief plaques. They make effective focal points and, free-standing or wall-mounted, can be the pivot of a layout.

Old lead water tanks, copper washing pots, cast-iron baths and troughs can be used as unusual, decorative plant containers.

Hanging wirework baskets are cheap, lightweight and look delightful when planted with a mixture of colourful annuals. They come in several sizes and a wide choice of colours, and can be galvanized or plastic coated. Hanging baskets for fixing on to overhead structures, and half-baskets for mounting on walls, come in real or reproduction wrought iron as well as wirework. They are heavy when filled and should be fixed to strong metal brackets and hooks.

Wall-fixed wrought-iron manger planters can hold individual pots, or be lined with moss and plastic and planted directly. Black-painted metal hoops in various sizes attached to metal backing can be fixed to walls and hold pots of upright or trailing plants, outdoors or inside. Wrought-iron planters, with ornate scrollwork, come in several widths and can be fixed across the base of a window, or on to a wall. Free-standing wrought-iron planters are ideal for patios, basement areas and balcony gardens.

times available. This type of fencing is functional rather than decorative but can be made more attractive if it is covered with climbing plants.

Painted iron railings made of vertical bars topped with spikes or arrow points are traditional in Victorian gardens. They are attractive and long-lasting, but costly and need regular repainting. Wrought-iron gates are popular, too, and can be combined with iron railings, brick walls or hedges.

Watchpoints

☐ All metal furniture lasts longer if it is brought under cover for the winter. Heavy iron types can be left outside as long as they are painted regularly.

☐ Lightweight metal furniture is easy to move, but less stable than heavier types and may twist or distort on uneven paving.

▶ **Plant stand** Victorian-style metal plant stands take up little ground space and are ideal for displaying a profusion of flowering bedding plants. Such stands are portable and can be moved to cheer up dull corners. Every winter they should be given a fresh coat of paint.

▼ **Weathervane** A bright red weathervane stands like an exclamation mark in a tunnel of trees. At the same time it guides the eye towards an abstract sculpture at the end of the walk.

▲ **Recycled metal** A whimsical collection of old metal utensils is grouped around the cast-iron wheel of a piece of industrial machinery. Wood and metal harmonize with the softer forms of foliage and flowers and make good containers for pots of bedding plants.

▶ **Lead cupid** Raised on a stone pedestal, this small lead statue makes a stunning focal point against an ivy-covered background. Lead is extremely heavy but easily damaged; antique sculptures are very expensive.

☐ When metal furniture is placed on a lawn, ensure that the feet are broad enough not to sink in. It is a nuisance to move furniture for mowing, and it is probably better to decide on a permanent position.

☐ Once paint or plastic coating is scratched or cracked, non-galvanized metal will corrode.

☐ Ornate metal furniture collects dirt and is difficult to clean. Do not place it under sycamores or limes, which exude sticky honeydew.

☐ Metal plant containers can create toxic conditions for plants. And ferrous metals, such as iron and steel, rust and corrode when wet. It is therefore sensible to use a polythene or butyl rubber liner, or a rigid plastic inner container. Alternatively, treat the inside of the metal container with rubber- or bitumen-based paint.

GARDEN GATES

**A timber or metal gate can be welcoming
or forbidding, an ornamental entrance to a garden
or a functional barrier to keep out intruders.**

A garden gate traditionally marks the entrance to a garden in the same way that a front door marks the entrance to a home. Security, privacy and decoration are some of the different reasons for having a gate.

There are several variations in styles, materials, sizes and finishes. In addition to the standard models, gates can also be made to order locally by blacksmiths or carpenters.

Security and privacy

Gates range from industrial-style barriers, meant to exclude all outsiders, to more ordinary types which simply keep small children and pets from straying. Whatever the intent, a gate is just one part of a larger boundary which is only as strong as its weakest point. A totally secure gate set in a privet hedge or low wall, for example, offers little security. Gates under 1.5m (5ft) high can usually be climbed, and hedges, unless heavily thorny or prickly, can be breached.

Side gates are often high, solid and sturdy, with top and bottom bolts, to deter intruders. If children and pets use the garden, a gate with a self-closing device is a sensible choice. A stop post and hook ensure that the gate can, on occasions, be left open.

As well as keeping pets in, you may wish to keep neighbouring animals out – gates with open work at low level can be breached by smaller breeds of dogs and, if you live in the country, by rabbits.

Gates made from solid panels of wood that obscure vision are ideal for providing privacy, while lacy wrought iron or open trellis-work give a filtered view of the outside world from the garden, and vice versa.

Gate styles and sizes

Many gates combine practicality

▼ **Picket fence** A plain white-painted picket fence with matching gate is in keeping with a country cottage. It defines the boundary without enclosing the front garden.

gates is awkward and presents a traffic hazard, consider fitting remote control gates which can be operated from inside the car.

A gate looks peculiar if it is taller than the wall or fencing on either side. A low gate set in a high boundary, however, can appear friendly and welcoming.

Timber and metal gates come in a range of sizes suitable for most uses. Ready-made, they measure 90cm (3ft), 1m (3¼ft) and 1.2m (4ft) wide; and 90cm (3ft), 1.2m (4ft) or 1.5m (5ft) high.

Side gates are often in the form of a garden door, for security. Though similar in width to ready-made front gates, they are available in heights of 1.6m (5½ft), 1.8m (6ft) or 2m (7ft).

For a driveway, there are 2.4m (8ft), 2.7m (9ft), 3m (10ft) and 3.5m (12ft) wide gates.

When measuring gate widths, allow for supporting posts or piers.

Gate posts and piers

A gate is never seen in isolation – the adjacent posts or piers are always part of the picture. Generally, the posts or piers should be

◄ **Wrought-iron gate** A massive stone wall demands an equally imposing gate. Custom-built in wrought iron, it is maintenance-free – and expensive.

with good looks, and are built for a lifetime of service.

Ideally a gate should be in keeping with the rest of the boundary, garden and house, and the simpler it is, the more likely it is to fit in with its surroundings. However, ornate, wrought-iron gates can complement the richly detailed exteriors of Victorian or Edwardian houses, while country cottages may call for simple, rustic gates.

Matching the material and style of the gate to any adjacent fencing is generally a safe policy, and many manufacturers offer matching gates, in several sizes, as part of their ranges of fencing. Do not, however, camouflage the gate; make sure that the path, posts, latch or hinges indicate clearly where the gate is.

If you are disabled, or live on a busy road where stopping to open

▶ **Timber gate** Solid gates and fences ensure complete privacy in the garden. A carefully placed plant container points visitors to the entrance.

bulkier – though not necessarily higher – than the gate.

Wooden gates are best hung from stout wooden posts (a minimum of 10cm/4in square for small gates, and considerably larger for driveway gates). The post caps should be rounded or angled to shed rain.

Generously proportioned brick or stone piers are appropriate for both wooden and metal gates. Five- or seven-bar agricultural-type iron or tubular steel gates sit comfortably within metal posts.

Materials

Timber gates are relatively inexpensive. They are available to match popular styles of timber fencing: close-boarded, feather-edged, larch lap, ranch-style post and rail, picket, palisade and rustic. They come in several heights and are made of pressure-treated or untreated wood. Some are available as self-assembly kits.

Hardwoods, such as oak, iroko or sweet chestnut, are the most expensive, but last longer than softwoods. However, softwoods are lighter in weight and easier to hang. They should be well seasoned and must be treated with a timber preservative. If you want a

▲ **Visual symmetry** Two white-painted wrought-iron gates, one set in a boundary wall of stone boulders, the other in a tall hedge, are strong focal points in a formal garden layout.

▼ **Clever asymmetry** A minor detail, such as the gentle curve on a plain gate, can have major visual impact when, as here, it breaks a rigid straight-sided pattern of stone-clad piers.

▲ **Double gates** Wrought-iron gates are durable and unlikely to rust. Aluminium gates are cheaper and usually enamelled in black primer; mild steel gates are also less expensive and are available with a rust-proof finish.

▼ **Gate posts** Timber posts for garden gates should be a minimum of 10cm (4in) square and made of hardwood or pressure-impregnated softwood. Some gates come complete with posts, to be set in hardcore and concrete.

▶ **Agricultural gates** Brick piers make sturdy posts for wide gates across a driveway. They should be erected on firm foundations of concrete, with hinge supports and gate fittings built in as the brick courses rise. Alternatively, face-fixing plates can be fitted to the completed brickwork.

Agricultural timber gates come in standard widths, from 2.4m (8ft) to 4.5m (15ft).

▼ **Gate ornament** A cross-piece gives a decorative effect to a traditional five-bar gate across a driveway. It matches the white-painted picket fence and side gate and looks attractive in an urban setting, but offers little privacy and only limited security.

and barley-sugar-type twists. Some manufacturers offer extension pieces, which can be fitted to adjacent pillars if the gateway is an unusual size.

Tubular steel gates are considerably cheaper. They are lightweight and maintenance-free, but do have industrial or agricultural overtones. Thermal movement can sometimes be a problem with close-fitting metal gates. In very hot weather they may expand, and in prolonged cold weather they can shrink, just enough to prevent the gate from closing properly.

Gates made from hollow-sectioned PVC components are sold by some fencing manufacturers. They are lightweight, rot-proof, easy to erect and maintenance-free, needing only an occasional wash with soapy water. They are inherently weaker than timber or metal gates and do not stand up to heavy use.

◄ **Ornamental gates** Local blacksmiths can forge individual designs for gates and other metal ornaments. Costs vary according to the type of metal and the amount of labour.

painted finish, make sure that the preservative is compatible with the paint. All painted wood needs regular repainting.

Solid wood gates, made of rows of slats fitted to horizontal crosspieces and single or double diagonal braces, offer the greatest security. 'Combination' gates, with a solid lower part and an open decorative top, are a useful compromise; traditional five-barred wooden gates look attractive but offer little security.

For a rustic style there are woven osier, wattle or reed gates, as well as waney-edge lap, straight lap and interwoven wood. These, like the fencing and screens they match, are inexpensive but relatively short-lived.

Wrought-iron gates are available in genuine iron, mild steel or aluminium. The styles of wrought-iron gates vary from the simple Victorian type with straight vertical bars topped by 'arrow heads', to curved scrolls

► **Moon gate** A hand-crafted, wrought-iron gate makes a spectacular entrance to a formal garden, attracting passers-by with its intriguing shape and the fascinating views through it.

TIMBER AND STONE BRIDGES

**Bridges and stepping stones across natural
streams, ponds and lakes are practical as well as
charming additions to large water features.**

Natural streams, gullies or drainage ditches where the water is more than a step or jump across need to be crossed by a bridge or a series of stepping stones. Large pools and ponds can also be spanned by bridges, and look wonderful, especially on still and sunlit days when the bridge is reflected in the water. Bridges also provide a platform from which to view the garden from a different perspective, and offer shelter and shade to fish.

Bridges should have a reason for their location. They should be part of a path system and span an area of water or boggy ground wide enough to justify their presence. A bridge spanning a pool that could easily be walked round or stepped over looks out of place.

Suitable sites

Think of bridges and stepping stones as paths through water. As with a path across a lawn, the route should appear sensible – as short and direct as possible and, unless there is a genuine obstacle, in a relatively straight line. While gentle curves, such as those following the contours of a bank, can be attractive, avoid sharp curves or diversions unless they are absolutely necessary.

The crossing place of a large, informally shaped pool can be made to seem shorter by reducing the water surface with a bog garden. Conversely, a bog garden or dense planting of water marginals, such as hostas, astilbes and willows, can visually extend a small pool and give some justification to the size of the bridge that spans it.

Stepping stones

Stepping stones blend easily into the landscape. They are suitable

---

▼ **Rustic bridge** A narrow bridge across a natural pond blends perfectly with the scenery in a country garden. Rustic softwood poles are suitable only for small bridges and are not particularly durable.

▲ **Stepping stones** A path of natural stone slabs continues its smooth line across a narrow stream. The transition from stepping stones to lawn path is level and unforced.

◄ **Wooden bridge** Sawn planks of treated hardwood make sturdy and durable bridges. Handrails are a sensible safety device as fallen leaves and rain make wood slippery.

Almost any suitably sized concrete or natural stone paving slabs can be used as stepping stones, across the lawn, for example, and then over the water. Rough surfaces are the safest.

Stepping stones are more hazardous than a bridge. The closer a stepping stone is to the surface of the water the better it looks, but movement in the water, or a stiff breeze, can lead to wet stones and feet. Ideally, the stones should protrude at least 5cm (2in) above the water.

Choosing bridges

A bridge needn't be elaborate or expensive. At its simplest, a bridge can be a couple of railway sleepers, planks of timber, or a single stone slab across a ditch. A small very ornate bridge can look like overdone icing on a cake.

for shallow water and can be exciting in flowing streams; they are unsuitable where the water level fluctuates dramatically.

Stepping stones should be about 45cm (1½ft) square and set at comfortable intervals. The occasional extra-large stone, or two paving slabs butted together, act as resting places and, if repeated,

can create a pleasant rhythm. The upper and lower sides of stepping stones made from natural boulders should be relatively flat, for sure footing. Such stones, varying in size and placed in seemingly random clusters, can give a natural rockfall effect. Additional boulders on the banks would reinforce this effect.

Unlike most other garden features, ready-made bridges are rarely available. For any bridge spanning more than 1.8m (6ft) professional advice should be sought. Bridges with deep foundations, one or more central piers or an arch spanning the water will also need professional design and construction.

The style of the bridge should mirror the style of the garden. A bridge can be flat or humped, although a small humped bridge with steeply angled ramps is awkward to walk on.

The height of a bridge above water depends on the height of the banks, on whether the water is still or moving, and on any fluctuation in the amount of water that passes beneath it.

Some bridges can be constructed with little disturbance; others may involve damming, draining or

---

▶ **Stream crossing** Two planks butted together make a simple but effective crossing over a narrow stream. Held in place by boulders, the wooden bridge weathers attractively.

▼ **Stone bridge** Access to a large-scale rock garden above a stream is via a bridge of crazy paving stones. With its central arch, such a bridge is an ambitious and expensive project, best left to the professionals.

diverting of the water. All this adds to the expense, and can leave the garden looking messy for some time afterwards. If any large machinery is required, wide access to the garden is essential. The heavier the machinery, the more damage it does to the lawn.

Basically, a bridge is a costly and time-consuming project. However, it is also a permanent feature which, if well constructed and maintained, can be a valuable addition to house and garden.

Materials

Use natural or natural-looking materials that fit comfortably into the garden setting. In a formal garden with a square or rectangular pool, geometrically cut and dressed stone is appropriate for the foundations of bridges.

Where possible, use local materials, such as York stone paving, Welsh slate or Cotswold stone,

though cost or availability may be prohibitive. In areas with no suitable local materials, treated softwood, hardwood, stone or brick can be used, as can concrete in a neutral colour with a rough aggregate finish. Ideally, match the material to other paving or walling in the garden.

Wood is a popular choice for bridges, particularly the unsawn, rustic type. However, even when treated with a timber preservative, this sort of softwood is short-lived and only looks appropriate in a truly rustic setting. Hardwood bridges with sawn, open-slat decking are sensible in most sites. They fall within the skills of many handymen and are suitable for both formal and informal settings. Railway sleepers are thick, sturdy and long-lasting, provided that any cut surfaces are treated with a timber preservative to prevent rot.

▲ **Wading stones** Large boulders look natural in shallow ponds and streams. The upper surface should be fairly flat and rough for foot safety and reach at least 5cm (2in) above the water.

Brick of any sort is expensive, both in the cost of materials and labour, but brickwork piers supporting a stone, concrete or wooden walkway can be most attractive. Make sure the bricks are the frost-proof type and, if seeking the advice of a builder's merchant, make clear that the bricks will be saturated.

One large stone slab used to span a small stream is both attractive and practical, though its weight is such that several people, or even a small crane, will be needed to position it. A stone bridge built in the traditional manner, with courses and mortar, is very expensive and skilled labour and design are necessary.

GARDEN LIGHTING

**Outside light fittings have practical as well as
decorative effects, and there are a wide range of types
and styles to choose from.**

The type of lighting you choose for the garden depends on the effects you wish to achieve. Functional lighting is one of the most important considerations. For instance, you and any visitors need to be able to find the way easily to the front door on a dark night. Lighting here is especially important if there are steps or other obstacles, such as low walls or overhanging branches, to negotiate, or if the family includes young, old or disabled people.

Alternatively, lighting can be purely decorative. You could illuminate the attractive features of the garden – specimen trees, a rockery or fish pond, for example – so that they can be seen not only from the garden but from the house as well.

One drawback with outside lighting is that it attracts insects on summer nights. You can get round this either by siting the fittings some distance away from the sitting area or by buying a special ultraviolet light that attracts and kills insects.

Home security is of increasing interest to householders everywhere and lighting can be a deterrent – few would-be intruders will have the nerve to approach a well-lit house.

Whichever kind of lighting you intend to install, there are several points to bear in mind, since any use of electricity outdoors is potentially dangerous.

Wherever possible use safe, low-voltage lighting, confining mains-voltage lights to positions on the house wall, where they can be wired up easily and safely as an extension of the house wiring.

Do not attempt to run mains-voltage lights down the garden

▼ **Spotlighting** Well-placed lights illuminate a path and patio at night for safety. Other fixtures highlight attractive features, such as a weeping silver birch.

WALL-MOUNTED LIGHTS

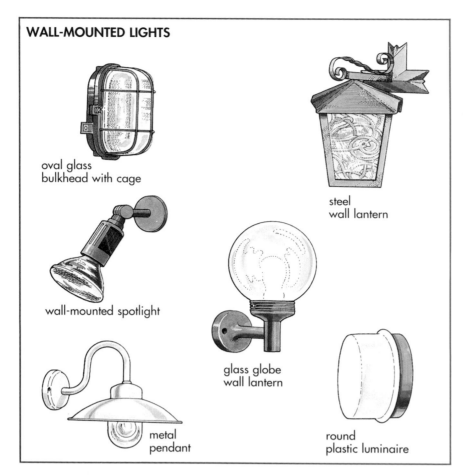

oval glass
bulkhead with cage

wall-mounted spotlight

metal
pendant

steel
wall lantern

glass globe
wall lantern

round
plastic luminaire

to the house – outside the front door, for example, or across a patio – choose a wall-mounted light fitting.

The simplest and cheapest kind is a bulkhead light, consisting of a baseplate and a translucent cover. Various styles are available, from nautical versions with a protective wire grille to sleek cube lights with plastic covers, which can also incorporate the house number.

Wall-mounted lanterns are more decorative than bulkhead fittings. The cheapest types – globe lights – have a spherical diffuser. More expensive versions imitate traditional carriage lamps and are available in different finishes with clear or coloured glass.

Reproductions of old-fashioned lamp post fittings may be worth considering if they suit the style of house; they are usually expensive.

Safety lights are suitable for lighting a garden path without illuminating everything else. Small bollard lights set along the side of a path are ideal as they cast a low-level beam without glare and are relatively unobtrusive during the day. Ground-level

unless you are a very experienced DIY electrician. A separate circuit must be run from the main consumer unit and this should be protected by a special safety device known as a residual current circuit breaker.

It is not recommended to run lights via extension flexes plugged into the house wiring. A temporary set-up – coloured festoon lights at Christmas or around a patio for a party, for example – is possible during dry weather only, unless the lights are weatherproof. Dismantle them as soon as possible after use.

Types and styles
There is a wide range of garden lighting. The best way of finding out what is available is to visit a specialist lighting showroom.

All fittings should be suitable for outdoor use, and should be marked as such. If in doubt, check with the retailer before buying.

For general-purpose lighting over a broad area of ground next

▶ **Low-voltage lights** Ideal for lighting paths and steps, low-voltage kits usually comprise two or four lights on spikes, connected to the electricity supply in a nearby outbuilding.

downlighters work in a similar way, casting light in a downwards direction only. They can also be used to good decorative effect if placed in flower beds and borders.

General background illumination can be achieved with almost any type of light. Simple bulk-heads or lanterns can be mounted on sturdy posts or walls (but not on fences, where the wiring could be damaged and exposed if the fence blew down).

Festoon lighting is suitable for lighting up the patio or garden for a party, or to illuminate an outdoor Christmas tree. This consists of a chain of individual lights set on a long flex, which is draped round trees or across a house wall and plugged into an outdoor or indoor socket.

Low-voltage kits
Low-voltage lighting sets are safe and inexpensive to run. They come in kit form complete with two or four lights (usually in the form of spike fittings), either mini-post lanterns or mini-flood-lights, run via a low-voltage cable from a transformer sited in the house or in an outbuilding. The fittings are mounted on spikes to be positioned in flower beds and borders, with the cable between them. Low-voltage cable can safely be left lying on the surface of the soil, but you can also bury it in a shallow trench as long as you remember that it is there.

Use mains-voltage spotlights to highlight individual features. They throw a narrow, directional beam of light, which can be aimed precisely. The fittings can be wall or post mounted, or fitted on spikes so that they can be concealed at ground level.

Pool lighting
An illuminated pool can make a highly attractive feature, especially if it has a fountain. Low-voltage

▲ **Pool lighting** A garden pool looks spectacular lit up at night. The lights can be submerged or float on the surface, and low-voltage lighting kits, with waterproof connections, are fairly easy to install.

fittings are the safest – they work in much the same way as garden spikes, except that the lights are usually supplied already wired to the low-voltage cable to ensure waterproof connections.

Security lighting
Floodlights can be installed high up on the house walls. They are not particularly attractive fittings, and standard types can be expensive to run because they take high-wattage bulbs – often up to 500W, in either GLS (general lighting service) or tungsten halogen types. Smaller and cheaper mini-floods may be adequate. Floodlights can be programmed to a time clock or photocell.

▲ **Temporary lighting** Multi-coloured cone flares can be positioned exactly where they are needed – along a path or around a patio. They last for up to six hours and withstand light winds.

▲ **Outdoor candles** Garden candles come in a wide range of shapes and sizes, in plain foil or ornamental containers. They burn for several hours, and many contain insect repellents.

▲ **Garden flares** Versatile and inexpensive, garden flares are available in a range of sizes and designs. They are perfect for outdoor occasions and are more wind-resistant than candles.

There are also special security lights which are linked to a detector and switch on automatically for a pre-set period if anyone enters the field of vision.

Using outdoor lighting
When it comes to getting the best from garden lighting, the first thing to bear in mind is that you need nothing like the light levels used indoors – a 40W bulb looks like a searchlight in the dark. It is advisable to start off with a few lights and to fit larger bulbs or extra fittings as necessary.

Avoid glare – either directly from the fitting, or by reflection from white-painted walls, patio doors or a garden pool. Adjust the positions of the light fittings accordingly. Use opaque diffusers where possible, or choose lights with bodies that direct light only upwards or downwards.

When highlighting garden features such as specimen trees, keep the light fitting itself at a low level so that it shines upwards at the object being illuminated. Place the light between the viewer and the object, to avoid shadows.

Take care when using coloured bulbs in spotlights. Yellow turns plants pale and wan, while red makes leaves look brown, and

▲ **Night into day** A combination of wall-mounted lights and ground fittings throws subdued illumination over a terrace. Properly installed, lighting can make an outdoor room into a place for entertaining during fine weather.

blue bulbs give a strange, unearthly light. Green is the most successful, since it brings out the natural colour of most foliage.

Experiment with the best light positions before installing them permanently. Wire up the fittings temporarily with an extension flex, or use portable indoor light fittings, and get a helper to hold the light in various positions while you check that it illuminates what it should and gauge the effects of the shadows. Then mark out the chosen positions, ready for the permanent wiring to be installed.

Low-voltage cables can be left lying on the soil surface or can be buried in shallow trenches. However, mains-voltage cable must be buried underground and should either be armoured (this is expensive on long runs) or else consist of ordinary PVC-sheathed cable laid in an impact-resistant plastic conduit. In either case, the installation should be carried out by a qualified electrician.

GARDEN FURNITURE

**Stylish furniture is the finishing touch that
can transform a garden from a plant showcase into a
comfortable outdoor living room.**

Most people prefer comfortable garden furniture to sitting on the ground. Whether a single deckchair for a balcony or tiny roof-top retreat, or a co-ordinating table and chair set, garden furniture eliminates the problems of wet and hard ground; and of armies of ants taking a fancy to food and drink.

Garden furniture near the house allows for spur-of-the-moment breaks and quick meals. It gives children somewhere to read or play, and entertaining in the garden is far more enjoyable for guests and hosts alike if there are comfortable seats and handy tables.

Adequate but uninspiring garden furniture can be given a new lease of life with a fresh coat of paint or new seat cushions. Starting from scratch, consider first the pros and cons of the various types and styles on offer.

Cost and maintenance
Cost is obviously important, but it pays to buy the best quality and materials that you can afford. The most expensive is not necessarily the best – you may be paying extra for a fashionable brand name, and DIY and garden centres with large stocks and rapid turnovers keep prices lower. Cheap and poorly made garden furniture, though, does not last. It is better to buy one good piece, with a guarantee, and add to it as money becomes available than to buy several flimsy pieces for the same price but with a shorter life-span.

Consider the age and style of the house and the layout of the garden: formal or informal; old-fashioned or modern; sophisticated or semi-wild. Garden furniture should reflect or contrast with that style, yet there are no hard and fast rules. Victorian furniture, for example, can be attractive in a modern garden; and modern, tubular metal furniture can add spice to a country-cottage garden.

As a general rule, and particularly in a small garden, choose one theme and stick to it. The simpler the furniture, the less likely it is to look out of place.

Large gardens can take large

▼ **Plastic furniture** Although less attractive than natural materials, plastic is cheap, hard-wearing and easy to stack and store. Chiefly made in white, green, red and mauve plastic garden furniture is also available.

◀ **Romantic wrought iron** Reminiscent of a bygone age, wrought-iron furniture is immensely durable, though it needs frequent repainting. Aluminium is a lighter, less expensive alternative.

available pre-assembled. They are obviously less expensive than hand-crafted and custom-built furniture.

Styles of furniture
Garden seats range from folding canvas deckchairs to heavy cast-iron armchairs. Deckchairs and folding director's chairs, with wood or aluminium frames, are easy to carry and store, but deckchairs are difficult for the elderly and infirm to use, and can collapse if incorrectly erected. Double deckchairs are available, and some ranges have matching sunshades, folding benches and tables. Covers range from traditional canvas to cheap plastic.

There are also shiny aluminium folding seats, modern seats and armchairs of glassfibre or various shapes of preformed plastic and tubular steel. Some have adjustable back positions, others have armless seats or seats with right or left arms, so that sofa-style seating can be built up.

White-painted aluminium reproductions of Victorian, Regency and neo-classical seats range from simple to elaborate designs, with or without arms. Similar, but heavier and more expensive cast-iron seats are also available. Plastic-coated wire seats, in the style of Victorian wire plant stands, can be found;

pieces of furniture, and even several groups of furniture in separate 'rooms', defined by internal hedges, shrubberies or walls. The smaller the garden, the fewer pieces of furniture it can comfortably accommodate. Always allow for circulation space around the furniture.

Consider the purpose of the furniture and establish priorities when space or money is limited. If you plan to entertain outdoors, a table and upright chairs are more important and useful than loungers and swing seats.

With a dry shed, garage or basement for storage, the choice is wider than if the furniture has to remain outdoors, exposed to the weather, all year round. Heavy-duty, weather-proof plastic covers are available and offer good protection against winter ravages. Lightweight, folding furniture is easier to carry and store than

heavy, solid furniture, although some rigid seats and tables are stackable.

Consider how much maintenance will be needed, how much time you are prepared to spend on upkeep, and how soon the furniture is likely to need replacing.

Some garden furniture is available in kit form; other types are

▶ **Classic bench** Traditional styles suit most gardens, and a simple bench in cast iron and wood has a certain elegance. Available in kit form, such benches need regular maintenance.

they are neither particularly comfortable nor durable. There are also informal, woven willow tub chairs, in child and adult sizes, and woven 'peacock' thrones.

Sturdy slatted wooden armchairs are available to match traditional wooden benches. Slatted wooden seats can have upright or comfortably curved backs; some have steel or aluminium frames and legs. Garden stools and bar stools are available, but they can be awkward to sit on.

Loungers are made of wood, expanded resin or lightweight metal frames, with fitted cushions. Loungers can have up to seven adjustable back positions and may have adjustable height; some convert from chaises-longues to armchairs. Many have integral foot rests and/or sun shades, others have separate foot stools, which can also serve as small tables. Loungers on wheels are easy to move and most fold flat for easy storage.

◄ **Timber furniture** White-painted wood has a clean, solid look. Hardwoods, like teak, oak and iroko, are expensive but will last a lifetime. Softwoods, such as pine and larch, are less durable and should be treated every two years with a wood preservative. Ideally, all wooden furniture should be stored under cover in winter.

▼ **Teak furniture** Natural wood blends perfectly with any garden scene and comes in a variety of designs and sizes. Prices vary, but solid teak furniture is never cheap. Left in the open throughout the year, the natural colour deepens with age; algae should be removed with a stiff brush and the wood should be rubbed down with a suitable furniture oil.

moved around the garden easily. Reproduction Victorian park benches, of cast iron and wood, are also available.

Benches with backs and arm rests are more comfortable than those without, and some have folding flaps on the arm rests for placing drinks.

Tables are made in the same range of materials and styles as benches and seats, and many fold up or can be stacked for storage. Sizes range from tiny, bistro-type round tables for two, to generous dining tables, with extra leaves for expansion.

Slatted or perforated table tops prevent puddles and increase the life of the furniture. Solid slate, stone and even marble are virtually indestructible, though pale marble may stain.

Circular tables take up less space for the number they seat than oval, square or rectangular

▲ **Wickerwork chairs** Attractive to look at and comfortable to sit on, wickerwork furniture is expensive, with a limited life-span. Left in the open for any length of time, wickerwork will deteriorate and lose its shape.

▶ **Sun loungers** Light and easy to move around, tubular-framed furniture is ideal for lazy, sunny days. It is relatively inexpensive, has good resistance to wear and folds flat for storage.

Upholstered seats are usually more comfortable than hard ones, but fabric cushions, such as cotton or viscose, should not be left out in the rain. Waterproof plastic cushions do not breathe and cause bare skin to sweat and stick to the plastic. Upholstery is sometimes included in the list price, but is often an optional extra. Off-the-peg upholstery covers and replacement fabric for deck and director's chairs are available in canvas, painted cotton, reversible cotton and various plastics.

Benches and tables

Benches are mainly two- or three-seater versions of garden seats in the same range of materials and styles. Rectangular and curved benches are sold, the latter to fit circular tables.

Simple, rectangular, slatted hardwood park benches are widely available, and some models have built-in wheels and handles, wheelbarrow style, so they can be

ones. Some garden tables have a central hole for a sun umbrella.

Certain ranges of garden furniture include small, low, occasional tables, drinks and coffee tables, and two-tiered trolleys. Some tables have adjustable feet, to give a level surface on bumpy ground. If table and chairs are bought separately, there should be at least 25cm (10in) clearance between the seat and the underside of the table for leg room.

Glass-topped garden tables are only beautiful if spotlessly clean, and present too much of a safety risk to be recommended.

Combined seats and tables include traditional wooden picnic tables, which take up little space, but can be awkward for those sitting in the middle of the bench. Some picnic tables have detachable and tilting seats. Outdoor dining suites, with matching table, side chairs, arm chairs or

stools, are designed to fit neatly together and make maximum use of table space.

Furniture accessories

Sun umbrellas can be free-standing on their own base, or be an integral part of a table or lounger. They have stainless steel, aluminium or wooden poles to fit into plastic bases filled with water or sand for balance. Most sun umbrellas can be adjusted to several angles. Fabrics include plastic and weather-proofed canvas, in various colours, patterned or plain. Some have fringed, scalloped valences, or optional light fittings.

Swing seats, or gliders, come with or without adjustable fabric hoods, and with high or low backs. They consist of a metal frame with upholstery, and are offered as part of larger ranges.

Hammocks of rope netting or cotton canvas are suspended in the branches of a tree or between two trees by cords. Hammocks should be securely fixed, and taken down and stored when not in use.

Furniture materials

Wicker, bamboo and cane furniture ranges from cheap to expensive. It is relatively short-lived,

▲ **Modish look** Collapsible director's chairs are the perfect solution where storage space is limited. Less robust than other designs, the chairs are easy to move around in the garden and can also be used indoors. The heavy-duty canvas takes a long time to dry out, and the chairs should be brought under cover in wet weather.

and, ideally, should be stored after each use, though it is often left out all summer. If painted, it needs regular repainting – more often if left in the sun, which causes the material to shrink and cracks the paint.

Metal furniture includes cast and wrought iron, though these are now largely replaced by aluminium. Lightweight and less expensive, aluminium is usually coated in a baked, white polyester-powder finish guaranteed against corrosion.

Stainless steel has a long life but is very expensive and can look tawdry unless regularly cleaned. Painted metal needs regular repainting with an anti-corrosive paint; black and white are the traditional colours. All metal furniture has a potentially long life if well maintained, but it is best overwintered under cover.

but are life-time investments; the latter range from cheap to expensive. Among the hardwoods, teak, oak and iroko last indefinitely and need little maintenance if left to weather naturally. They can remain outdoors all year round and offer the best long-term value for money. If oiled to retain their colour and preserve the grain, they should be treated regularly and stored under cover in winter.

Softwood, such as pine, is shorter lived and needs frequent treatment with a wood preservative. Rustic work of untreated, unpeeled logs quickly rots; furniture made from peeled and varnished rustic poles lasts slightly longer. Painted softwood needs repainting every few years and is best stored under cover in winter.

Painted furniture

White-painted garden furniture, if well maintained, looks fresh and bright, especially in a shady garden, and complements all colour schemes. Green is also popular for painted garden furniture, because it blends in with grass and plants. While very dark green (like black) does tend to disappear visually, some green paints can look harsh.

▼ **Patio set** Preformed plastic garden furniture often comes with a sun umbrella and optional matching chair cushions. They make seating more comfortable but should not be left outside during rainy weather.

▲ **Deckchairs** Lightweight, and taking up little storage space, deckchairs remain favourite garden furniture. Frames are made in wood or aluminium, traditionally with canvas covers. Cheaper models with plastic covers are sticky and uncomfortable in hot weather.

Plastic is generally cheap, and ranges from the flimsy to longlasting. Apart from washing it down (especially white plastic) all types should be maintenance-free. Glassfibre furniture is lightweight, easily cleaned, permanent in colour, but expensive. Some plastics are treated with an ultraviolet stabilizer, to preserve colour; others quickly fade. Some plastics become brittle and crack in sunlight, others are unaffected. All plastic furniture is best stored indoors over winter.

Wood includes hard and soft woods. The former are expensive

INDEX

Dimorphotheca 9
Dogs 36-7, 38
Dogwood 28, 32
Doronicum 26
Dovecotes 36, 64, 128
Dry-stone walls 91
Dustbins, container plants 120

E

Eccremocarpus scaber 47
Echeveria 73, 122
Echinops banaticus 13
Edgings 141-6
Eremurus elwesii 28
Erica carnea 121
Espaliers 16, 58-61
Eucalyptus 68
Eucomis 74
Euonymus 122
Euphorbia 13, 28, 72
Evening primrose 90
Evergreens 78-9, 138

F

Fan training 58-9
x *Fatshedera lizei* 70
Fatsia 71, 72, 73, 80, 82, 83, 120, 123
Fences 45, 49, 150-1, 153
Fennel 13, 19, 27, 71, 89, 90, 91, 92, 93,
   96, 98, 103
Ferns 29, 78, 80, 86, 120, 121, 123, 124,
   138
Festoons 62
Feverfew 13, 24, 28, 91, 96
Fig trees 72, 83, 122, 134
Fish 37, 38, 80
Flame creeper 47
Flares 166
Flax 23
Fleabane 13
Floodlights 165
Focal points and features 39-86
   arbours and pergolas 51-6
   centrepieces 77-80
   containers 67, 69, 73, 75, 76, 82
   corners 81-6
   cottage gardens 14
   fans and espaliers 57-62
   herb gardens 90
   ornamental buildings 63-6
   plants 67-9, 71-5
   positioning 69-71
   trelliswork 40-50
   wild gardens 29
Foeniculum vulgare 13, 27, 96
Foliage
   coloured 27
   in containers 122
   herbs 93-7
Follies 66
Forget-me-not 24, 28, 83, 121, 122-3, 132
Fountains 80, 84, 85, 126, 134
Foxes 34
Foxglove 8, 13, 26, 27, 28, 38, 139
Foxtail lily 28
Freesia 74
French beans 16, 20
Fritillaria 22
Frogbit 22
Frogs 33-4
Fruit trees 12, 16, 18, 33, 59, 60, 122, 139
Fuchsia 71, 73, 75, 76, 121, 123, 150
Furniture 113, 167-72
   in corners 81, 83-4
   metal 147, 148, 149-50, 151-2, 168-9, 171
   rustic 135-7, 140
   wooden 169, 172

G

Gardener's garters 11, 13, 78
Garlic 22, 24, 91, 92, 104
Gates 138, 148, 153-8
Gazebos 52, 64-6, 84, 136
Geranium 13
Glassfibre furniture 172
Glassfibre ornaments 131
Globe artichokes 19-20
Globe thistle 13, 72
Goat's rue 117
Godetia 123
Golden rod 38
Gourds 20, 62
Granite setts 141, 142-3
Gravel beds 96
Ground-cover plants 83
Growing bags 17
Guelder rose 22, 33
Guinea pigs 37, 38
Gunnera manicata 29, 68
Gypsophila 13

H

Hammocks 171
Hanging baskets 83, 122, 123, 150
Harlequin flower 74
Hawthorn 12, 28, 77
Hazel 28, 33, 72
Heartsease 92
Heather 28-9, 79, 121, 123
Hebe 72
Hedera 27, 44, 47, 121
Hedgehogs 22, 34-5
Hedges
   arches in 62
   corners 86
   cottage gardens 12, 14
   dwarf 145
   herb gardens 89
   potagers 15
Helichrysum 75, 94, 98, 121, 122
Hellebore 22, 83, 121
Helxine soleirolii 78
Hemerocallis 28
Herbs 87-112
   in containers 19, 122
   cottage gardens 9, 19
   growing 89-98
   knot gardens 19
   wild gardens 28
Hermodactylus tuberosus 74
Heuchera 13, 28
Holly 12, 26, 28, 32, 33, 62, 79, 138
Hollyhock 9, 13, 139
Honesty 13, 28, 32
Honeysuckle 9-12, 14, 22, 28, 38, 41, 47,
   51, 54, 61, 62, 64, 72, 79, 83, 121, 122, 139
Hops 47
   golden 28, 45, 64
Horehound 93
Hornbeam 59, 62
Horseradish 104
Hosta 13, 28, 66, 72, 80, 82, 86, 121, 159
Houseleek 120
Hurdles 139, 140
Hyacinth 121, 122
Hydrangea 22, 47, 83, 123
Hydrocaris 22
Hypericum 'Hidcote' 27
Hypochaeris radicata 22
Hyssop 91, 92, 104

I

Ice plant 38
Ilex aquifolium 138

Indian shot plant 73
Iris 12, 22, 26, 28, 29, 72, 74, 78, 98, 122
Irish ivy 47
Isatis tinctoria 93
Ivy 26, 27, 32, 47, 59, 72, 80, 81, 83, 120,
   121, 122, 123, 127, 134, 138, 143, 150,
   152

J

Jacob's ladder 26, 27
Jasmine 26, 47, 53-4, 62, 83, 117, 122, 139
Jerusalem artichoke 19
Judas tree 72
Juniper 67, 79

K

Kitchen gardens 15-20
Knautia arvensis 22
Knot gardens 19, 87, 90
Knotweed 27, 32

L

Laburnum 59, 60, 62, 122
Lady's mantle 10, 13, 14, 25, 26, 27, 82,
   140
Lamb's tongue 28
Lamium 28, 128
Larkspur 13
Lathyrus latifolius 26
Laurus nobilis 100
Lavandula 97
Lavender 9, 10, 12, 15, 28, 32, 38, 87, 90,
   91, 93, 97, 98, 145
Lawns
   cottage gardens 9, 12
   edgings 141, 142, 145
   herb 91
   meadows 22, 23, 27
Lead, decorative metalwork 131, 149,
   150, 152
Leeks 16, 17
Lemon balm 19, 89, 91, 93, 94, 96, 98, 105
Lemon verbena 93, 98, 105
Lettuces 16, 17, 18, 20
Leucanthemum vulgare 22
Levisticum officinale 106
Lewisia 122
Lighting 113, 163-8
Ligularia dentata 29
Lilac 28
Lily 22, 76, 120
Lime trees 59, 62, 152
Ling 28-9
Linum usitatissimum 23
Lobelia 72, 75, 85, 86, 116, 121, 146
Lonicera 12, 13
Loosestrife 27
Loungers 169-70
Lovage 92, 93, 106
Love-in-a-mist 139
Lungwort 28, 32
Lupin 13
Lychnis 22, 28

M

Macleaya cordata 28
Madonna lily 14, 125
Magnolia 44, 72, 122
Mahonia 22, 72, 79, 82
Mallow 13, 23, 120
Malus 22, 60, 77
Malva sylvestris 23
Mangers 150
Manure 9

ACKNOWLEDGEMENTS

Photographer's credits
Agence Bamboo 137(b), 139(b); Sommer Allibert 167; Heather Angel 21-22, 23(t), 32(t), 33, 34(t), 35(t), 64(b), 100(b); Barlow Tyrie Ltd 169(b); Linda Burgess 50(bl), 116-117(b), 120(tl); Brian Carter 102; Eric Crichton 8-15, 18, 25-27, 52(t), 65, 69(b), 83(b), 86(b), 96(b), 107, 109, 111, 112, 116(bl), 120(br), 127(t), 128, 129(t), 130(b), 132, 133(t), 135, 141-142, 143(t), 146(br), 150(b), 151(t), 152(b), 155(t), 156(t), 157(t); E.C.C. Quarries Ltd 63; Garden Comfort 170-171(b); Garden Picture Library (B Carter) 31(r), 66(t), 86(t), (H Dijkman) 126, (N Francis) 50(t), (J Glover) 6, 40, (M Heuff) 32(b), (A Kelly) 152(t), (J Pavia) 42-43(b), (Perdereau/Thomas) 20, 42(tl), 44(t), 45(t), 70(t), (D Russell) 156(b), (JS Sira) 76(tl), (W Stehling) 162, (R Sutherland) 45(b), 46, 54, 82, 83(t), 84(b), 85(b), 148(tl), 163, 169(t), (N Temple) 70(b), (Brigitte Thomas) front cover; (S Wooster) 75(t), 124(b), 127(b); John Glover 1, 55(b), 67, 72, back cover; Derek Gould 90(c),
161(t); Jerry Harpur 41, 89, 90(b), 91-92, 93(b), 125, 130(t), 137(t), 161(b); J Harpur/J Plummber 85(t); M Heuff 48, 56(t), 100(t), 116(t), 117(tr), 120(tr), 170(tl); Hozelock-ASL Ltd 164; Pat Hunt 94; Jacqui Hurst 115; Inklink 157(b); Insight Marketing Services Ltd 66(b); Lamontagne 23(b), 36(t), 43(tr), 56(b), 57, 60(b), 61, 74(t), 93(t), 108, 131, 136(t), 138(t), 146(bl), 147, 148(b), 148-149(t), 155(b), 172(t); Larch-Lap Ltd 53, 154(b); Andrew Lawson 17(t), 24(t), 36(b), 75(bl), 95(b), 129(b), 136(b), 138(b), 160(t); M Leach 34(b); G Leveque 59(t); S & O Mathews 68-69(t), 98, 139(t), 140(t), 154(t); Tania Midgley 19, 68(tl), 73, 74(b), 77-80, 122, 123(b), 124(t), 150(t); National Trust (E Crichton) 68(b); Natural Image (Bob Gibbons) 16(b), 59(b), 140(b), (J Meech) 31(l); Clive Nichols 2-3, 4-5, 76(tr,b), 114; Nova Garden Furniture 172(b); Frank Odell Ltd 166(tl,c,b); Hugh Palmer 47, 168(t); Phillippe Perdereau 117(br), 159, 160(b); Clay Perry 51, 52(b); Photos Horticultural 16(t), 17(b), 37(t), 38(b), 58(t), 81, 84(t), 95(t), 103, 105, 106, 143(b), 146(t), 158; Annette
Schreiner 49; Cindi Simon 50(br); Harry Smith Collection 35(b), 38(t), 44(b), 55(t), 133(b), 153; Stapley Water Gardens 165; C Ternynck 28-30; Elizabeth Whiting & Associates 24(b), 88, 96, 97, 123, 134(t), 151(b), (K Dietrich-Buhler) 71(b), (M Dunne) 171(tr), (Jerry Harpur) 58(t), 60(t), 62, 75(br), (Andrew Lawson) 71(t); Wickes Building Supplies Ltd 166(tr); P Woloszynski 64(t); Steve Wooster 134(b), 168(b).

Illustrators
Paul Cox/Reader's Digest 100(b); Elisabeth Dowle 101(t), 102(b), 103, 105(b), 109, 110, 111(b); Shirley Ellis/Reader's Digest 99(b), 100(t), 101(b), 104(t), 106; Collin Emberson/Reader's Digest 99(t), 104(c); John Hutchinson 105(t), 118-119, 164; Donald Myall/Reader's Digest 102(t), 104(b); Reader's Digest 107, 108; Kathleen Smith/Reader's Digest 111(t), 112; Gill Tomblin 90, 121.

Index compiled by Hilary Bird

Printing & Binding PRINTER INDUSTRIA, GRÁFICA S.A. BARCELONA
Separations COLOURSCAN OVERSEAS CO PTE LTD, SINGAPORE; Paper PERIGORD-CONDAT, FRANCE

53-012-1

KU-586-410

01132

01132

www design
flash

The Best Web Sites from around the World

www.rockpub.com/flashworld

ROCKPORT

BOOK
 Design: In Your Face New Media/Daniel Donnelly
 Cover: Daniel Donnelly
 Design Associate: Patrick Lang
 Strategic Design Consultant: David J. Link

 Production: Jesse Hall, Shoko Horikawa, Carolyn Short

 Introduction: Hillman Curtis

 Interns: Briana Martin, Robbie Reaves

 MSPI2: Mike Doyle, Jason Childs, Reid Seibold

 SPECIAL THANKS:
 Editors: Don Fluckinger, Jeannie Trizzino

WEB SITE: www.inyourface.com
 Design: Daniel Donnelly, Jesse Hall
 Production: Shoko Horikawa

© 2002 by Rockport Publishers, Inc.

All rights reserved. No part of this book may be reproduced in any form without written permission of the copyright owners. All images in this book have been reproduced with the knowledge and prior consent of the artists concerned and no responsibility is accepted by the producer, publisher, or printer for any infringement of copyright or otherwise, arising from the contents of this publication. Every effort has been made to ensure that credits accurately comply with information supplied.

First published in the United States of America by:
Rockport Publishers, Inc.
33 Commercial Street
Gloucester, Massachusetts 01930-5089
Telephone: (978) 282-9590
Facsimile: (978) 283-2742

ISBN: 1-56496-906-1

Printed in China

www Design

flash

The Best Web Sites from around the World
www.rockpub.com/flashworld

www des

90
NORTH AMERICA

A

SOUTH AMERICA
90

AFRICA AUSTRALIA AUSTRIA BELGIUM BRAZIL CANADA CZECH REPUBLIC DENMARK FRANCE GERMANY GREECK

n:flash

3 SITES FROM AROUND THE WORLD

EUROPE
30

ASIA
16

MIDDLE EAST
84

0

AUSTRALIA
24

350 — 450
DESIGN 350

ISRAEL ITALY JAPAN MEXICO NETHERLANDS RUSSIA SINGAPORE SWEDEN UNITED KINGDOM UNITED STATES

Flash. It's worldwide now. Pushing envelopes, design, and often frustration levels, all at the same time. If you are a particularly passionate person or perhaps an employee of Macromedia, you might call it a revolution. I suppose it is, though I hate to use a word as powerful as revolution in the same sentence with a product. A better way for me to describe it is as a door or a passageway.

The most important doors that Flash has opened for me personally are those that have led to where I am today. I was an employee of Macromedia back in '97 when they acquired the Flash technology. I remember very clearly having this box of what I thought was shareware dropped on my desk and having no idea what to do with it. In fact, it sat there for three or four days, quietly waiting to change my life.

After I began experimenting with Flash, I was hooked. Long enamored with the film title sequences of designers such as Pablo Ferro, Saul Bass, and Kyle Cooper, I suddenly found myself, as a graphic designer, capable of incorporating the same effects into my work. I was suddenly able to zoom, animate, bounce and spin things around for no reason other than aesthetic flair. And at first, that's what I did.

But it wasn't long before I learned, as the title designers I admired surely had, the value of restraint. In fact, it was through struggling to find ways to design motion graphics that could work without download bars that I learned about repetition, pacing, and economy. Experimenting with Flash and making mistakes taught me, more than anything had before, how to focus my work and shed any element that isn't absolutely necessary. Too much of anything, I soon realized, whether fonts, 3D elements, movements, colors, or text, not only affects a design's online performance, it more importantly, dilutes and confuses its message.

Flash also opened doors for me at Macromedia, affording me greater leverage within the company. While I enjoyed my time there, however, I couldn't see myself designing executive slide shows forever, with one eye on my stock options and the other on the corporate ladder. I knew that I had another side, one that craved professional and creative independence. So I started my own business. And it may sound dramatic, but by opening my eyes to that other side, Flash opened the door to realizing my dream too.

I'm sure that everyone working with Flash has a great story about how it has affected their lives and work. But beyond the personal level, Flash has changed design, marketing, and business practices on a global level as well.

This book is about that global impact. It's about Flash's effect on the World Wide Web and the expanding community of designers who live in the world's great cities and its rural enclaves alike. It's about the future of an extraordinary tool. Flash is a global language, carried over a truly global medium, bringing together a global community of designers that, together, may learn, grow, and chart the course of Web design henceforth.

At the same time that I was becoming aware of other new Flash designers, they were becoming aware of me. I engaged in online discussions about the various strengths and weaknesses of my own and other designers' work. I offered and received suggestions from people all over the world that I knew only by name, with whom I communicated only online. And among us all was an unspoken camaraderie.

And there still is today. We are all united by a passion for great designs and new possibilities. But we're also united, as if members of a movement, by an expressive form that is

always in danger of censorship, standardization, and corporate whitewashing. As graphic artists, we have a great deal of control over these things. Though we often support ourselves doing work for corporations, for example, we can use Flash to speak between the lines. Through an ostensibly commercial design, we have the freedom to use color, movement, rhythm, and sound to infuse the project with art—a universal language that speaks louder than any marketing slogan.

The sites and designs in this book represent the great, vast community of Flash designers around the world. In their designs, I see a rich mixture of influences and innovations. I see the progression of ideas and style in the designers' work, both individually and as a group. This book reflects how those who constitute this international community influence each other. It embodies the evolution of their work, revealing how their ideas are shared and come through in each other's designs. And, finally, it proves the ability of Web design to transcend cultural and political boundaries to foster a pan-global creative relationship between everyone working in the field. With the cama-raderie I mentioned before, Flash opens the door to this global community in a way that few things can.

Because of its wide availability, however, Flash carries the threat of developing a certain global homogeneity. One can argue that there are somewhere around ten templates for Flash site design and when visiting any Flash site you can immediately identify the template. In other words, Flash looks like Flash, immediately and without hesitation. I have heard many times that "Flash all looks the same." And there is some truth to that. There are the gray Flash sites with big pointy 3D elements and fragments of grids, the sliding redraw picture sites all somehow tied to a Barneys site of two years ago, the clean, white minimalistic Flash sites, and of course the Japanese lunchbox layout Flash sites where everything is sectioned off and the different boxes fill with content upon rollover of navigation elements.

So where do we go from here? What new doors will Flash open for us? I can only speak for myself and give words to my intuition. I believe Flash—and more importantly—I believe those designers around the world using Flash to express themselves or to express the visions of their clients will grow the movements I am witnessing right now. The random and chaotic action script driven experiments, where animations animate themselves, differently every time—these *generative* works will grow, revealing patterns within the chaos. Those patterns will then reveal new ways in which to communicate that perhaps doesn't rely so much on language.

Furthermore, as Flash becomes ever more prominent in the field of visual media, those of us working with it will be able to transfer the skills we develop to other visual media—namely film and video. In turn, the existing languages of those media will be affected by Flash as well. In many ways, they have been already. We are on the cusp of a new era, in which elements of graphic, interactive, and motion design will meld with traditional, filmic narratives, creating a new visual language that spans all existing visual media.

This book is a testament to the power of a great graphic tool, one that is ever-evolving, ever-improving. As such, we who work with Flash have the luxury of always evolving and improving as well. And we do this as a community, one that transcends cultural, geographic, and language barriers. We're just beyond the first stage, though, and many of the possibilities Flash holds are still to be discovered. This book reflects a great start, and points to an even greater future.

D. Hillman Curtis

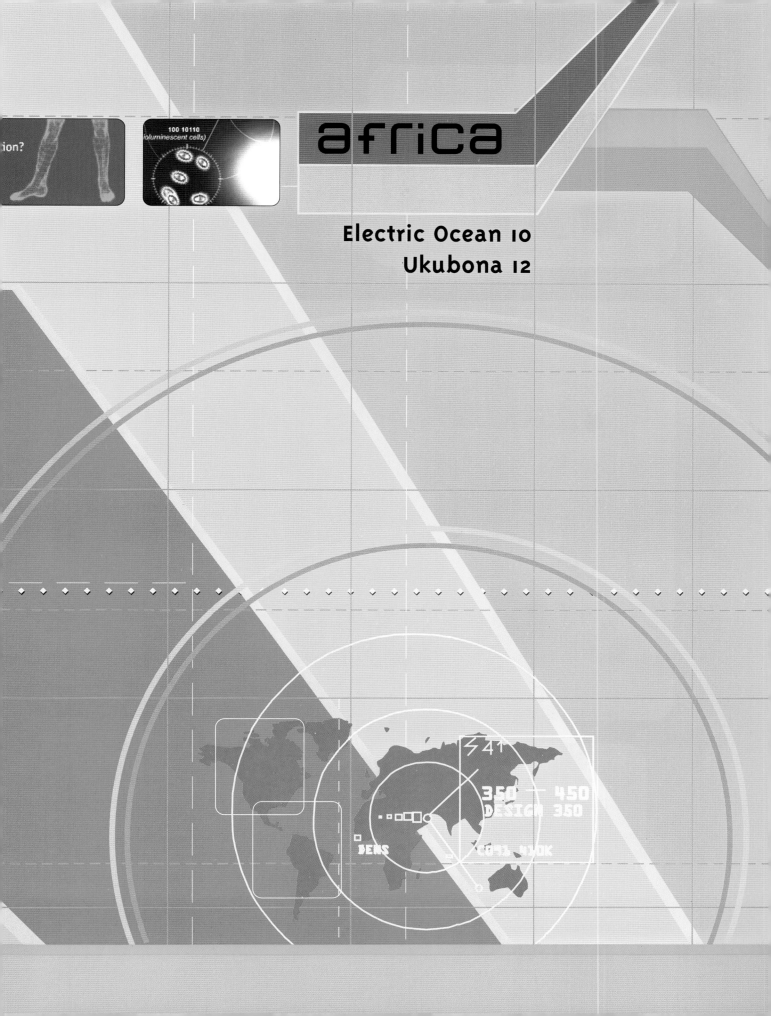

africa

Electric Ocean 10
Ukubona 12

100 10110
(luminescent cells)

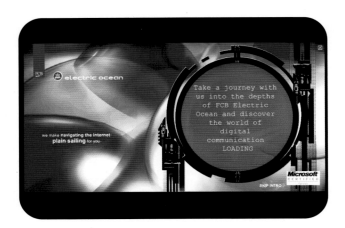

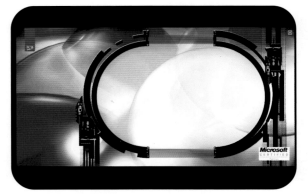

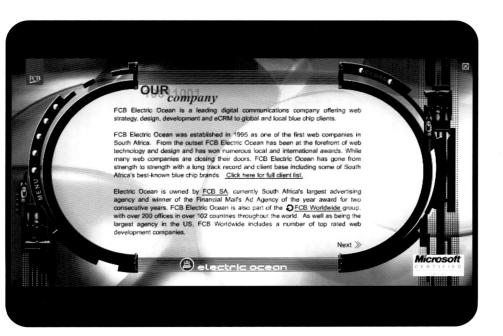

FCB Electric Ocean is a digital communications company owned by FCB SA, one of South Africa's largest advertising agencies. Electric Ocean's portfolio, shown here, features an interface that combines the visuals of an underwater scene with the structural mechanics of a submarinelike design theme for previewing their work. The design includes the pings and noises of an underwater experience and the hydraulic sounds of expanding and contracting equipment.

Using Flash animation to create a series of bioluminescent animated cells, the designers play upon the company's tag line, "A Source of Light in a Sea of Digital Communication." Clicking on the glowing cells initiates a pop-up window that begins to scroll as it reveals the strategies and comparisons between the company's technical expertise and the deep-sea phenomenon of bioluminescent light.

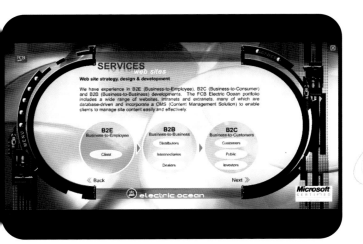

SOUTH AFRICA
www.fcbelectricocean.com

Project:	Self promotion portfolio
Design Firm:	FCB Electric Ocean
Design:	Pedro Pereira, Vincent Sammy, Jorice Langerman
Illustration:	Pedro Pereira, Vincent Sammy
Programming:	Bhauk Nana, Cabelo Moshapalo
Production:	Pedro Pereira, Diane Ritchie
Copy:	Michelle Solomon
Project Management:	Claire Taylor
Authoring Software:	Photoshop, Fireworks, 3ds max
Specs:	20MB (full site)
Language:	English
Special Features:	Screensaver

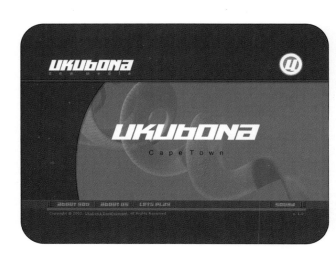

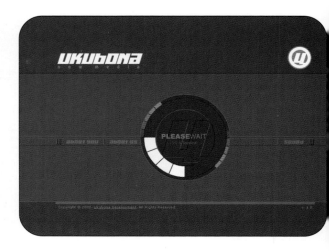

Ukubona is a design firm located in Cape Town, South Africa. The firm created its Ukubona.tv Web site as an interactive showcase of its high-end Web design featuring conventional HTML, broadband (streaming video) production, and Flash design.

The Ukubona site shows potential clients the company's Flash capabilities in designing a complete Flash site. Several areas within the site feature advanced ActionScripting techniques, such as the slider with a watchlike interface (facing page, top) that allows viewers to watch streaming video through a Windows Media Player, the "about us" scrolling "ring of success," and a 360-degree panoramic view of the company's offices (facing page, bottom).

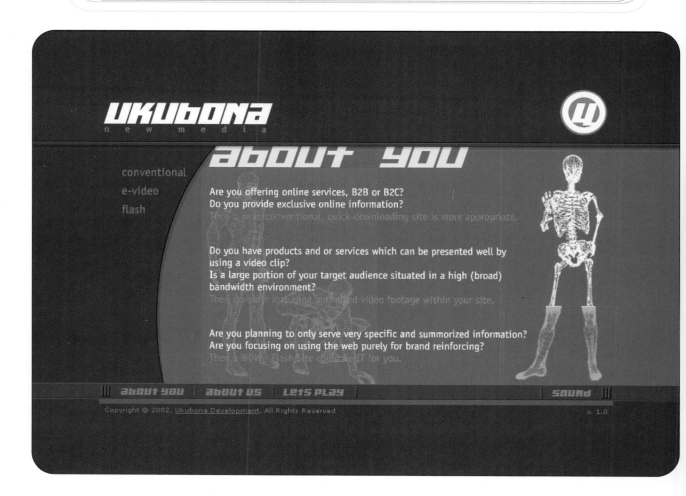

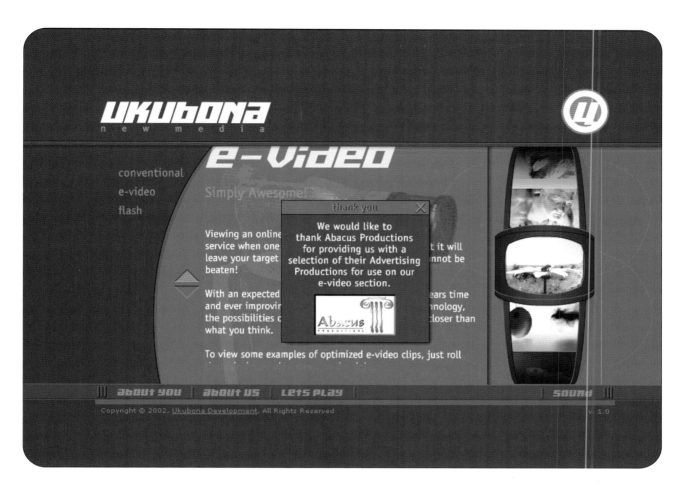

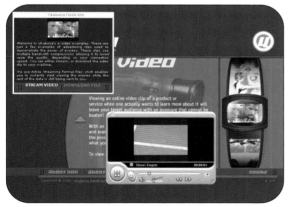

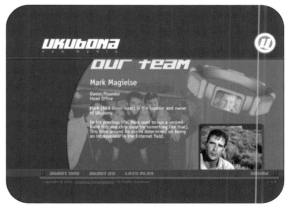

SOUTH AFRICA
www.ukubona.tv

Project:	Ukubona.tv
Design Firm:	Ukubona New Media
Design:	Alex Baroutsos, Garth Sykes
Photography:	Alex Baroutsos, Rakesh Chavda
Production:	Mark Magielse
Authoring Software:	Photoshop, After Effects, Premiere, 3ds max, Swift 3D
Specs:	800 x 600, 900KB, full screen
Language:	English
Special Features:	Streaming video

asia

water
re is always by our side

HONG KONG
www.itcatmedia.com/school

Project:	itCat Media Designer's School
Design Firm:	itCat Media Limited
Design:	Stephen Lo
Programming:	Perk Sze
Copy:	Joshua Nannen
Project Management:	Novita Leung
Authoring Software:	Photoshop, Poser
Specs:	800 x 600, 200KB
Language:	English

When itCat's designers began conceptualizing their online design school, they realized early that the quality of the site's design would be an important decision-making factor to potential students. To this end, rather than just provide static descriptions of course offerings to site visitors, they opted for a dynamic Flash Web site featuring the same high-quality design that they teach.

Colorful animated backgrounds, moving type, and 3D-rendered objects help to make this online new-media design school a distinctive and fresh alternative, particularly compared to HTML-based sites of similar training schools. The school also offers prospective students the chance to review the graphic and animated Flash projects that will be used for learning within the specific courses, such as animation, and interactivity.

JAPAN
www.adwave.co.jp

Project:	Self-promotional portfolio
Design Firm:	Adwave
Design:	Hitoshi Takahashi
Authoring Software:	Photoshop, Illustrator
Specs:	700 x 400
Special Features:	Music downloads
Languages:	Japanese, English

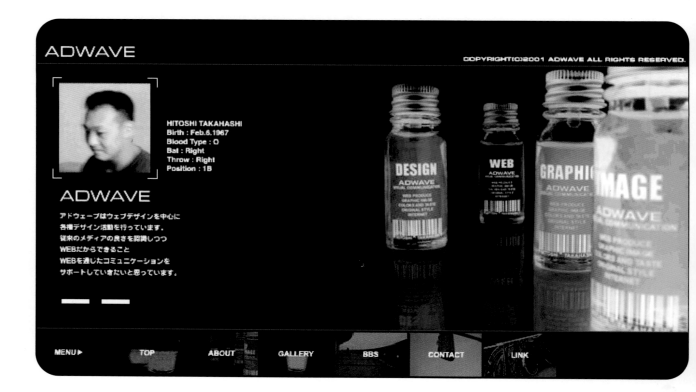

Adwave is a self-promotional site created by Flash designer Hitoshi Takahashi. The site showcases Takahashi's talent for designing clean, functional Flash interfaces, as well as an ability to add motion to type and graphics that rivals motion graphics work produced with higher-end programs.

Moving type is used throughout the portfolio as headlines and descriptive text, but the viewer is never subjected to an excessive number of effects such as those found in less creative, more gimmicky sites. Attention to detail and artistic expression can be seen in the Movie Gallery projects Takahashi has created, such as the Nature project (left). In this project, as with many of his works featured within this site, he combines slowly moving and fading photography with a storyline carried by elegant animated typography.

The most impressive elements of his site are the experimental typography projects featured in the Type Gallery. This area showcases four keyboard-activated experiences that allow viewers to create and manipulate full sentences, photo sequences, and individual letters by hitting keys on their keyboards and number pads.

These type sequences are ephemeral works of art, some dreamlike and some hard-edged, but remarkable in that the creator (Takahashi) and collaborator (viewer) are unknown to each other.

Sony Marketing Asia hired the Aretae firm to design and produce a Web site to promote the network capabilities of the Sony Walkman. To accomplish its goal of branding the product as a personal entertainment product for a younger demographic, the design firm created a site that focused on the Network Gadget as an e-lifestyle product.

Using vector drawings of tech-savvy Walkman users as the main focus, the designers at Aretae produced an HTML Web site with embedded Flash animations in different areas that show the characters relaxing or moving to the music as they use Sony technology. Combining HTML and Flash allows specific areas of the HTML site to be updated by traditional coding without involving Flash programmers or animators; at the same time the Flash animators can focus on specific Flash elements separately from the navigational elements of the HTML site.

©2001 Sony Marketing Asia Pacific Pte Ltd. All rights reserved. Terms of Use

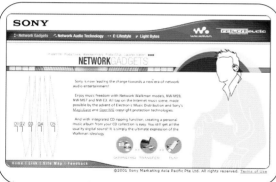

SINGAPORE
www.sony-asia.com.sg/networkaudio

Project:	Network Audio Entertainment
Client:	Sony Marketing Asia Pacific Pte. Ltd.
Design Firm:	Aretae Pte. Ltd.
Design:	Ivan Tan (AD), Adrian Chew, Tan Lei Yan, Charlene Leung
Illustration:	Ivan Tan, Adrian Chew
Programming:	Lim Mei Ling
Production:	Ng Ngee Fei
Authoring Software:	Photoshop, Illustrator, ImageReady
Specs:	800 x 600, 319KB
Languages:	English
Special Feature:	Games, screensavers, press releases

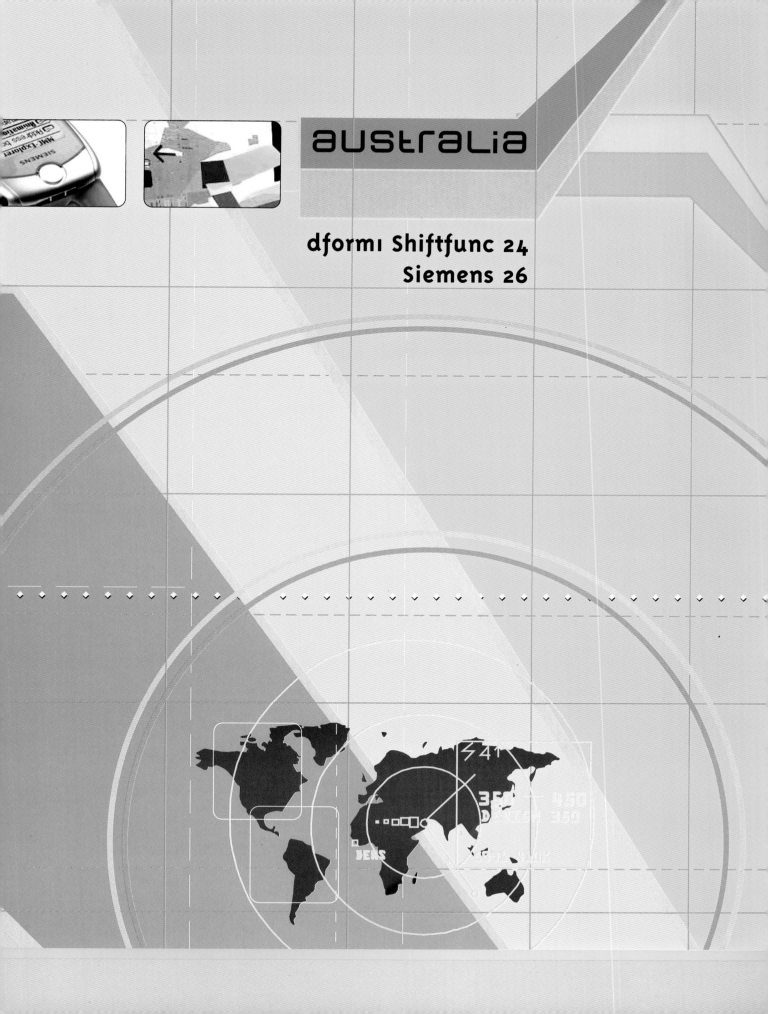

australia

dform1 Shiftfunc 24
Siemens 26

5

shiftfunc
dform1.

dform(one).shiftfunc. reunited.

After 5 years shiftfunc and dform(one) finally
managed to get their machines rolling again
and their minds synchronized. Honestly, they
forgot where they paused back in 95 but they
will continue from right here.

We're now open for freelance work, please
look through our portfolios:

→ Goto dform(one) visual portfolio
→ Goto dform(one) biography
→ Goto shiftfunc audio portfolio

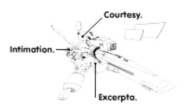

Courtesy.

Intimation.

Excerpta.

Just pet the robot and dig in...

dform(one) gotos:

| go ahead > | ⬍ |

shiftfunc gotos:

| go ahead > | ⬍ |

we love you:
mediatemple™ for supreme hosting
muce for the loading script

AUSTRALIA
www.dform1shiftfunc.net

Project:	dform(one) shiftfunc portfolio
Design Firm:	dform
Design:	Anders Schroeder
Sound Design:	Rasmus Kunckel
Authoring Software:	Photoshop, Illustrator, 3D Max, After Effects, Dreamweaver, SoundForge, Cubase, QuickTime Pro, ASP, PHP, Visual Basic, CGI, JavaScript, Generator
Specs:	770 × 606, 2MB, pop-up window
Special Features:	Wallpaper, original MP3s

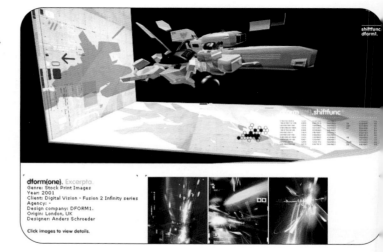

dform(one). Excerpta.
Genre: Stock Print Images
Year: 2001
Client: Digital Vision - Fusion 2 Infinity series
Agency: -
Design company: DFORM1.
Origin: London, UK
Designer: Anders Schroeder

Click images to view details.

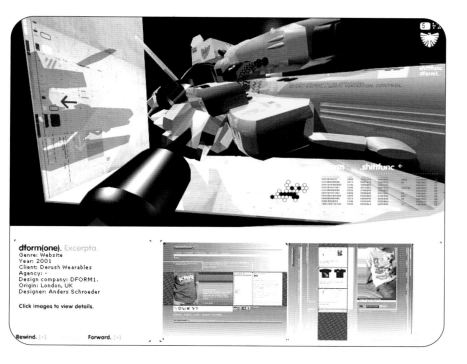

dform(one). Excerpta.
Genre: Website
Year: 2001
Client: Derush Wearables
Agency: -
Design company: DFORM1.
Origin: London, UK
Designer: Anders Schroeder

Click images to view details.

Rewind. [<]   Forward. [>]

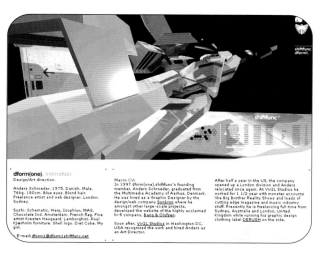

dform(one). Intimation.
Design/Art direction.

Anders Schroeder. 1975. Danish. Male. 76kg. 180cm. Blue eyes. Blond hair. Freelance artist and web designer. London, Sydney.

Sushi. Schematic. Warp. Isophlux. MAS, Chocolate Ind. Amsterdam. French flag. Fine artist Kresten Havgaard. Lamborghini. Poul Kjærholm furniture. Shell logo. Diet Coke. My girl.

E-mail: dform1@dform1shiftfunc.net

Macro CV:
In 1997 dform(one).shiftfunc's founding member, Anders Schroeder, graduated from the Multimedia Academy of Aarhus, Denmark. He was hired as a Graphic Designer by the design/web company Sunkron where he amongst other large-scale projects, developed the website of the highly acclaimed hi-fi company, Bang & Olufsen.

Soon after, Vir2L Studios in Washington DC, USA recognised the work and hired Anders as an Art Director.

After half a year in the US, the company opened up a London division and Anders relocated once again. At Vir2L Studios he worked for 1 1/2 year with monster accounts like Big Brother Reality Shows and loads of cutting edge magazine and music industry stuff. Presently he is freelancing full time from Sydney, Australia and London, United Kingdom while running his graphic design clothing label DERUSH on the side.

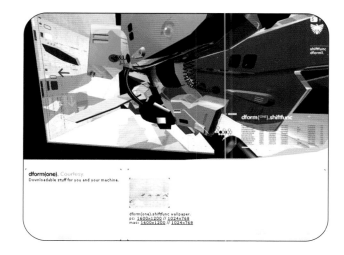

dform(one). Courtesy.
Downloadable stuff for you and your machine.

dform(one).shiftfunc wallpaper.
pc: 1600x1200 // 1024x768
mac: 1600x1200 // 1024x768

Dform(one) shiftfunc is a prime example of the creative design process taking place within a global and virtual environment. Anders Schroeder is a Flash designer working in Sydney, Australia, while his partner Rasmus Kunckel is a sound designer in Aarhus, Denmark. Together, they have formed a design collaborative that pushes the envelope of how Flash and audio can be combined to create a cutting-edge site.

The portfolio shown here showcases Schroeder's recent print and Web work in a stark interface that incorporates a powerful entourage of ActionScripting, HTML, and high-end software applications such as 3D Max and After Effects to accomplish the look and feel of a spacecraft.

As the site loads, sound effects and high-tech imagery reminiscent of a spaceship's viewing screen flash and scroll, finally revealing a 3D spaceship. The most dynamic element of the site's design is the use of the 3D ship as a navigation tool (as well as a navigation metaphor). To navigate, viewers roll over specific areas of the ship as it floats, vibrates, and shudders within the space dock. When viewers click a navigation link, the ship rotates and spins as it moves forward and loads information into the frame below. To add realism to the ship, the designers included multiple light sources to cast shadows from the floating ship.

AUSTRALIA
www.siemens.com.au/sl45

Project:	Siemens SL45 mobile phone
Client:	J. Walter Thompson Sydney
Design Firm:	Deepend Sydney
Design:	Ashleigh Bolland, Toby Grime
Illustration:	James Furey, Leon Rosenberg
Programming:	Ashleigh Bolland, Silas Rowe
Production:	Kate Theakston (Deepend), Karen Exton (JWT)
Audio:	Rob St. Clair
Authoring Software:	Photoshop, Illustrator
Specs:	300KB per module, total: 5MB
Language:	English

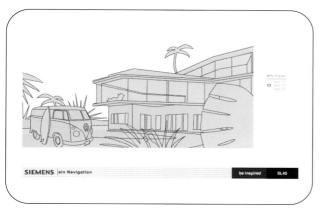

SIEMENS | ain Navigation

be inspired   SL45

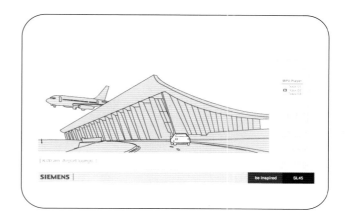

| 8:00am Airport Lounge |

SIEMENS |

be inspired   SL45

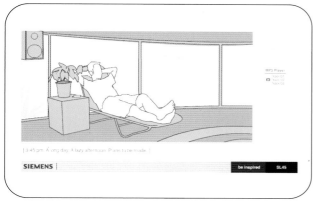

| 3:45pm A long day. A lazy afternoon. Plans to be made. |

SIEMENS |

be inspired   SL45

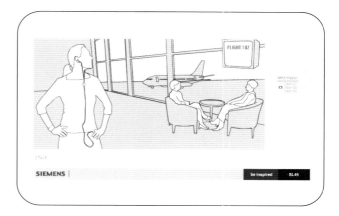

FLIGHT 102

| Nick |

SIEMENS |

be inspired   SL45

| With the built in MP3 player James listens to tunes whilst he waits ... |

SIEMENS |

be inspired   SL45

| 11:00 am The morning after a big night out. Cafe revival. |

SIEMENS |

be inspired   SL45

Deepend's design of the Siemens SL45 mobile phone Web site promotion reflects the cellular company's commitment to provide advanced mobile services for users, while also reinforcing Siemens' move to penetrate a young adult style- and fashion-conscious market.

Using vector-based line drawings of characters acting out scenes from everyday situations, the designers work to create a relationship between the mobile phone user in the scenario and the viewer by showing how cool it is to use the company's high-tech products and services.

The style of the site highlights the device's key selling point to its young audience by focusing on its MP3 player function. Modern, hip music clips accentuate the scenes as viewers watch the characters interact with the phones.

To stem the irritation that occurs from the wait for large file downloads, the designers offer a Flash game that viewers can play (facing page, bottom) as the files load.

europe

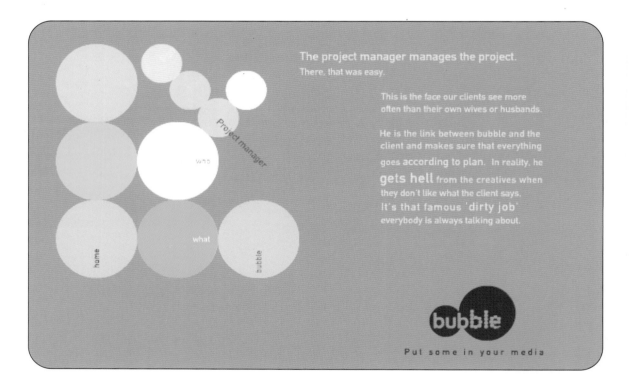

www.creativeclub.be: "Talk to many designers and they'll tell you that on the visual side, Webdesign needs a kick up the arse. One welcome trend is the use of hand-drawn illustration styles online..."

(Create Online issue 019 Winter 2001)

Online 01/11/01
▶ CANVAS
In progress 11/10/01
▶ Chris & Phil
In progress 18/09/01
▶ Clinsource
Online 15/09/01
▶ BRANTANO

For Whoopee!
▶ Subscribe now

bubble

The project manager manages the project.
There, that was easy.

This is the face our clients see more often than their own wives or husbands.

He is the link between bubble and the client and makes sure that everything goes according to plan. In reality, he gets hell from the creatives when they don't like what the client says. It's that famous 'dirty job' everybody is always talking about.

bubble

Put some in your media

BELGIUM
www.bubble.be

Project:	Bubble portfolio
Design Firm:	Bubble Interactive Media
Design:	Ilse Pierard
Illustration:	Ilse Pierard
Programming:	Bubble Digi-Work
Authoring Software:	Fireworks, Dreamweaver
Language:	English

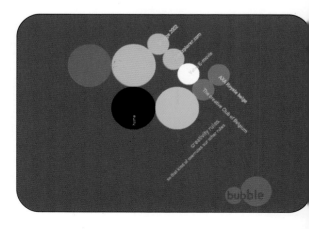

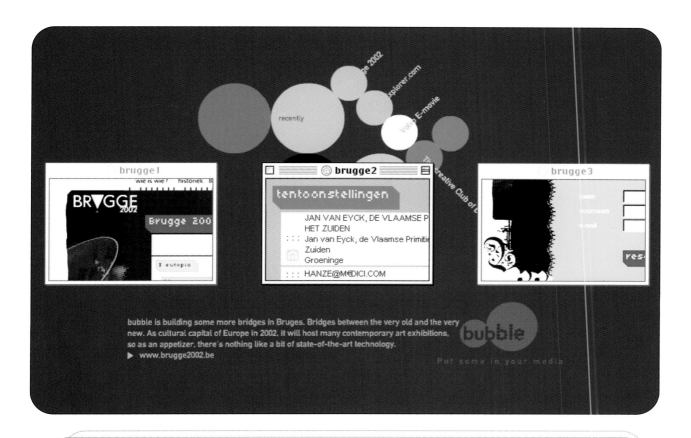

Bubble is a design firm located in Gent, Belgium. Its portfolio site shown here is a study in minimalism and demonstrates the less-is-more theory when it comes to design. Basic bubble shapes are the main navigational icons used throughout the site; when the viewer moves a cursor over a bubble, text appears inside each one, which in turn lets viewers know where the link will take them.

Flash shape-tweening morphs one bubble into another and another (below right), giving the bubbles cell-like motion as they split and divide to form the various interface screens.

While many sites embed Flash animation into HTML pages, the designers at Bubble have made a Flash-only site that uses JavaScript pop-up commands to position HTML portfolio boxes in a row when portfolio links are clicked.

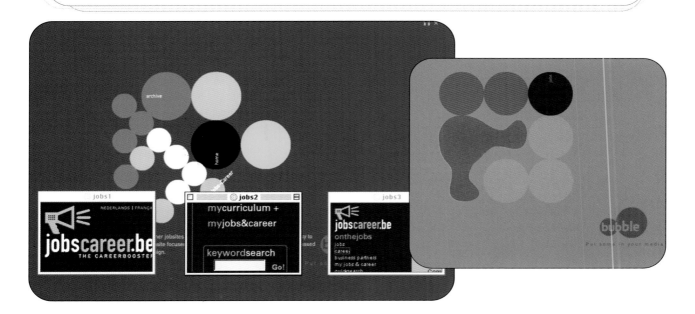

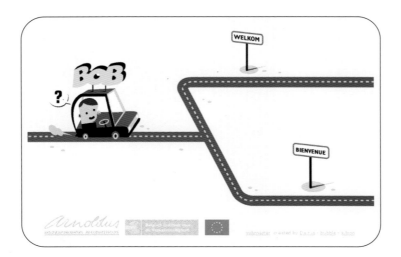

BELGIUM
www.bob.be

Project:	Bob
Client:	BIVV
Design Firm:	Bubble
Design:	Peter Dekens (CD), Steve Reggers (typography)
Illustration:	Steve Reggers
Programming:	Kurt van Houtte
Authoring Software:	Photoshop, Illustrator
Specs:	5MB (full project)
Languages:	Dutch, French

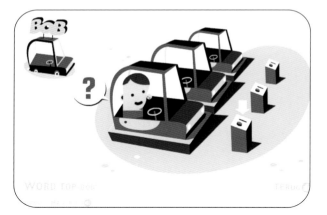

Though the Bob Flash site was created by Bubble in 2001, the Bob character was developed in 1995 by Belgian advertising agency DeKie. The campaign to stop drinking and driving has made Bob one of the most successful characters in Belgian advertising. Bob is now synonymous with the designated driver who agrees not to drink at parties, and who makes sure everyone gets home safely.

The site features the Bob character driving along a road that takes him past different areas, such as the Bob Information booth, a Bob banner site where viewers can download a banner to promote the campaign on their personal Web site, a Bob drive-in theater where a QuickTime video commercial awaits, a Flash game area to test your driving skills, and information about the Bob Bus that stops at cafés and parties to test alcohol levels and inform people about the campaign.

The navigation incorporates ActionScripting that allows the viewer to use the forward and backward keys to move Bob's car along the road and through the site. Viewers stop along the way to click on icons and experience the various areas.

Des jeux, encore des jeux!

Kid City is a virtual Flash-animated city that offers children an educational and fun way to discover the various services, products, and entertainment opportunities available in a big city. The Kid City site features a museum, city hall, movie theater, hotel, train station, park, and other areas to explore.

Before entering the city, viewers are offered a Flash or HTML site to choose from. When the Flash site is chosen, an animated character on a go-cart hurries over green hills toward the city.

The main interface is the layout diagram of the city, which shows a flattened, almost one-dimensional aerial shot of the buildings. When the viewer rolls the cursor over any of the building icons, a 2D-vector drawing of each building pops up to reveal an entrance. Clicking on a building takes the viewer to a specific page with an embedded Flash file at the top, and HTML text below.

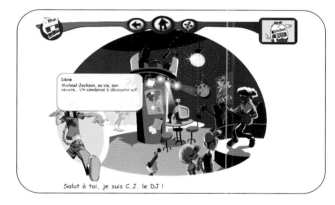

Salut à toi, je suis C.J. le DJ !

BELGIUM
www.kidcity.be

Project:	Kid City
Client:	Eduline
Design Firm:	Digital Age Design/Eduline
Design:	Renaud Collin, Rae De Weerdt, Cedric Danaux
Illustration:	Renaud Collin, Damien DeBieve
Programming:	François DeJardin, Emeric Florence
Additional Team:	Averpode and Belgacom Skynet
Authoring Software:	Photoshop, Illustrator, SoundEdit 16
Specs:	800 x 600
Languages:	French, Dutch

The Tatra Mléko site is a Flash promotion for the Czech Republic's Tatra milk producer. The introduction begins with two children's cartoon characters gliding through space and then landing on Earth in a flying saucer. After landing, the children use their transporter (located at the top of each screen) to explore the six different areas of the site to discover how milk is processed. Though the Milk Factory site is primarily an advertisement to sell milk, the fun of interacting with the animated characters (freeing the cows from the milk truck), and playing with animated machinery or searching for clues to the workings of different objects, can almost make you forget that you're being sold a brand.

The designers at Deepend, Prague have done well to create a branded experience that incorporates basic ActionScripting, such as the draggable transporter, and a large selection of quirky and enjoyable Flash animated characters. Other elements that stand out are a competition for creating your own comic and the choice of experiencing the project in several different languages.

CZECH REPUBLIC
www.tatramleko.cz

Project:	Tatra Mléko
Client:	Mlekarny Hlinsko, s.r.o.
Design Firm:	Deepend, Prague, s.r.o.
Design:	George Ihring
Illustration:	George Ihring
Programming:	Riccardo Zamurri, Lukas Jirka
Production:	Milan Chvojka
Audio:	Martin Kappel (DJ Kaplick)
Copy:	Martin Panek
Authoring Software:	Illustrator
Languages:	Czech, English

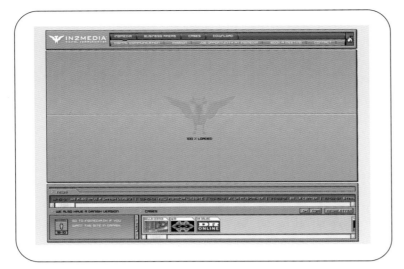

DENMARK
www.in2media.com

Project:	In2Media portfolio
Design Firm:	In2Media
Design:	Pelle Martin Christiansen
Copy:	Kent Hansen
Illustration:	Jon Knudsen
Programming:	Kim Lynge, Kasper Rasmussen
Authoring Software:	Photoshop, Illustrator, ColdFusion
Specs:	600 x 800
Languages:	Danish, English

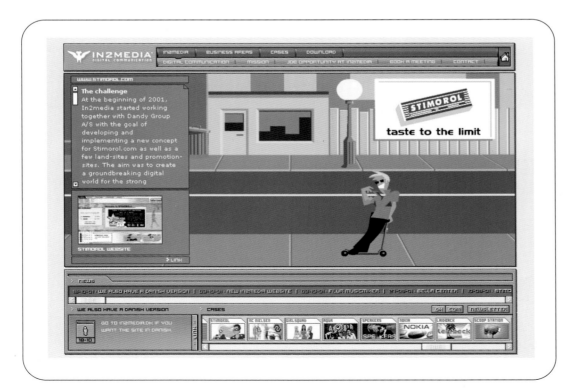

In2Media's portfolio showcases the company's work in a bold, solid interface with a metal framework. The top frame is focused on the business links: About Us, Mission, and Jobs. The bottom frame features case studies and thumbnail links to its portfolio of work. Finally, the large middle frame showcases images of work for various clients.

Other portfolio Web sites use smaller pop-up windows to show client work, but In2Media has chosen to showcase its work in the best possible light, sometimes using the original Flash imagery from the projects at actual size or showing animated Flash features of specific elements from the projects.

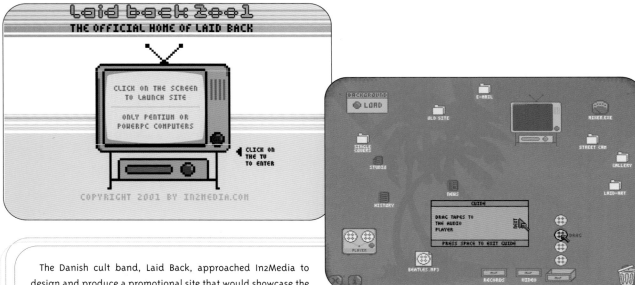

The Danish cult band, Laid Back, approached In2Media to design and produce a promotional site that would showcase the band's music and videos from the 1980s. To create a juxtaposition between the band's '80s-era music and its high-tech digital presence, the In2Media designers created a navigational interface that joined the two.

The combination of designing a computer screen with classic icons such as a reel-to-reel tape player, an old television set, and a mixer were just a few of the interactive elements integrated into the site. Other dynamic elements include drawers that open to allow music reels to be dragged to the tape player, vinyl albums that can be listened to by choosing various tracks, and music videos showing the band in its prime.

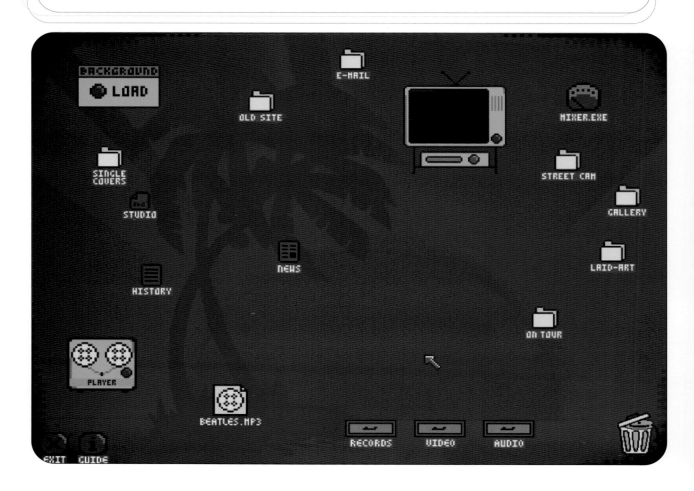

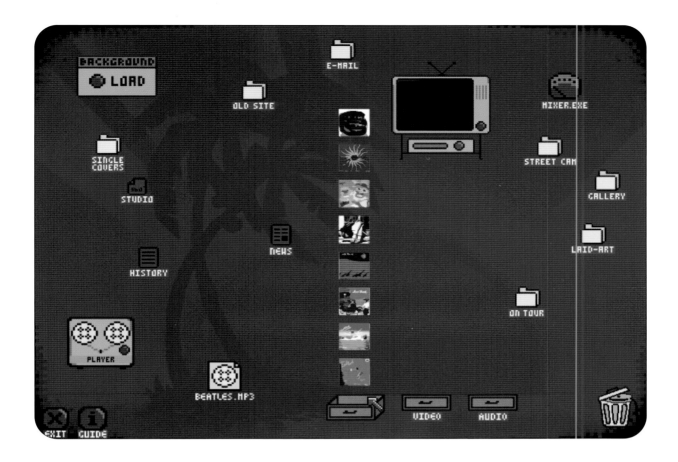

DENMARK
www.laidback.dk

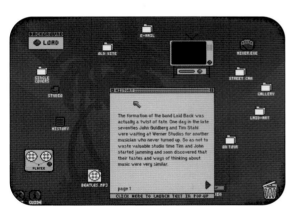

Project:	Laid Back music site
Client:	Laid Back
Design Firm:	In2Media
Design:	Kasper Rasmussen, Jon Knudsen
Authoring Software:	Photoshop, Illustrator, Cool Edit
Specs:	190kB (full screen)
Languages:	English

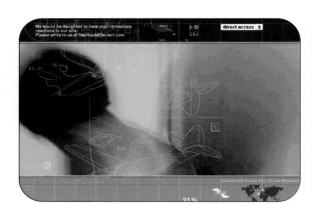

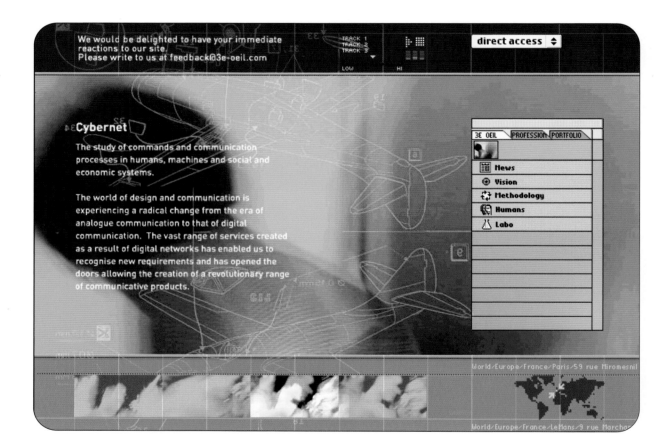

Troisième Oeil's Flash portfolio showcases the French design firm's work in a beautiful and skillfully designed interface that gives viewers the idea that they are looking into a world that is still under the touch of its creator's hand. Blueprintlike motifs, organic and inorganic imagery blurred into the background, and segmented video sequences of subways, high-speed film loops, crowd scenes, and other video imagery randomly load into the screen's lower half.

The navigation centers around an ActionScripted, draggable window that links to all of the main content. Once inside the body of the site, scrolling windows that feature small Flash demos of its client work can be viewed. One unique Flash element is the use of a full screen window in the background, with the main Flash interface in the foreground. This style of JavaScript pop-up window is used often—what makes the Troisième Oeil site unique is the Flash animation that the designers have embedded into the background window. Placing the main Flash window on top of another full screen image adds a new layer of depth to the design.

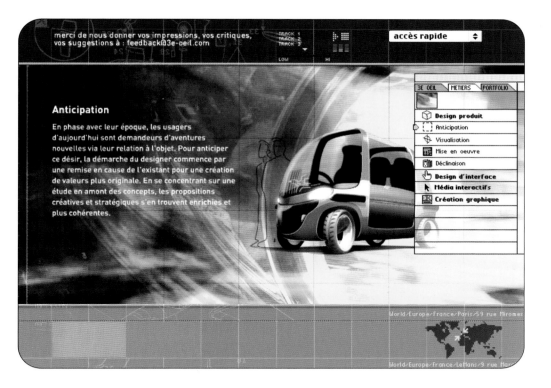

merci de nous donner vos impressions, vos critiques, vos suggestions à : feedback@3e-oeil.com

accès rapide

3E OEIL   METIERS   PORTFOLIO

Design produit
 Anticipation
 Visualisation
 Mise en oeuvre
 Déclinaison
Design d'interface
Média interactifs
Création graphique

Anticipation

En phase avec leur époque, les usagers d'aujourd'hui sont demandeurs d'aventures nouvelles via leur relation à l'objet. Pour anticiper ce désir, la démarche du designer commence par une remise en cause de l'existant pour une création de valeurs plus originale. En se concentrant sur une étude en amont des concepts, les propositions créatives et stratégiques s'en trouvent enrichies et plus cohérentes.

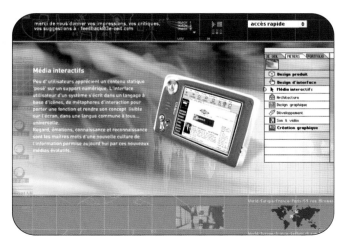

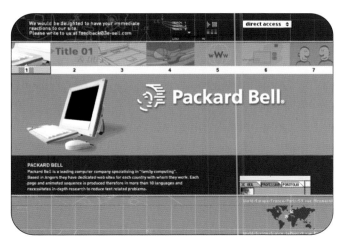

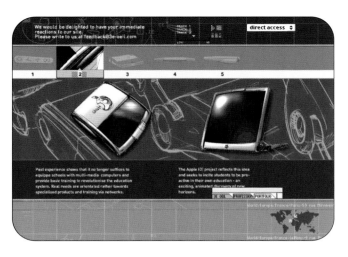

FRANCE
www.3e-oeil.com

Project:	Troisième Oeil portfolio
Design Firm:	Troisième Oeil
Design:	Chris Maresco Lecouble
Illustration:	Chris Maresco Lecouble
Programming:	Philippe Szymansky
Photography:	Chris Maresco Lecouble
Authoring Software:	Photoshop, Director, HomeSite, QuickTime VR
Specs:	800 x 600 (full screen)
Languages:	French, English
Special Features:	Wallpaper

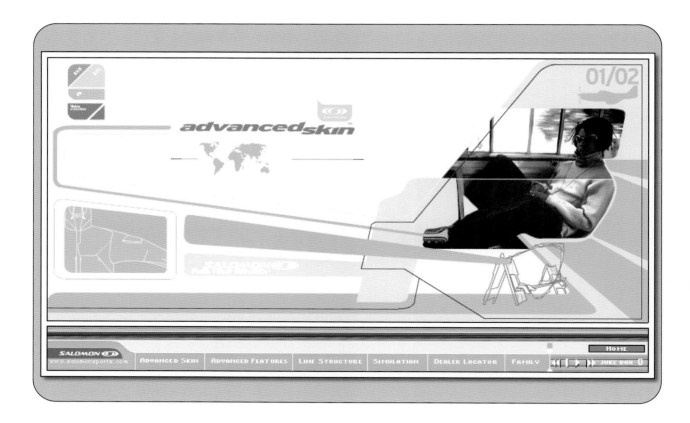

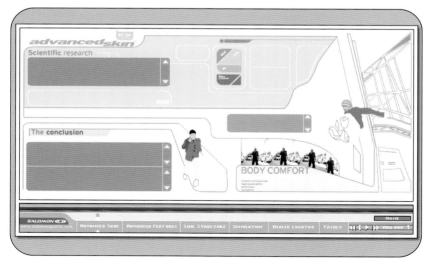

STL-551W

space

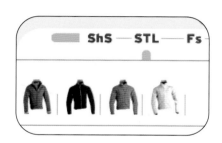

ShS — STL — Fs

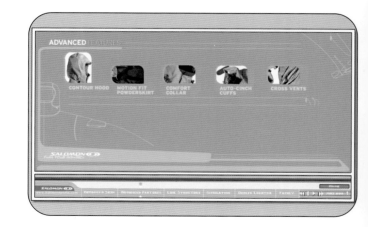

The Salomon Style Advanced Skin site introduces the high-end apparel collection from Salomon Sports to the target audience of active, outdoor enthusiasts who want comfort and style even while enduring extreme weather conditions.

The site is a fully interactive brochure that allows visitors to view the entire line of clothing, to mix and match outfits in Flash simulations, download wallpapers and screensavers, to view a photo gallery of the Advanced Skin team showing off the outfits, and to browse a photo gallery of extreme skiers captured in extreme places.

The navigation bar is located at the bottom of all screens for ease of use and quick access, while additional animated sequences and links within the various departments are designed around the respective vector-based drawings and photography. Viewers are given the choice of three subtle and unobtrusive background audio loops as they browse the site, and button sounds cue viewers that a link is active.

The project successfully incorporates a high frame rate throughout. This allows image scrolling and sliding, as well as interface loading to happen quickly and smoothly—essential for a target audience that already craves speed on the slopes.

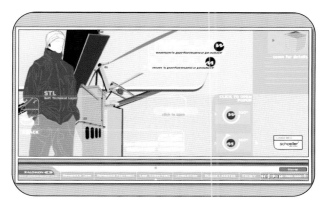

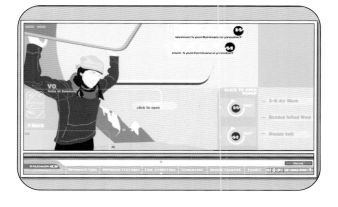

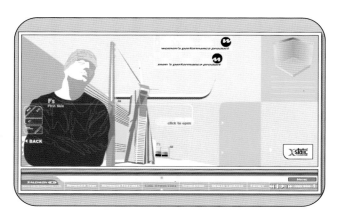

FRANCE
www.salomonstyle.com

Project:	Salomon Style: Advanced Skin
Client:	Salomon Style
Design Firm:	Xcess Lab
Design:	Phil Vergez, Numa Mouazan
Art Direction:	Phil Vergez
Illustration:	Numa Mouazan, Mathie J.
Programming:	Numa Mouazan
Music:	Reno
Specs:	600 x 800
Authoring Software:	Photoshop, Illustrator
Languages:	French, English, German, Finnish, Spanish, Japanese

Uzik, the Underground Zone of Interactive Kontent, is a French design group composed of in-house designers and freelancers located in Paris. Its team focuses on developing print and interactive content for the entertainment industry, with an emphasis on music projects. The Flash loading screen for Uzik's portfolio opens with an image of a silhouetted, bikini-clad woman that switches to a posterized version of the final image. The Flash movie clip image randomly blurs, fades, and flickers, evoking the feel of stills from a music video shoot. The group has produced work for well-known musicians such as an e-card for Madonna, flyers for Björk, and a Web project for Warner Music France.

The navigation for the site consists of one row of links across the top of the screen and secondary project links within each portfolio section. The projects themselves are located at the bottom of the screen within an area that opens and closes to reveal new content when links are clicked.

FRANCE
www.uzik.com

Project:	Uzik portfolio
Design Firm:	Uzik
Design:	Uzik Team, Frank Borato (freelance)
Programming:	Pierre Antoine Aubourg
Production:	Jean-Marie Tassy
Authoring Software:	Photoshop
Language:	English
Special Features:	Screensavers, Interactive Remix animations

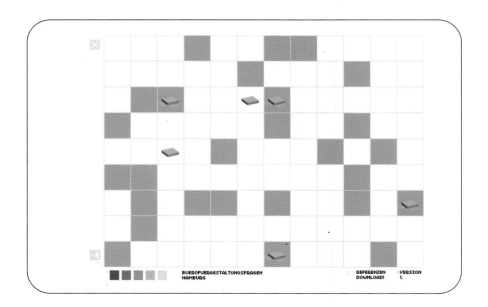

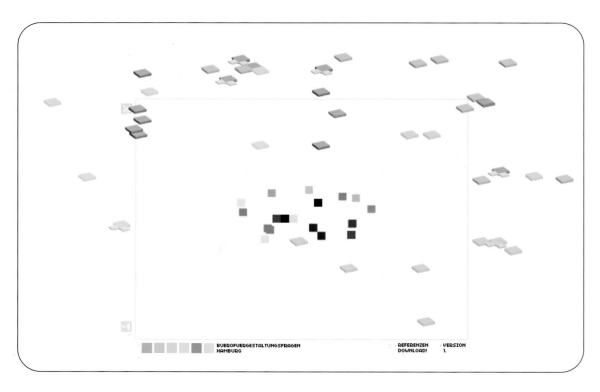

GERMANY
www.gestaltungsfragen.de

Project:	Gestaltungsfragen
Client:	Büro für Gestaltungsfragen
Design Firm:	Fork Unstable Media GMBH
Design:	Daniel Goddemeyer
Project Management:	Sandra Lülgens
Audio:	Klaus Voltmer
Programming:	Daniel Goddemeyer (Flash), Klaus Voltmer (Backend)
Authoring Software:	Illustrator, Fireworks, Freehand
Language:	German

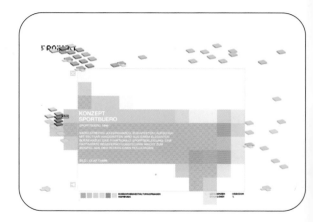

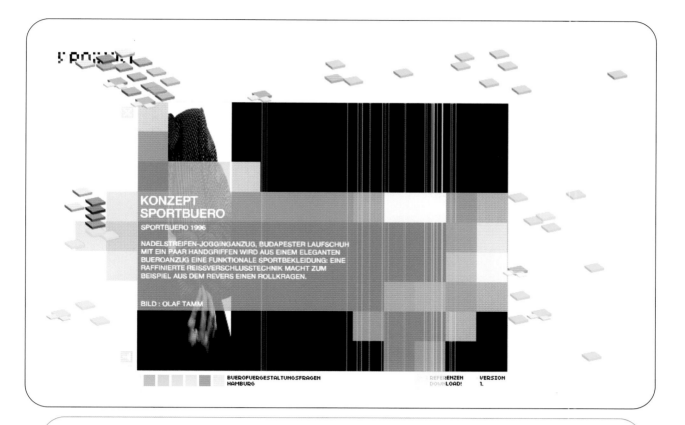

The Gestaltungsfragen industrial design studio wanted an online solution that offered the studio complete flexibility for future updates to its site. It also wanted a templated system that they could adapt themselves: one that included sound, animation, and experimental navigation. The studio also wanted Fork Unstable Media—the agency in charge of the design—to create a navigation system to contexualize the nature of the studio's work: modular architecture.

The Gestaltungsfragen site is built around building block elements that can expand or contract depending on the amount of content the studio wants showcased in the portfolio. The animated blocks form navigation categories when a specific block is clicked on, then offer further information from the portfolio upon clicking on one of the secondary blocks.

The blocks are in a constant state of movement, stopping only when the cursor rolls over them to reveal the link text and when they have been clicked on for a deeper exploration of the portfolio.

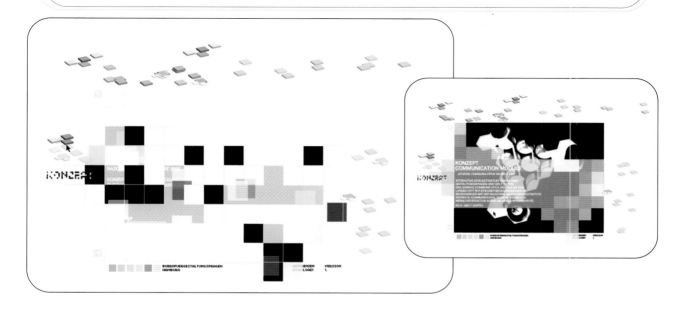

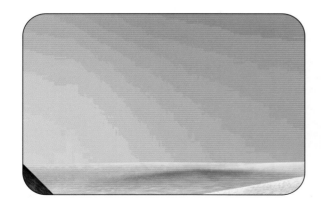

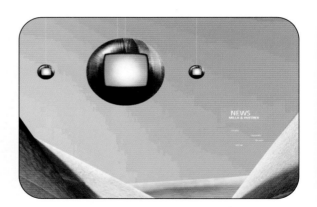

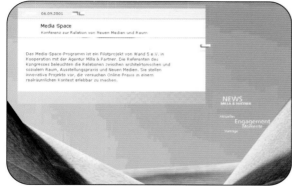

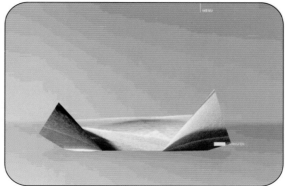

The interface of the Milla Flash site is a beautifully rendered organic structure that dynamically re-forms as viewers click on navigation icons leading to six areas. Exploration in these areas reveals windows into the event-management agency's world of business and its philosophy.

Diffus, the German design firm responsible for the design and realization of the project, used animated objects such as the unfolding flower (below) and animated light and color combined with atmospheric sounds to form a surreal landscape. Despite the playful and exploratory approach to displaying Milla's information, the navigation is easy to understand and use, and content is offered plainly and without unnecessary complication.

GERMANY
www.milla.de

Project:	Milla & Partner (Stuttgart)
Design Firm:	diffus—Büro für Mediengestaltung
Design:	Christian Weisser, Holger Pfeifle
Programming:	Andreas Schlegel, Uli Schöberl
Photography:	Chris Christensen
Audio:	Bastian Hollschwandner
Authoring Software:	Photoshop, Fireworks, Freehand
Language:	German

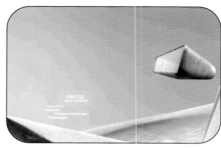

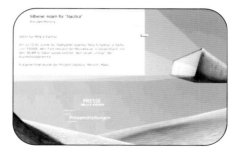

The Moccu portfolio offers an entertaining animation and navigation experience using high-level ActionScript programming to create random actions of animated elements, from clouds floating across screen to the movements of Mick, the site's mascot.

The site incorporates pre-loaders that show the Flash content loading before action starts, a performance check of the viewer's processor capabilities, and loading of the movies from Flash libraries using ActionScripting.

The style of the interface's design and the playful and cartoonlike color palette permeates the site and can be seen within the various projects featured in the portfolio section. Additional characters done in the robotesque style of Mick can also be found in the portfolio area.

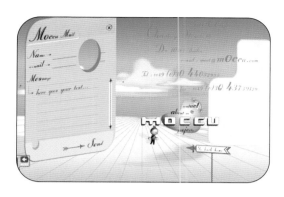

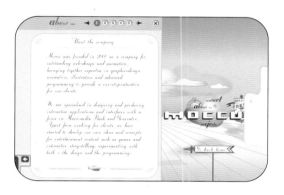

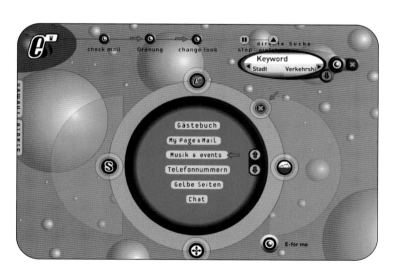

GERMANY
www.moccu.com

Project:	Moccu
Design Firm:	Moccu
Design:	Heiko Freier, Christoph Petersen, Jens Schmidt
Illustration:	Heiko Freier, Christoph Petersen, Jens Schmidt
Programming:	Thomas Walter, Bjoern Zaske
Authoring Software:	Photoshop, Illustrator, Freehand, SoundEdit 16
Language:	English

Welcome! I'm pretty amused you've chosen me as your pet assistant – and not that horny dumb rabbit

GERMANY
www.petgo.de

Project:	Petgo portfolio
Design:	Pet Gotohda
Illustration:	Pet Gotohda
Authoring Software:	Flash
Specs:	760 x 540
Language:	English

Welcome! I'm very happy you've chosen me as your pet assistant – and not that lousy stinking dog

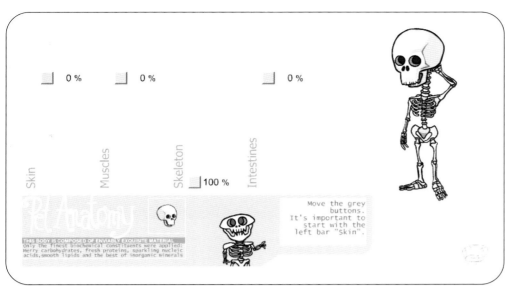

0 %   0 %   0 %

Skin   Muscles   Skeleton   100 %   Intestines

Pet Anatomy

THIS BODY IS COMPOSED OF ENVIABLY EXQUISITE MATERIAL
Only the finest biochemical constituents were applied:
Merry carbohydrates, fresh proteins, sparkling nucleic
acids, smooth lipids and the best of inorganic minerals

Move the grey
buttons.
It's important to
start with the
left bar "Skin".

All about Pet

An aspiring young
man manoeuvers
his way into
the heart of
a heteropteran.
A classic story
of ambition and
betrayal!

Pet Gotohda

N STOP SQUINTING SCEPTICALLY AT THE SCREEN LIKE THAT!
we are daring to look nifty, so deal with it.
come to the pleasure dome of a bug under influence
a man with entomophobia. Enjoy the drinks!

Petgo.de's designer, illustrator, programmer, and producer Pet Gotohda states his design imperative best: "Like a truffle pig, I like to explore sites; it enthuses me to stumble upon hidden and not-so-hidden features." With this concept in mind, he created a portfolio of his animated illustrations as a kind of pop-up book where the curious viewer can rummage around and discover the quirky and humorous characters that exist throughout the site.

Fun is definitely at the forefront of the Petgo site, but underneath the humor is an extremely skilled illustrator and Flash programmer who knows ActionScripting well. An example of his ActionScripting skills can be seen in the Pet Anatomy section of his site where the viewer can explore the anatomy of a character by adjusting opacity through slider bars to hide and reveal layers of skin, muscles, skeleton, and intestines.

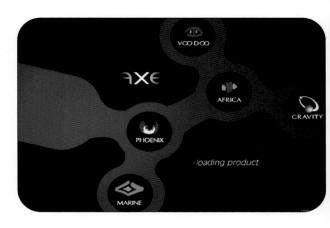

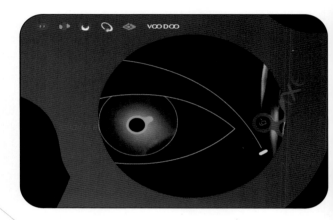

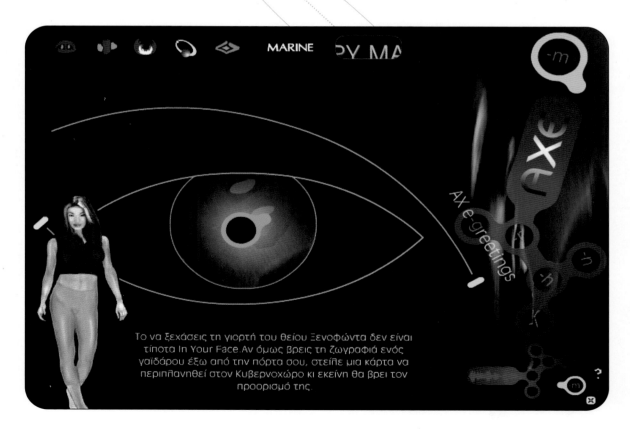

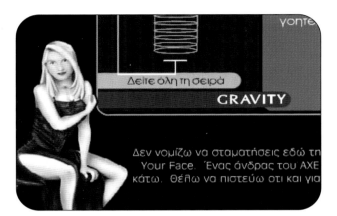

Unilever, a maker of men's body-care products, hired the em(phaze) design firm to create a Flash site that would target its products to a male audience. The site was designed with the product's tag line in mind, "Use it, and women will crawl at your feet."

To appeal to voyeuristic male viewers, the designers created an interface hosted by four virtual hostesses. Before entering the site, viewers choose one to accompany them throughout the site.

To gather information and create a profile of each viewer for Unilever, the designers incorporated pop-up questions that appear throughout the experience. Each time a question is answered correctly, the hostess removes a piece of clothing— a wrong answer and the hostess puts the clothing back on.

While navigating the site, viewers are also offered cinema and music guides, e-cards, horoscopes, a product gallery, and contests to enter.

GREECE
www.axe.gr

Project:	Unilever Hellas/AXE
Design Firm:	em(phaze)
Design:	Alexiou A. Vassilis
Illustration:	Stavros Papadakis, Odysseas Kontis
Programming:	Alex Coutsogiannopoulos
Authoring Software:	Photoshop, Illustrator, Dreamweaver, MYSQL, PHP
Special:	E-cards, wallpaper, screensavers, cursors, themes
Language:	Greek

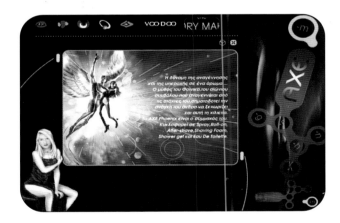

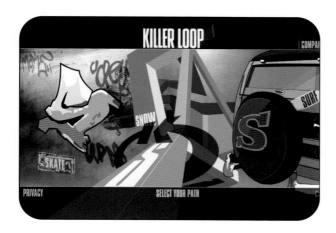

Killerloop's Flash site serves to strengthen the apparel manufacturer's position in the market as a leader and resource for those who embrace extreme sports: snowboarders, skateboarders, and surfers. Deepend SRL designed and produced this online community site to encompass the vision, philosophy, and lifestyle of the target audience.

Each of the four areas (surf, skate, snow, and store) was designed with distinct icon elements that introduce and characterize the different realms. The surf station is characterized on each screen by the Woodie, the surfer's vehicle of choice in the '50s and '60s. The snowboarding environment reflects the stylish, hard-nosed nature of the sport with a matrix of sharp angles and twists conveying a sense of speed and risk. The dominant feature of the skate area is the wall, which has names of legends etched into its surface, and animated skaters shooting across the screen performing skateboard acrobatics.

The store and community areas offer merchandise, downloads, and interviews to keep viewers occupied and returning. Deepend demonstrates its ability to combine outstanding graphics, animation, and technology in a site that loads rapidly and is accessible and usable.

ITALY
www.killerloop.com

Project:	Killerloop
Client:	Benetton
Design Firm:	Deepend SRL
Design:	Jim Morgan, Sarah Grimaldi, Andrea Mazzocchi
Illustration:	Maxo Ruggiero
Programming:	Riccardo Zamurri, Carlo Pascoli, Daniel La Nave
Production:	Riccardo Zamurri, Mike Harrison
Music:	Edoardo Cianfanelli
Authoring Software:	Photoshop, Illustrator, iMovie, QuarkXPress, Cleaner
Specs:	740 x 480
Language:	English
Special Features:	Wallpapers, screensavers, postcards

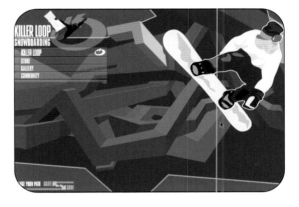

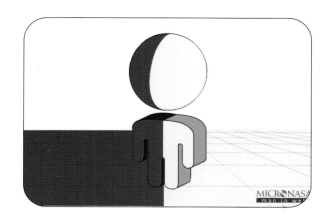

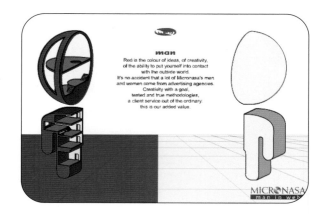

man

Red is the colour of ideas, of creativity,
of the ability to put yourself into contact
with the outside world.
It's no accident that a lot of Micronasa's men
and women come from advertising agencies.
Creativity with a goal,
tested and true methodologies,
a client service out of the ordinary:
this is our added value.

MICRONASA
man in web

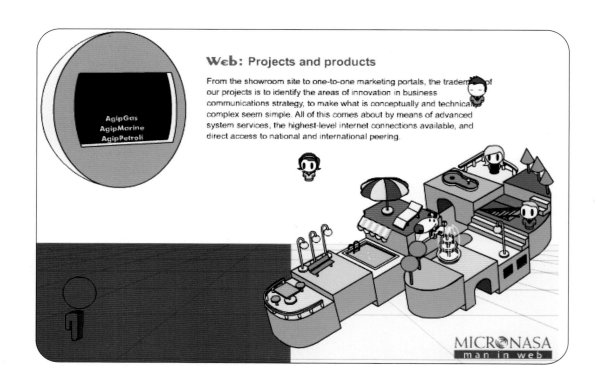

AgipGas
AgipMarine
AgipPetroli

Web: Projects and products

From the showroom site to one-to-one marketing portals, the trademark of
our projects is to identify the areas of innovation in business
communications strategy, to make what is conceptually and technically
complex seem simple. All of this comes about by means of advanced
system services, the highest-level internet connections available, and
direct access to national and international peering.

MICRONASA
man in web

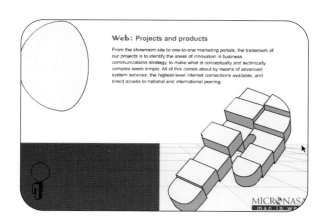

Web: Projects and products

From the showroom site to one-to-one marketing portals, the trademark of
our projects is to identify the areas of innovation in business
communications strategy, to make what is conceptually and technically
complex seem simple. All of this comes about by means of advanced
system services, the highest-level internet connections available, and
direct access to national and international peering.

MICRONASA
man in web

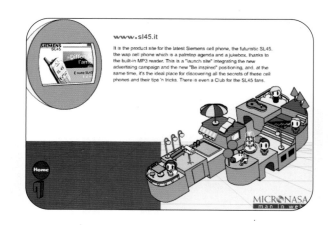

www.sl45.it

It is the product site for the latest Siemens cell phone, the futuristic SL45,
the wap cell phone which is a palmtop agenda and a jukebox, thanks to
the built-in MP3 reader. This is a "launch site" integrating the new
advertising campaign and the new "Be inspired" positioning, and, at the
same time, it's the ideal place for discovering all the secrets of these cell
phones and their tips 'n tricks. There is even a Club for the SL45 fans.

Home

MICRONASA
man in web

The Micronasa site opens with an animated half-red, half-blue icon figure representing the duality of the Italian design and marketing agency; one half human—"man," and the other technology—"Web."

Entering the site splits the man icon apart and offers viewers the option of choosing either area. Clicking on the right half, the Web: Projects and Products area, transforms the half-icon into a rooftop where toylike people wander. Rolling the cursor over a little person displays client images in the half-round monitor, which is actually the backside of the man-icon's head.

Clicking on the left side takes the viewer to the Man area of the site, where the viewer can find out about the culture of the company. This side shows the more humorous and personable elements of the agency, such as a cupid shooting the arrow of interoffice love into the rear of an employee, little people parachuting from an airplane flyby, or a technician electrocuting himself at a computer.

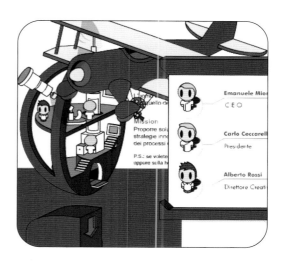

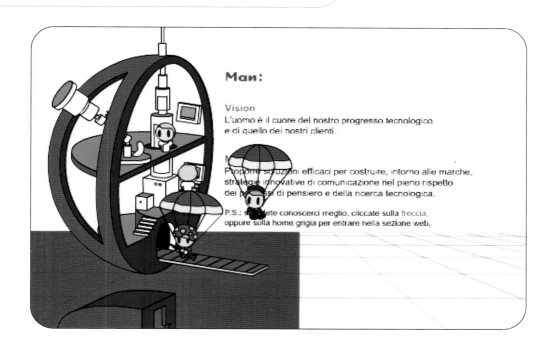

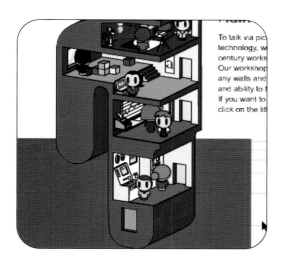

ITALY
www.micronasa.it

Project:	Micronasa SRL
Design Firm:	Micronasa SRL
Design:	Alberto Rossi (CD), Massimiliani Izzo, Enrico D'Elia, Eleonora D'Erme, Marco Quintavalle, Liliana DiCarlo, Gabriele Bichiri, Davide Cardea, Massimo Galgani
Illustration:	Enrico D'Elia
Programming:	Massimiliano Izzo, Renato Medini, Eleonora D'Erme
Production:	Samantha Spagnuolo, Fulvio Mezzo, Andrea Giovannetti
Authoring Software:	Photoshop, Illustrator, Freehand, Dreamweaver, Screentime
Specs:	800 x 600, 450kB (main interface)
Languages:	Italian, English
Special Features:	Icons, wallpaper, games, screensavers, tales

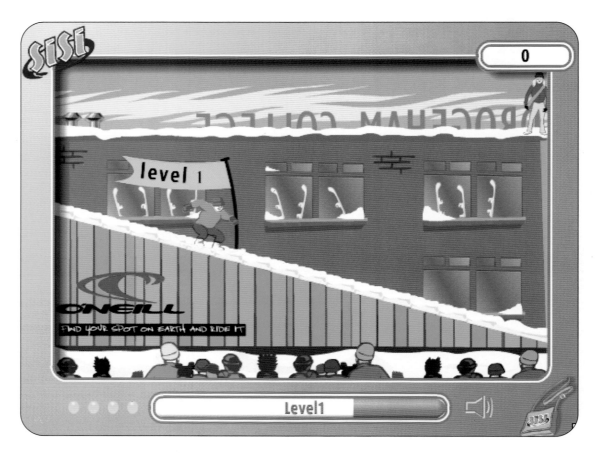

Tijd tot het volgende niveau

Het Zoen-spel

The Sisi orange drink site promotes a Dutch soft drink, and the company targets students between the ages of thirteen and nineteen years old. The design firm PPGH JWT—Colors, also based in The Netherlands, chose a virtual school environment to promote the Sisi product. The site opens with visitors choosing either a male or female character to serve as a host who leads them through the halls of the school and introduce the different areas, such as the music room, cooking class, concierge, or snowboarding training area.

To entice viewers into bookmarking the site and returning on a regular basis, the designers incorporated a number of games. Many of the games are updated on a monthly basis, and new games are added regularly. Viewers are also able to check the school roster and see who the high scorers are for each of the games.

The Saturday-morning-cartoonlike illustrations work well as vector drawings and offer a fast download for viewing all areas. Two navigation modes move the viewer through the school: The first is a scrolling virtual environment complete with billboards, a Sisi orange drink vending machine, and an Elvis character waiting in front of the music class; the second is a bookbag that opens when clicked on to reveal icons that will take the viewer directly to the chosen area.

Level 1

NETHERLANDS
www.sisi.nl/drogeham/archief.htm

Project:	Drogeham College
Client:	Vrumona (Sisi Brand)
Design Firm:	PPGH JWT—Colors
Design:	Orchidee Brasz, Dimitri Michels, Sander Kessels
Illustration:	Erik Krick
Programming:	Sander Kessels
Production:	Sander Kessels, Martyn Amendt
Authoring Software:	SoundEdit 16
Language:	Dutch
Special Features:	Bulletin board, SMS

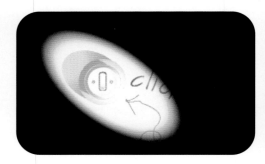

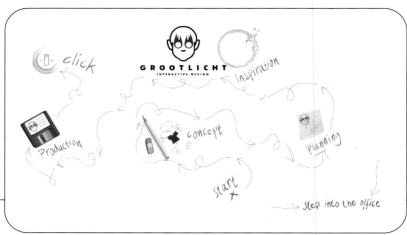

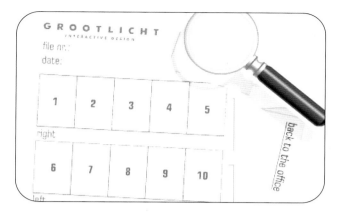

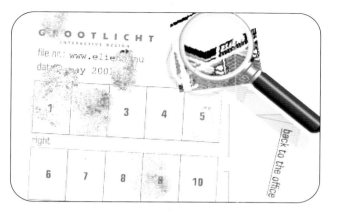

The Grootlicht portfolio site showcases the company with an interface that uses icons and navigational elements that could be considered "neo-retro," evoking design tools of yesteryear that many young new media designers have never used, and Flash designers in particular might never find anywhere near their computers. Incorporating objects such as floppy disks, pencils, scissors, and a film reel, the designers have created a humorous and, for some older designers (i.e., in their late 30s), a mode of navigation that is easily recognizable and intuitive.

The interface is reminiscent of CD-ROM design from the early 1990 and is a nice alternative to the raster lines and Flash vector drawings that are now common on the Web, as well as being imitated in print design and television.

NETHERLANDS
www.grootlicht.com

Project:	Grootlicht portfolio
Design Firm:	Grootlicht Interactive Design
Design:	Ivo van de Grift
Specs:	790 x 400, 3MB, (full screen)
Authoring Software:	Photoshop, Illustrator, Dreamweaver, Painter, Cool Edit
Language:	English

NETHERLANDS
www.spelerij.nl

Project:	De Spelerij amusement park promotion
Client:	VOF. De Spelerij
Design Firm:	Grootlicht Interactive Design
All Design:	Ivo van de Grift
Illustration:	Ivo van de Grift, Hester van de Grift
Programming:	Ivo van de Grift
Photography:	Ivo van de Grift, Lisete Photography
Authoring Software:	Photoshop, Dreamweaver, Cool Edit, CorelDraw
Specs:	740 x 450, 245KB, (fullscreen)
Language:	Dutch
Special Features:	Interactive games, sticker collecting

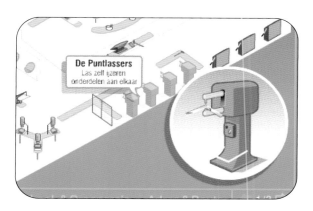

Spelerij is a Dutch amusement park. In contrast to traditional amusement parks (particularly those in the United States), Spelerij brings both children and adults together to experience play and learning at the same time. The park is filled with bizarre objects made from old machinery, a puppet theater, and a Uitvinderij, a unique workplace where children can create with materials such as wood, fabric, paper, and metal.

The Spelerij Flash site was designed and produced by the Dutch design firm, Grootlicht. Grootlicht designer Ivo van de Grift created the site in 2000 using Flash 3, before the ActionScripting in Flash 4 and 5 made programming for smaller file sizes much easier. The majority of the site features Flash vector graphics, with a minimum of bitmapped graphics to keep file sizes low. The updated site was switched to Flash 4—even though Flash 5 was being used—to make sure the site was compatible with the majority of browser plug-ins. Flash 4 gave van de Grift several advantages over Flash 3, such as the ability to replace complex movie clips with simpler ones and to replace conventional tweened animation with ActionScripting to accomplish the same processes.

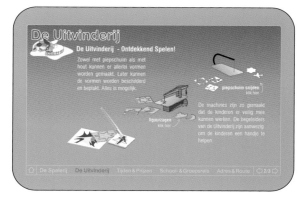

RUSSIA
www.conclaveobscurum.ru

Project:	Conclave Obscurum
Design Firm:	Art Lebdev Studio
Design:	Oleg "cmart" Paschenko
Photographers:	Oleg "cmart" Paschenko, Thomas Swan, Birdy
Authoring Software:	Photoshop, Illustrator, BIAS Peak, BIAS Deck
Specs:	450kB (main interface)
Languages:	Latin, Old English, Old Middle German, Old French
Special Features:	Audion skin

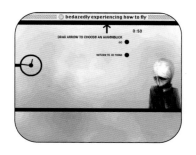

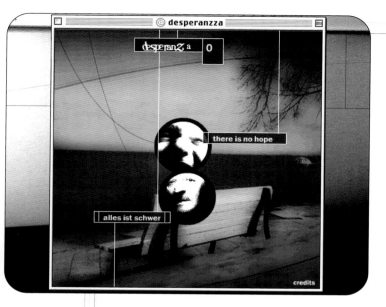

Conclave Obscurum is an exploration into the haunting and eerily artistic visions of Russian Flash designer Oleg Paschenko. The site is a collection of experimental narratives that offer viewers a look at Paschenko's illustration and story-telling abilities, while also showcasing his Flash animation and ActionScript programming skills.

Paschenko's JPEG illustrations of blurred alienlike characters jitter their way throughout the site. Realistic shadows add depth and mood to the characters, while mysteriously dark music and audio effects reminiscent of a David Lynch sound-track pull the project together.

Exploration is key to navigation of the site. While the basic navigation of arrows and rollover titles is easily accessible, there are no defined navigation bars or instructions on how to navigate the many areas. In some instances, this would detract from the overall experience of the project, but it can easily be forgiven here because of the large number of beautiful and mysterious images Paschenko delivers to the viewers as they browse through the site.

Within the portfolio area of the site (below), Paschenko showcases more traditional work for companies such as Epson. Even here, the interface is edgy, using pop-up windows overlaying a navigation palette of a half-hidden face and a Flash animation of crows flying out of a dark, dense forest of trees.

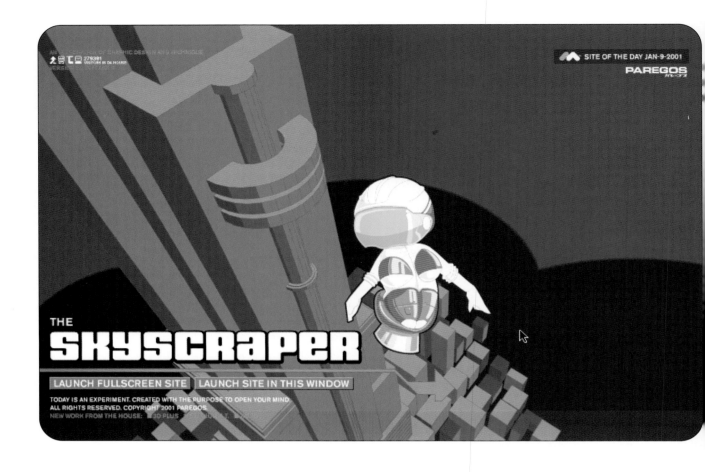

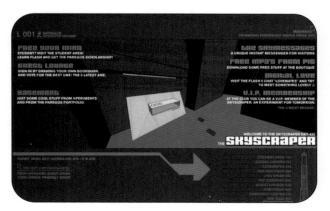

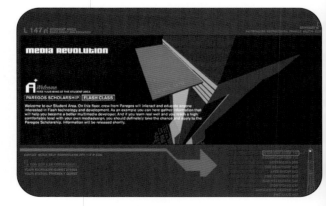

URLS: WWW.JENETT.COM · WWW.ZUPER.COM · WWW.ZX26.COM · WWW.UNCOLLECTIVE.CA · WWW.SUPERBE.ORG · WWW.YEAHBABE.ORG

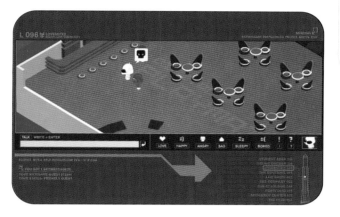

With the launch of The Skyscraper in late December 2000, Paregos Mediadesign—located in Stockholm, Sweden—pushed its repertoire of Flash skills to the limit. In The Skyscraper there are twelve floors to visit, and on each level, viewers can experience unique creative and technical approaches to Flash interactivity.

All of the floors in the Skyscraper offer animated explorations; Lovemates (facing page) is a fun and interactive chat room that operates on the concept of viewers entering a space-age lounge and communicating with other robotlike avatars, while the Soundcorner allows viewers to play music clips on piano keys while listening to the accompanying music.

The basic graphics are built in 3ds max and Swift 3D, with vector art also created in Macromedia Freehand and Flash. The Skyscraper contains, among other things, a Flash school for learning specific elements of the application and a music machine.

SWEDEN
skyscraper.paregos.com

Project:	The Skyscraper
Design Firm:	Paregos Mediadesign AB
Art Direction:	Robert Lindstrom
Illustration:	Daniel Stolpe
Programming:	PM Nordkvist, Klas Kroon
Production:	PM Nordkvist, Klas Kroon
Music:	Paregos
Authoring Software:	Photoshop, Freehand, 3ds max, Turbine (backend)
Specs:	740 x 480
Language:	English
Special Features:	Wallpaper, games, music, tutorials

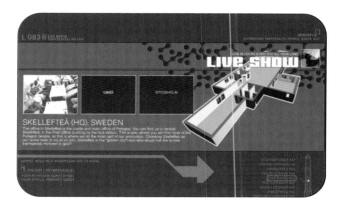

LOCATION DATE   TEMPERATURE HUMIDITY WIND   OUTLOOK
LONDON 21/1/2002   7°   81%   S   OVERCAST

CONTENTS
LESSRAIN: PORTFOLIO NEW TEAM JOBS CONTACT

WEBSITE   SCREENSAVER
FISH   EYES ONLY

LANGUAGES
ENGLISH DEUTSCH FRANÇAIS ESPAÑOL ITALIANO ΕΛΛΗΝΙΚΑ 日本語

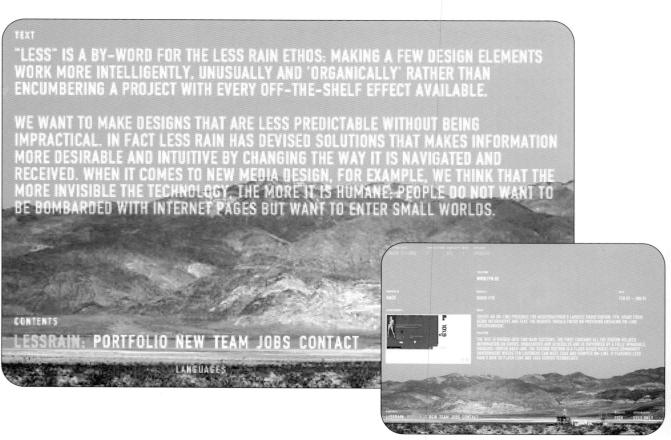

TEXT

"LESS" IS A BY-WORD FOR THE LESS RAIN ETHOS: MAKING A FEW DESIGN ELEMENTS WORK MORE INTELLIGENTLY, UNUSUALLY AND 'ORGANICALLY' RATHER THAN ENCUMBERING A PROJECT WITH EVERY OFF-THE-SHELF EFFECT AVAILABLE.

WE WANT TO MAKE DESIGNS THAT ARE LESS PREDICTABLE WITHOUT BEING IMPRACTICAL. IN FACT LESS RAIN HAS DEVISED SOLUTIONS THAT MAKES INFORMATION MORE DESIRABLE AND INTUITIVE BY CHANGING THE WAY IT IS NAVIGATED AND RECEIVED. WHEN IT COMES TO NEW MEDIA DESIGN, FOR EXAMPLE, WE THINK THAT THE MORE INVISIBLE THE TECHNOLOGY, THE MORE IT IS HUMANE: PEOPLE DO NOT WANT TO BE BOMBARDED WITH INTERNET PAGES BUT WANT TO ENTER SMALL WORLDS.

CONTENTS
LESSRAIN: PORTFOLIO NEW TEAM JOBS CONTACT

LANGUAGES

The designers at Less Rain set two goals for themselves when designing their company portfolio site: identify a visual style that represents Less Rain and design a simple, functional online presence.

The result is a colorful, photographic approach with a touch of reality. By animating the smaller details of the JPEG images, such as the rotating radar antenna in the middle of the desert, and incorporating audio sounds from nature; the ocean, seagulls, and crickets, the viewer's search for reality cues is satisfied.

The quick-loading site has maximum visual impact without the Flash bells and whistles that work well in many other applications.

The site is constantly connected to a weather information site and responds with updated weather information on the main screen.

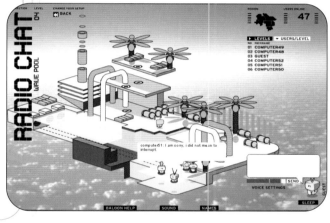

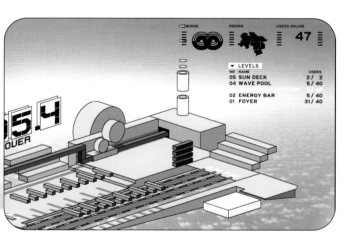

UNITED KINGDOM
www.lessrain.co.uk

Project:	Less Rain portfolio
Design Firm:	Less Rain
Design:	Lars Eberle, Carsten Schneider
Programming:	Thomas Meyer, L. A. Martinez, Vassilios Alexiou
Photography:	Sonja Mueller, Ronald Dick, Andrew Cross
Authoring Software:	Photoshop, Director, Freehand
Specs:	800 x 600
Languages:	English, German, French, Spanish, Italian, Greek, Chinese
Special Features:	Screensavers

UNITED KINGDOM
www.nesquik.co.uk

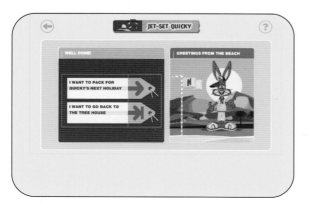

Project:	Nesquik pan European Internet strategy
Client:	Nestlé
Design Firm:	Zentropy Partners Ltd. (UK)
Design:	Andrew Mason (AD)
Illustration:	Andrew Tonkin (Interaction Designer)
Programming:	Matthew Greenhaleh
Technology Direction:	Fabio Fabrizio, Andrew Leszczynski
Project Managment:	Tom Wason
Account Direction:	Tim Watson
Authoring Software:	Photoshop, Illustrator, Director, XML technologies
Specs:	800 x 600
Languages:	English, Danish, Finnish, French, German, Hungarian, Italian, Norwegian, Portuguese, Spanish
Special Features:	Games, sticker collecting

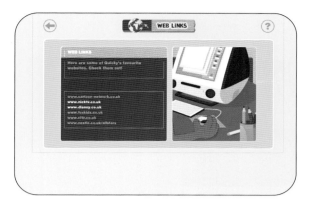

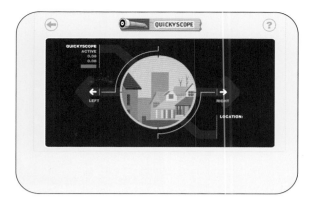

The Nesquik pan-European Internet strategy, created for Nestlé by Zentropy Partners, is a Flash site developed to promote the brand throughout the European market. The concept uses innovative Flash and XML technologies to produce a site that appeals to computer-literate children and enhances the perception of Nesquik as a fun chocolate-milk-drinking experience.

From the home page of the site, children can build and customize their own tree houses by choosing from more than 3.7 billion personalization options. After choosing the Tree house Builder link, viewers can customize their tree houses (below), including the telescope sticking out of the roof, colors and patterns of the house, and extras such as the ladder and windmill.

As an incentive for children to return to the site, the designers included Flash games and activities such as the interactive virtual stickers that can be found while exploring the various areas of the tree house and placed in a sticker album. Stickers are released on a monthly basis, and plans are in the works to add sticker-trading functionality to the site in the near future.

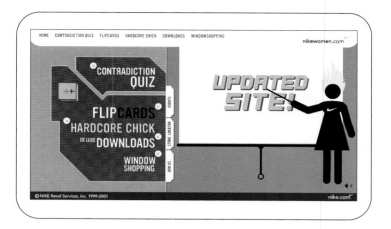

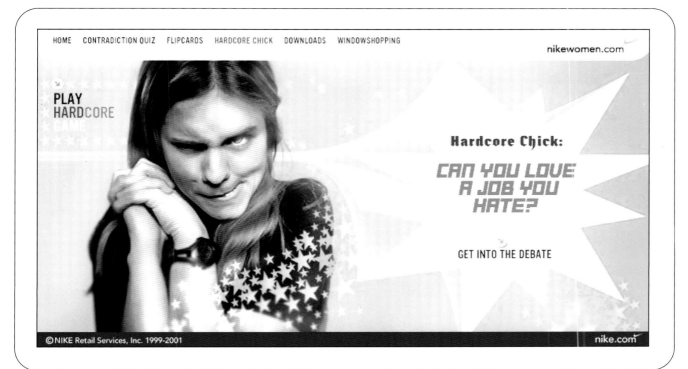

For the Hardcore Chick competition Web site, the AKQA agency created two characters—the "arsehole male" and the hardcore chick—who compete on a virtual rowing machine game to see who wins. After defeating the "arsehole," the user is prompted to e-mail three friends who will vote on whether their friend is hardcore—increasing the reach of the viral marketing campaign.

Tongue-in-cheek humor is the foundation of the site, with interactive experiences such as the Contradiction Quiz (He's a loser...but sexy, and I Love My Job...Hate My Job). There are also downloadable elements: wallpaper, e-mail cards, and a Flash-animated window shopping experience where viewers can take a look at Nike clothing and shoes.

UNITED KINGDOM
www.nikewomen.com

Project:	Nike Hardcore Chick competition
Client:	Nike Europe
Design Firm:	AKQA
Design:	James Hilton, Paul Kennerley
Photography:	David Clerihew
Programming:	Emile Swain, Guy Kilty, Matten Elwin
Production:	Ajaz Ahmed
Authoring Software:	Photoshop, Poser, 3ds Max
Specs:	380 x 760, 300KB streaming
Languages:	English, Spanish, French, Italian, German
Special Features:	Wallpaper, interactive game, e-cards, screensavers

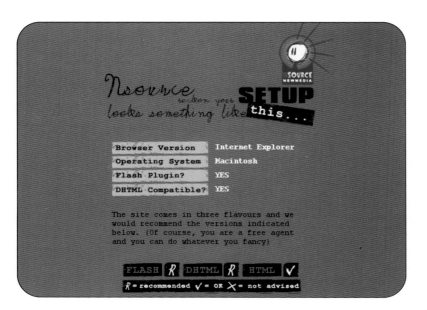

UNITED KINGDOM
www.nsource.co.uk

Project:	NSource portfolio
Design Firm:	NSource
Design:	Dan Dineen
Illustration:	Bryn Dineen, Dan Dineen
Programming:	Sam Allen, Bryn Dineen
Production:	Bryn Dineen
Authoring Software:	Photoshop, Freehand, HomeSite
Specs:	640 x 440, 392KB
Language:	English

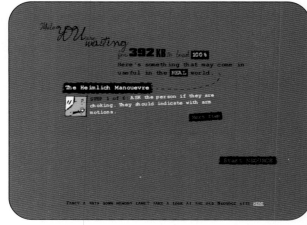

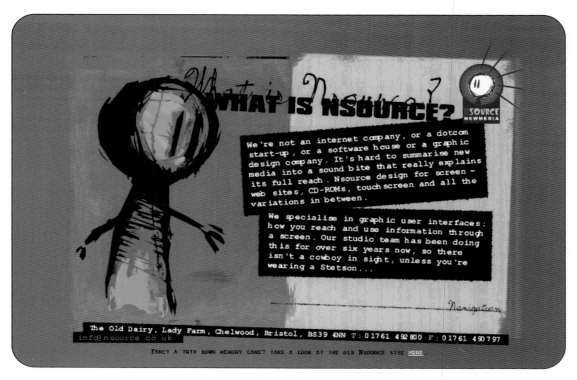

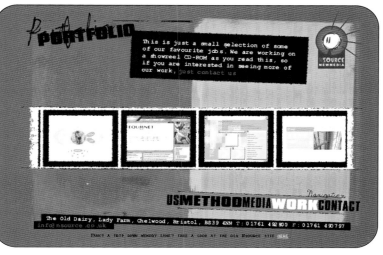

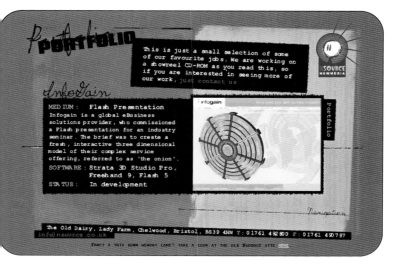

The Nsource site offers viewers a look at the steps and business methods the company uses to complete a project and also gives viewers a look at the work they've produced for various clients. The designers wanted to convey their sense of humor throughout the site, accomplishing this by creating playful illustrations and including humor in the written text. Content and characters are situated around a cartoon-like interface. Rough, hand-drawn, illustrated figures introduce viewers to various sections of the portfolio.

A bright red color palette augmented by contrasting oranges and yellows help set a dynamic and upbeat tone; bold black text blocks contrast with the rest of the interface and make it easier for viewers to find their way around the content.

Together, the tilted text blocks, eroded imagery, and rough-edged borders keep the theme of the illustrated interface going throughout the site.

To keep the design clean and uncluttered, Flash navigation is hidden until the viewer moves the cursor over the Navigation text. When the viewer moves the cursor away, the link becomes hidden once again.

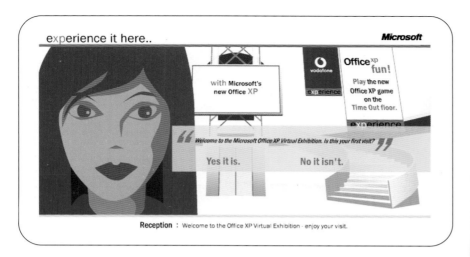

UNITED KINGDOM
www.akqa.com

Project:	Office XP Virtual Exhibition
Client:	Microsoft
Design Firm:	AKQA
Design:	Nick Holder, Miles Unwin
Copy:	Jamie Shohet
Programming:	Emile Swain, Faheem Razak
Production:	Franca Cumbo
Authoring Software:	Photoshop, Illustrator, Director
Specs:	800 x 600, 3.2MB
Language:	English
Special Features:	Video downloads, interactive game

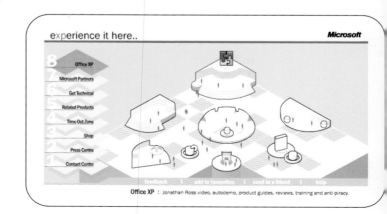

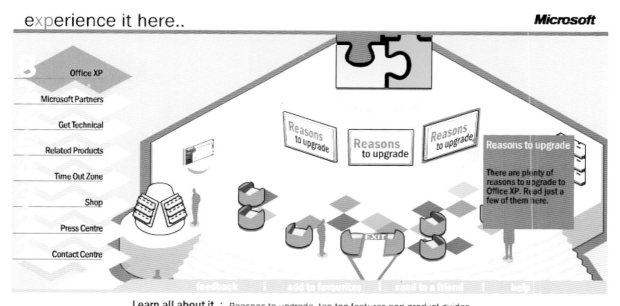

experience it here.. **Microsoft**

Office XP
Microsoft Partners
Get Technical
Related Products
Time Out Zone
Shop
Press Centre
Contact Centre

Reasons to upgrade
Reasons to upgrade
Reasons to upgrade

Reasons to upgrade
There are plenty of reasons to upgrade to Office XP. Read just a few of them here.

EXIT

feedback | add to favourites | send to a friend | help

Learn all about it : Reasons to upgrade, ten top features and product guides.

The Office XP Virtual Exhibition was developed as a promotional tool for the release of Microsoft's Office XP productivity software suite. The team at AKQA wanted site visitors to have the feel of attending a real product launch exhibition. To give the site this feel they started with a hostess to greet viewers at the entrance, offering them a lift to various floors of the exhibition. An elevator "lift" preloader was designed to disguise the loading time of the site once viewers choose to enter.

As with real exhibitions, the designers knew viewers would get tired of navigating through the large amount of content, so they created a Time Out floor for those surfers whose fingers got too tired of "walking" and who were ready to take a break. On this floor, viewers could send e-mail and play a custom Flash animated XP game.

Viewers also had the opportunity to enter a drawing for one of many different PC prizes after accumulating enough XP points during their time in the exhibit.

Contact centre : For general and technical help.

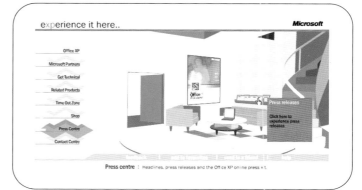

Press centre : Headlines, press releases and the Office XP online press kit.

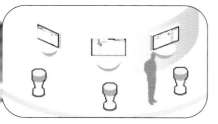
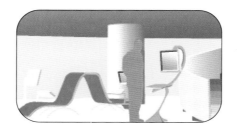

2 collection (to e *here*.

back   next

MIDDLE EAST

Ayala Bar 84
Batsheva 86

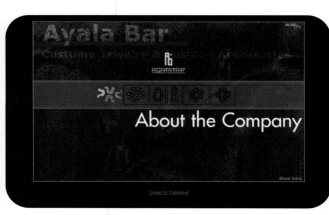

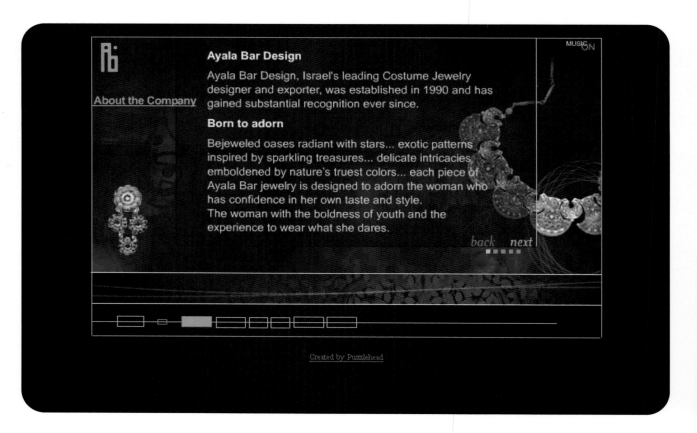

ISRAEL
www.ayalabar.com

Project:	Ayala Bar Design
Design Firm:	Puzzlehead Communication Design
Design:	Oren Moshe, Emanuel Paletz, Zoe Moshe
Programming:	Sagi Chizik
Photography:	Ben Lam
Copy:	Rena Cronental
Music:	Muso Productions
Authoring Software:	Photoshop, Image Ready, Freehand
Language:	English

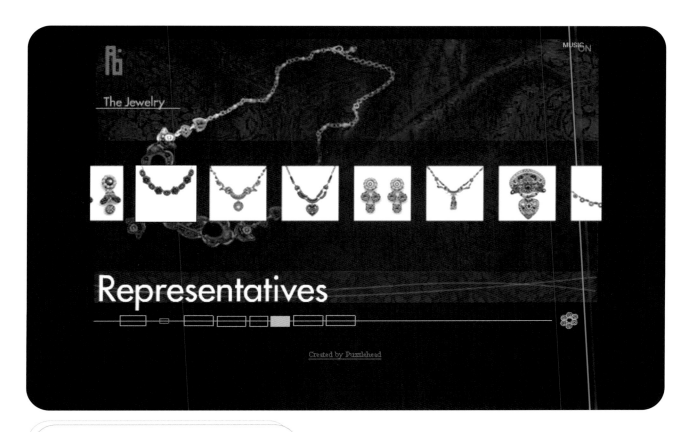

The Jewelry

Representatives

Created by Puzzlehead

The Web site for costume jewelry designer Ayala Bar incorporates a rich color palette of deep primary colors against a black background. The liberal use of black helps to accentuate both the jewelry and the fine fabric that each piece is photographed against on the main screens. The colors used within the interface, and the textures of the fabrics give the site a sensual and mysterious feel.

The animation implemented on each screen is secondary to the product visuals; only subtle, moving lines and geometric shapes float within the backgrounds and navigation bar. The navigation of the site consists of one bar across the bottom of the screen, and "next" and "back" links for moving through the content.

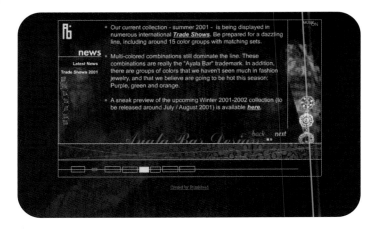

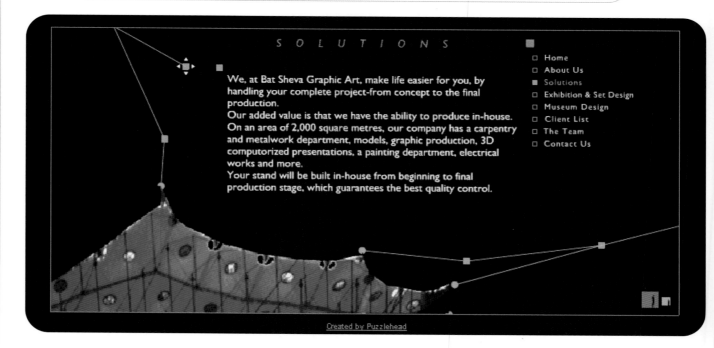

Bat Sheva is one of the oldest exhibition design companies in Israel. Its Web site, created by Puzzlehead, was designed to convey a sense that the company is creative, cutting edge, up-to-date on the latest technologies, and not afraid to integrate them into its work.

Its portfolio allows viewers to interact with different Flash elements, such as the Solutions graphic (below) that can be stretched and moved around the screen. These structural graphics suggest a 3D space using perspective and Flash to emulate a 3D environment.

The art direction for the site draws on imagery from the world of theater lighting and stage design to create a virtual stage upon which the user explores, experiences, and learns.

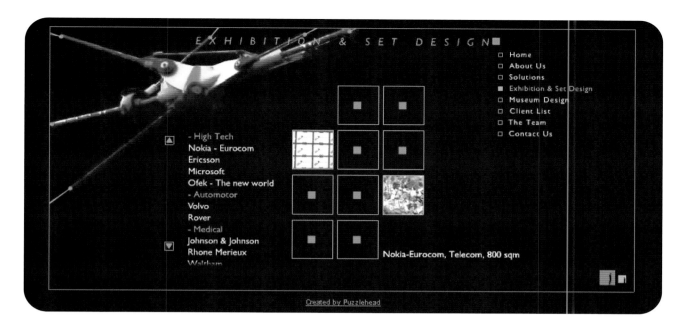

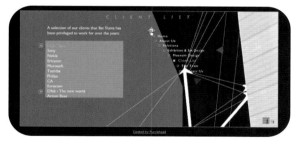

ISRAEL
www.batshevagraphic.com

Project:	Bat Sheva Graphic Art Ltd.
Client:	Bat Sheva Graphic Art Ltd.
Design Firm:	Puzzlehead Communication Design
Design:	Oren Moshe, Emanuel Paletz
Programming:	Sagi Chizik, Dimitry Kashket
Authoring Software:	Photoshop, Image Ready, Freehand
Language:	English

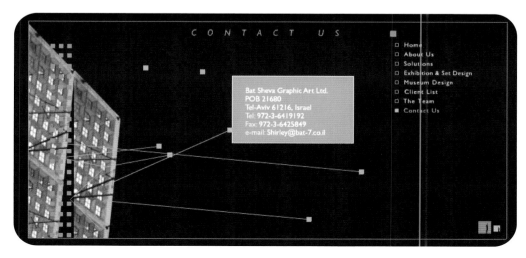

north & south america

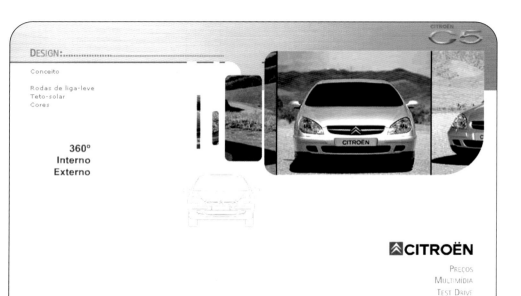

The Brazilian Citroën C5 Web site, designed by the Rumba Comunicaçao agency, was developed to give viewers an in-depth look at the technology, security, and comfort of the automobile manufacturer's 2001 model.

Visitors to the site experience the car and all its amenities by navigating through feature areas such as design, technology, and security. Actual navigation buttons are limited to a row across the bottom of the screen and those used within the Flash animations to showcase various aspects of the car.

A high frame rate was used to speed the animated segues from one section of the site to another, while mask-transitions showing only certain areas of the car help to create the feel of movement and speed for this sleek site.

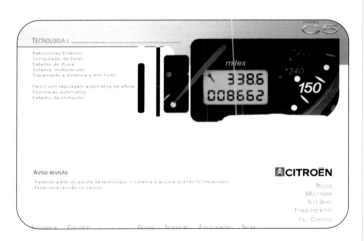

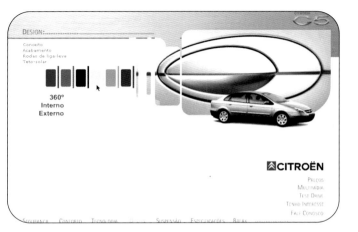

BRAZIL

www.citroenc5.com.br

Project:	Citroën C5
Client:	Citroën Brazil
Design Firm:	Rumba Comunicaçao Ltda.
Design:	André Cury
Illustration:	André Cury
Programming:	Caio Sartori
Production:	Caio Sartori
Audio:	Lua Web
Special:	Wallpaper, advertising, videos
Authoring Software:	Photoshop, Director, HomeSite, QuickTime VR
Language:	Portuguese

Velocity Studio is a full-service design agency located in Ontario, Canada. Its Flash portfolio site is a visually stunning example of the work it designs and produces for print and new media clients.

Vibrant images of male and female models are combined with 3D-rendered backgrounds and objects to create surreal virtual worlds where organic and inorganic forms seem to merge. Extreme lighting—of both people and objects—plays a major role in the design of the site's photographic images.

Several Flash elements add to the experience of exploring the site; floating squares react and follow the viewer's cursor as it is moved within the horizontal axis of a square. When the cursor falls directly upon a square, the button expands to show the section's title. Other elements are the translucent, ethereal spinning objects that can be seen against the static backgrounds of several sections, and the stark, sudden transitions that close and open to reveal a new section of the portfolio.

CANADA
www.velocitystudio.com

Project:	Velocity Design Studio portfolio
Design Firm:	Velocity Design Studio
Design:	Marco DiCarlo, Eric Vardon, Shane Stuart
Illustration:	Marco DiCarlo, Eric Vardon, Shane Stuart
Programming:	Eric Vardon, Donato DiCarlo
Photography:	Shawn Simpson, David Ruposo
Clothing Design:	Ben Soares
Makeup:	Heather Toskan
Hair:	Rocco and Dorisa Cervan
Authoring Software:	Photoshop, Illustrator, Dreamweaver, LightWave 3D
Specs:	654 x 583, 210KB
Language:	English
Special Features:	QuickTime animations, wallpaper

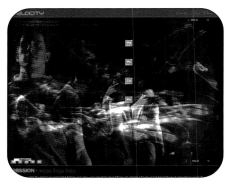

MEXICO
www.grupow.com

Project:	Fecundacíon de Ideas Interactivas
Design Firm:	W Interactive Media
Design:	Miguel Calderon
Illustration:	Roberto Espero
Programming:	Alejandro Villarello
Photography:	Fernando Valdés
Production:	Ulises Valencia, Roman de la Fuente, Juan Carlos Mantilla
Copy:	Marcela de La Cruz
Authoring Software:	Dreamweaver, Freehand, Fireworks, SoundForge, 3D Studio Max, Fractal Painter
Specs:	800 x 600, 900KB
Language:	Spanish

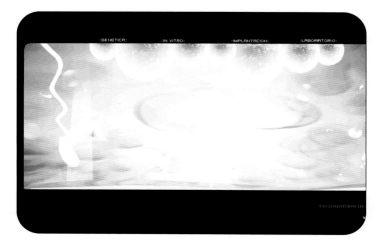

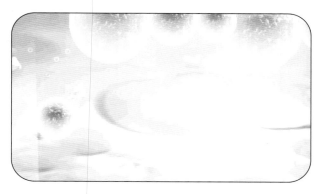

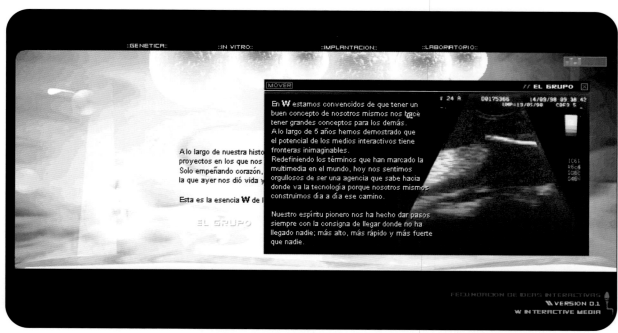

En **W** estamos convencidos de que tener un buen concepto de nosotros mismos nos hace tener grandes conceptos para los demás.
A lo largo de 5 años hemos demostrado que el potencial de los medios interactivos tiene fronteras inimaginables.
Redefiniendo los términos que han marcado la multimedia en el mundo, hoy nos sentimos orgullosos de ser una agencia que sabe hacia donde va la tecnología porque nosotros mismos construimos día a día ese camino.

Nuestro espíritu pionero nos ha hecho dar pasos siempre con la consigna de llegar donde no ha llegado nadie; más alto, más rápido y más fuerte que nadie.

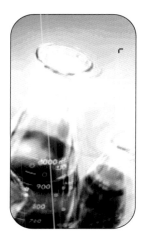

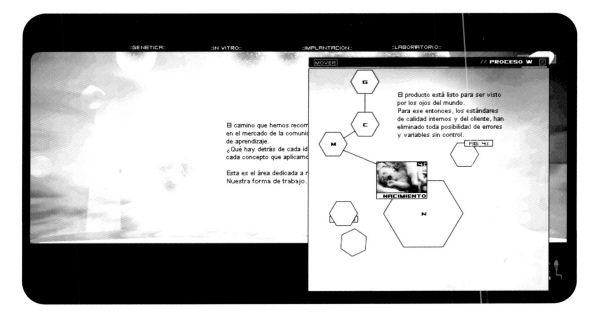

As the creator of the Fecundacíon de Ideas Interactivas Web site writes, "Spermatozoides and ovules are rarely seen on the internet." This is especially true when used in the context of a design firm's portfolio. W Interactive Media's Flash portfolio can surely be considered a unique exploration into the philosophies and work that the firm produces.

The main navigation area of the site is a virtual uterus, where ova detach from the top of the screen and are surrounded by sperm after the user clicks one of the four portfolio links. Once a single sperm enters the ovum, the next stage begins and the viewer is taken to a specific area of the portfolio. The W Interactive designers have artfully and tastefully incorporated the ideas of conception and birth throughout the site, developing parallels with the process of birthing ideas by using mock ultrasound imagery for the About Us section and genetic coding diagrams for interpreting the company's design processes. The use of music and audio gives viewers the feeling of being in an environment where something special is taking place.

Axiom Studio delivers **compelling design** to define and enhance our clients' brands through the use of **superior design**, in-depth research and advanced technologies. We offer a complete suite of services to build and support your **communications** strategy across all media including: **print, web, kiosk, dvd** and **wireless.**

1.800.54.AXIOM :: eBranding for the eConomy

Located in Philadelphia, Pa.. Axiom Studio serves clients on a **national** and **international** basis. Our **clients include** organizations in the financial services, professional services, and information technology markets that seek **high quality design** and creativity that can span a range of platforms.

Axiom Studio Incorporated
441 North 5th Street   Philadelphia, PA 19123
T: 215.509.7686   F: 215.509.7688   info@axiomstudio.com

1.800.54.AXIOM :: eBranding for the eConomy

Axiom Studio was founded with the **goal** of providing an **intensely creative** environment to foster the **best** in digital **design** for all media. We have built our company by ensuring that our **customers'** expectations are consistently **exceeded**. This has lead to the best kind of growth possible: **through word of mouth.**

Axiom Studio has built strong development partnerships with leaders in the creative and information technology industry to ensure world-class quality and results.

1.800.54.AXIOM :: eBranding for the eConomy

Axiom Studio's Flash portfolio features the company's client work and business theories using a clean, uncluttered interface. Smooth animated transitions of photographic imagery guide the viewer from one area of the site to another. Animation is used minimally and is focused on the left side of the screen throughout the project to maintain continuity.

The background on the clickable navigation buttons at the left doesn't simply highlight, but flares from black to orange, then subsides back to black. On other screens, clickable text links change to a shade in between the darkest tone of the active link and the lighter tone of inactive text. The portfolio area continues the clean and frequent use of white space to showcase the various clients for which the company has produced work.

our team:

Jeanne Macijowsky

Education: BFA Des
Inspiration(s): Davi
Margo Chase, My C
Passions: Striving t
which Adds Another
of a Piece

management0

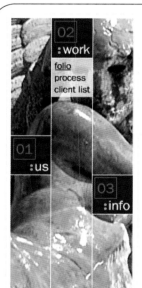

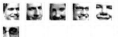

02
:work

folio
process
client list

01
:us

03
:info

folio:

solution: Our goal was to reinforce the brand and make Zave's work come alive, so we used Macromedia Flash to build the site with lots of movement. The Web site's subdued color palette allows their work to shine.

1.800.54.AXIOM :: eBranding for the eConomy

01
:us

03
:info

UNITED STATES
www.axiomstudio.com

Project:	Axiom portfolio
Design Firm:	Axiom Studio
Design:	Michael McDonald, Matthew Sasso, James Flaherty
Photography:	Zave Smith Photography, Michael McDonald
Programming:	Michael McDonald, Matthew Sasso, James Flaherty
Production:	Michael McDonald, Donald Fisher
Copy:	Donald Fisher
Authoring Software:	Photoshop, Illustrator, SoundEdit 16, Generator, BBEdit
Specs:	768 x 480
Language:	English

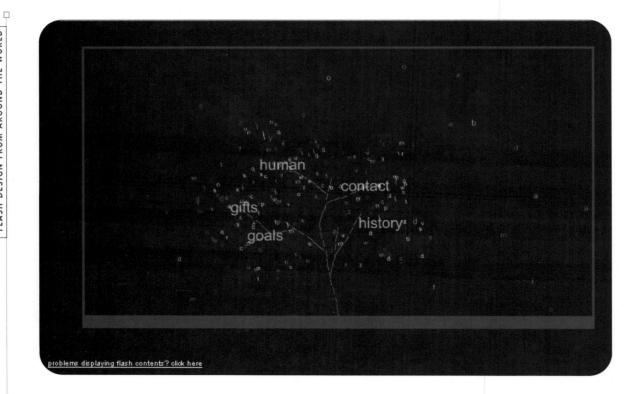

problems displaying flash contents? click here

lems displaying flash contents? click here

UNITED STATES
www.beingsmart.com

Project:	Being Smart portfolio
Design Firm:	Being Smart
Design:	Christine Smart
Authoring Software:	Photoshop, CorelDRAW, After Effects, Dreamweaver
Language:	English
Special Features:	Wallpapers, tutorials, font

Christine Smart designed her portfolio as a showcase for her Flash abilities and also as a medium to display her creativity, inspiration, and design philosophies.

The contents screen features a navigation "tree" blowing in the wind as letters of the alphabet (typographical leaves) blow randomly around the screen. An audio clip of gusty wind accompanies the visual to further enhance the feeling of nature.

The nature theme is carried throughout various areas of the site as organic imagery and subtle background textures move slowly around the screen. Smart's site is a playful and evocative look at the designer and her work.

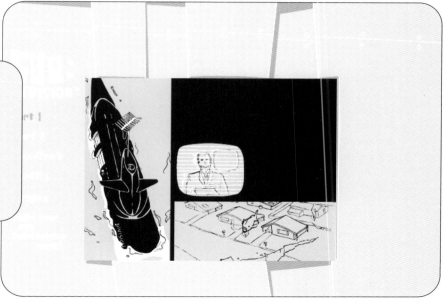

Jean-Paul Leonard, one of the creators of Sub:Division! says that the story is "sex, submarines, and Sears." Set in 1968, a group of suburban homeowners escapes a cata-strophic earthquake that sinks California. Their goal is to protect and eventually reclaim their now-underwater property.

The Flash animated story is set in two parts, the primary story and a faux merchandising layer (below) that displays 1960s-era consumer products, with descriptions that refer back to the primary narrative.

Leonard hopes the nostalgia invoked by the story will reach a broad audience or at least find a following of viewers who can appre-ciate the high-concept silliness of Irwin Allen-esque television redux.

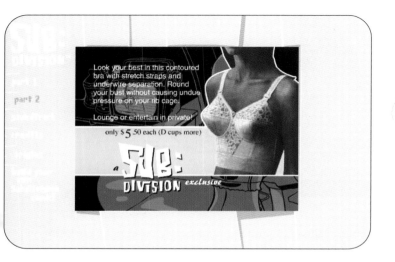

UNITED STATES
www.sub-division.net

Project:	Sub:Division!
Design Firm:	Angry monkey
Design/Illustration:	Jean-Paul Leonard
Production:	Kazandra Bonner, Sarah Strachan
Technical Development:	Marcus Brooks
Copy:	John-Paul Leonard
Animation Direction:	Nicole Weedon
Animators:	Monica Weedon, Roland Blanton, Michael Murphy, Ian Greeb, Kevin Chan
Music:	Michael Murphy
Sound Editor:	Jeff Darby, Earwax Productions
Dialogue Recording:	Bill Storkson
Authoring Software:	Adobe Streamline, pencil & paper
Specs:	420 x 316, 2.8MB (full project)
Language:	English

The Billabong-USA site was created by Juxt Interactive to promote the adventure sports clothing and equipment manufacturer's brand via an online presence. The project is divided into three sub-sites: surf, skate, and snow. Each section features Billabong-sponsored athletes as well as information about the various sports and a selection of the company's sport's apparel.

The most creative experimentation was in the featured rider section, which is constructed on the fly using Macromedia's Generator. Designed to be frequently updated, each new feature rider for the three sports received a different design treatment and unique navigational elements. Generator was used to insert JPEG images and embed text data into dynamic portions of the site and to create a new Shockwave file the moment the content-management database was edited or otherwise updated.

UNITED STATES
www.billabong-usa.com

Project:	Billabong-USA
Client:	Billabong-USA
Design Firm:	Juxt Interactive
Design:	Todd Purgason, Paul Nguyen, Josh Forstat, Jenn Redmond
Programming:	Brian Drake
Production:	Leanna Bush, Brandy Lee
Copy:	Tim Williams
Authoring Software:	Photoshop, Dreamweaver, Generator, SoundEdit 16, Freehand, Fireworks, GrooveMaker
Language:	English
Special Features:	Wallpapers

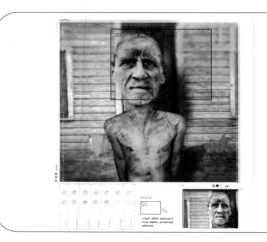

Brittlebones is an experimental playground created by designer Marc Stricklin. Stricklin uses the site to practice and hone his skills at Flash animation and programming and also as a vehicle to offer his views on various subjects relating to design and culture. Stricklin imbues many of his photographic montages and surreal images with a sense of sarcastic and wry humor, and each includes Flash animation or ActionScripting in one form or another. Draggable text blocks, bouncing and talking heads, and hidden content—such as tiny text that must be zoomed in upon to read—entice the viewer to dive in and explore the textural landscapes and photographic imagery.

Content overload could describe the viewer's mind after spending an hour or more browsing through the site, and an hour would be the short tour. As Stricklin succinctly says in one of his brief statements located in lightly screened back type in an autobiography section, "Its purpose serves none other than as a reason to display things I've created for the sake of creation."

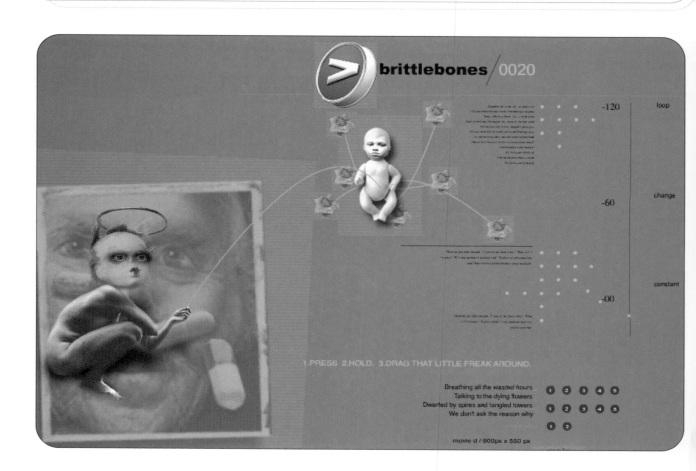

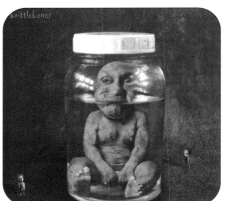

UNITED STATES
www.brittle-bones.com

Project:	Brittlebones
All Design:	Marc Stricklin
Authoring Software:	Photoshop, Dreamweaver
Language:	English

UNITED STATES
www.carbonhouse.com

Project:	Carbonhouse portfolio
Design Firm:	Carbonhouse, Inc.
Design:	James Sack (CD), Logan Watts (AD)
Programming:	Logan Watts
Photography:	James Sack, Logan Watts
Copy:	Brandon Uttley
Authoring Software:	Photoshop, Dreamweaver, Fireworks, BBEdit
Specs:	204KB (initial load), full screen
Language:	English

As a brand consulting firm, Carbonhouse decided the design of its site should be clear and understandable, yet push the limits of Flash to a point where form and function were not consumed by the urge to animate everything on the screen. The clean user interface designs Carbonhouse creates for its clients needed to be shown in its own visual branding. Carbonhouse wanted the user experience to be important but not the only thing the viewer took away when they were finished looking through the site. It was just as important that the viewers remember the content of the site.

Each screen of the site changes dramatically in the main horizontal area where content is displayed, but the navigation box—a sliding drop-down menu—stays constant through the navigation process. This drop-down menu is managed through ActionScripting and constrained on the horizontal axis. This allows viewers to move the slider from one end of the screen to the other but not to any other area of the screen.

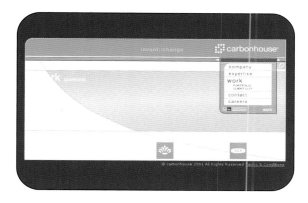

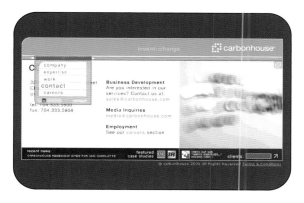

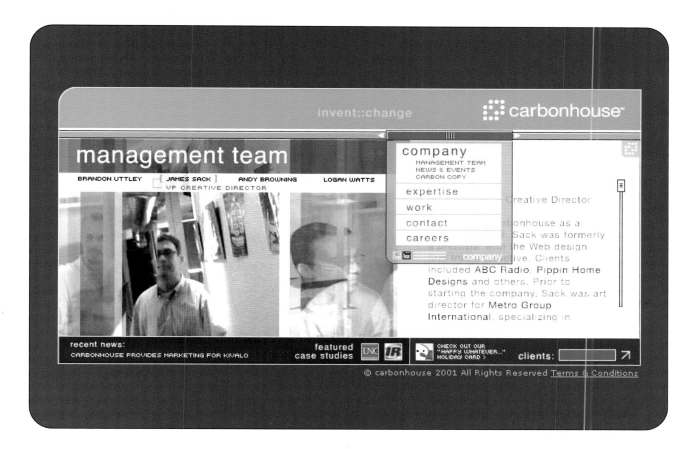

⬤DS9 *DEEPFATFRIED*

Since 1996, Oakland's enigmatic DEEPFATRIED has been releasing
slamming dancefloor tracks that hit like an 18 wheeler of funk.
Blending new school breaks, DnB, dub delays, hip hop flavor and mad
deep bass, DEEPFAT's sound has been described as "ghetto tech"
and "neuro-booty." 12 inch releases feature peak-hour tracks, while
CD and mp3 releases mix it up with groovy abstract downtempo.

You can find all their inspired compu_soul fiddling at http://deepfatfried.com

MP3_STREAMS

// DEEPFATFRIED LIVE ON KZSC_SANTACRUZ :
   MY LIFE HAS VALUE
// I AM AN ANDROID
// MADE YA STRONGER [PRE-RELEASE]
// DEEPFATFRIED VS. ANTIPOP - BLACK ACID
// DEEPFATFRIED VS. MC JAMALSKI - STICKS AND STONES

⬤DS9 : animal tested, mutha approved

Concentrated Audio Solution

Products are sufficiently animal tested before release for public consumption

At Diet Strychnine we understand the need to rigourously test our audio
tracks before releasing them to the public. At present we are in the midst
of conducting research at DS9 laboratories on how the Rhesus monkey
responds to our 12inch vinyl prototype of nu.skool breakbeats by
DEEPFATFRIED, entitled Chocolate Kisses and Gravy. Once we are
satisfied with its results, we will press it to wax for limited distribution.
Expected release date, 27th September 2001.

For your benefit we've provided a simulation of some of the physical effects
one might experience from listening to DS9 flavoured audio. Press the
numeric keys on your keyboard to initiate the simulation.

We also have a promotional subsite for the album, in which you can sample
the merchandise http://www.dietstrychnine.com/deepfatfried

Minimalism is key to DS9's Flash portfolio, which showcases a selection of the company's past work, its indie record label, and the alliance of free-lance designers who work with the company.

The site's navigation is limited to a single, rotating, moleculelike icon that follows the viewer's cursor around the screen. Clicking on the icon stops the motion and pulls up a hierarchical menu with links to the various sections.

Another dynamic Flash element featured within the site is an ActionScripted audio playback device that offers listeners a selection of the "DS9 flavored audio." Using the number pad on their computer's key-board, viewers press and hold a number to change the background audio loop. As the audio is being changed the chimpanzee in the testing cage also morphs using shape tweening.

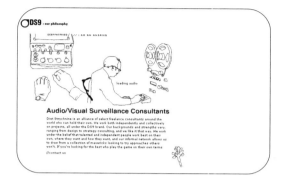

We also have a promotional subsite for the album, in which you can sample the merchandise http://www.dietstrychnine.com/deepfatfried

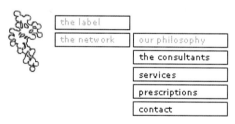

UNITED STATES
www.dietstrychnine.com

Project:	Diet Strychnine
Design Firm:	DS9
Design:	Sacha Sedricks
Production:	Derek Noonan
Music:	Deepfatfried (Crowe Morehouse, Nick Cain)
Authoring Software:	Photoshop, Illustrator, Swft 3D, Cubase, Reason, Pro Tools
Specs:	800 x 600
Language:	English
Special Features:	MP3 downloads (Deepfatfried)

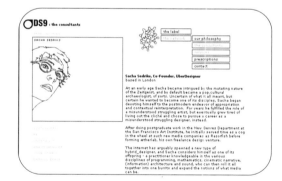

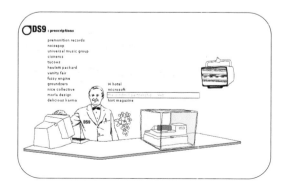

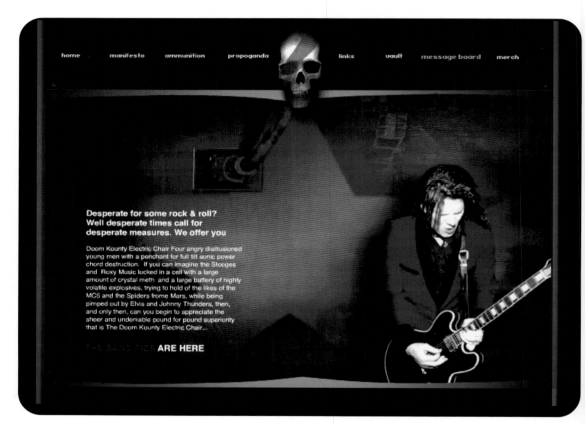

Desperate for some rock & roll?
Well desperate times call for
desperate measures. We offer you

Doom Kounty Electric Chair Four angry disillusioned
young men with a penchant for full tilt sonic power
chord destruction. If you can imagine the Stooges
and Roxy Music locked in a cell with a large
amount of crystal meth and a large battery of highly
volatile explosives, trying to hold of the likes of the
MC5 and the Spiders frome Mars, while being
pimped out by Elvis and Johnny Thunders, then,
and only then, can you begin to appreciate the
sheer and undeniable pound for pound superiority
that is The Doom Kounty Electric Chair...

THE BAND PICS **ARE HERE**

UNITED STATES
www.doomkounty.com

Project:	Doom Kounty Electric Chair
Design:	Marc Stricklin
Authoring Software:	Photoshop, Dreamweaver
Language:	English
Special Features:	Merchandise

Doom Kounty Electric Chair is a rock & roll band that is, as they state themselves in the Ammunition section of the site, "Four angry dissiollustioned young men with a penchant for full tilt sonic power chord destruction." Even if their style of hardcore rock & roll is not on the top of your music list, the site is worth a visit to explore the high-quality design and graphics.

Designer Marc Stricklin has created a Flash site for Doom Kounty Electric Chair that captures the essence of the band's attitude and philosophies. Stricklin enhances the site's atmosphere in some instances by incorporating extreme Photoshop imagery of skulls, weapons, and a blood-red color palette used throughout.

There are specific areas of the site that stand out among others, such as the Artillery section that showcases the band member's weapons of choice: guitars. Viewers enter the Ammunition area and then click further into the site to find a card game, complete with a smoldering cigarette butt. Clicking on a band member card transitions to a window that features the band's music and instruments.

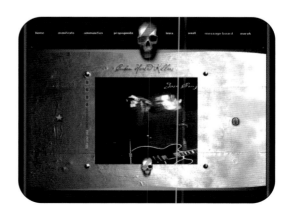

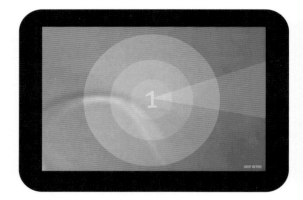

Convergent Moment 2001

Convergent animation of 20sec.
spot for web and broadcast.

Client: Fahrenheit Studio
and 48 Windows

Design and animation by
Fahrenheit Studio.
Music by 48 Windows.

◀ PREVIOUS PROJECT   **PLAY MOVIE**

1.3MB FLASH

PROJECTS

WEB/BROADBAND   PRINT GRAPHICS   INTERIOR DESIGN   MOTION GRAPHICS   CASE STUDIES   WHO WE ARE   CONTACT US

© 2000-2001 Fahrenheit Studio. All rights reserved.

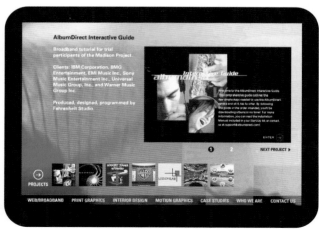

UNITED STATES
www.fahrenheit.com

Project:	Fahrenheit Studio portfolio
Design Firm:	Fahreneheit Studio
Design:	Dylan Tran, Robert Weitz
Photography:	Benny Chan, Robert Weitz
Production:	Dylan Tran, Robert Weitz
Music:	48 Windows
Authoring Software:	Photoshop, Dreamweaver, soundEdit 16, Pro Tools, Image Ready, After Effects
Specs:	600 x 400, 1.7MB (full project)
Language:	English

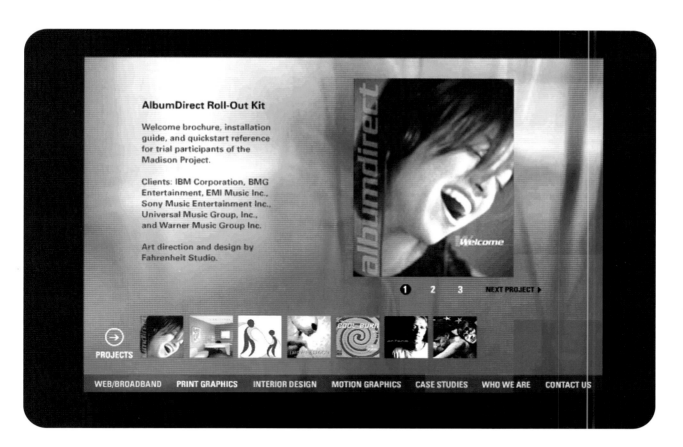

AlbumDirect Roll-Out Kit

Welcome brochure, installation guide, and quickstart reference for trial participants of the Madison Project.

Clients: IBM Corporation, BMG Entertainment, EMI Music Inc., Sony Music Entertainment Inc., Universal Music Group, Inc., and Warner Music Group Inc.

Art direction and design by Fahrenheit Studio.

1   2   3   NEXT PROJECT ▶

PROJECTS

WEB/BROADBAND   PRINT GRAPHICS   INTERIOR DESIGN   MOTION GRAPHICS   CASE STUDIES   WHO WE ARE   CONTACT US

Fahrenheit Studio's portfolio encourages viewers to interact: as the viewer moves the cursor across the circle icons, thumbnail images appear and musical notes of varying scale can be played.

Once the viewer enters the main portfolio area, a secondary navigation bar is located at the bottom of each screen, and large thumbnail images show a preview of the portfolio projects.

To further differentiate one area of the portfolio from another, the designers incorporated full-screen JPEG images of organic-looking shapes and colors as backgrounds.

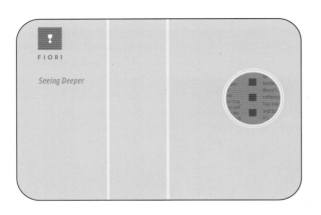

UNITED STATES
www.fioriinc.com

Project:	Fiori Inc.
Design Firm:	Paris France
Creative Direction:	Doug Lowell
Technical Direction:	Scott Trotter
Design:	Molly Sokolow
Programming:	Erik Falat, Sophie Schmidt
Photography:	Steven Bloch
Production:	Jason Davis
Copy:	Doug Lowell
Strategy:	Chuck Nobles
Authoring Software:	Photoshop, Illustrator, SoundEdit 16
Specs:	780 x 500, 250KB (streaming), pop-up
Language:	English

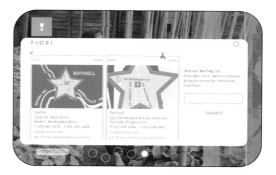

Fiori Inc. is an industrial design company that approached the design studio Paris France with the idea that they wanted to pursue high-end consumer electronic projects. At the time, Fiori didn't have a large portfolio of such projects to showcase, so Paris France designers focused on the company's research processes and featured the thoughts and feelings of consumers, which is an important issue in industrial design. The Flash site features two "real" people, Sophia and Erik, and reveals personal information about their lives. The profiles offer a voyeuristic look into the worlds of these two case studies.

Viewers to the site choose either Erik or Sophia and in both cases are taken to large, static scenes of each individual in a setting where there is more than meets the eye. Using masking and ActionScripting, the designers created a moveable viewing portal that, when moved around the scene, reveals a new image and descriptive content hidden away.

Other areas of the site are less dynamic but still offer a nicely designed look at Fiori's portfolio of projects, business philosophy, and the strategies of the company.

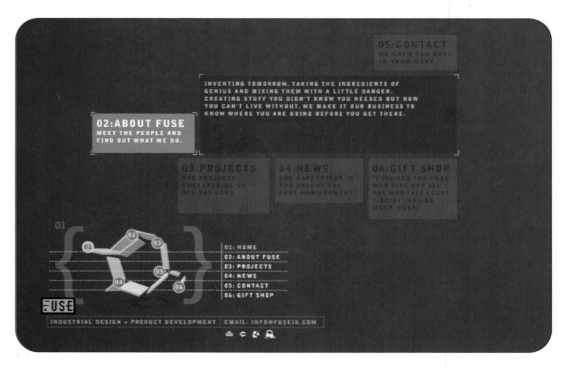

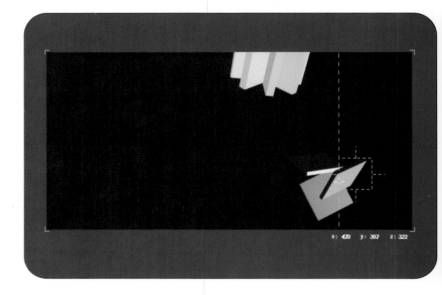

Project:	FUSE Industrial Design portfolio
Client:	FUSE
Design Firm:	Opus Creative
Design:	Stephen Landau, Don Gross
Illustration:	Stephen Landau, Don Gross
Programming:	Stephen Landau, Don Gross, Rich Joslin
Production:	Kristin Wulfestieg
Audio:	Eric Hedford, Scott Fox, Flooded Music
Authoring Software:	Swift 3D
Specs:	10.2MB (full project)
Language:	English

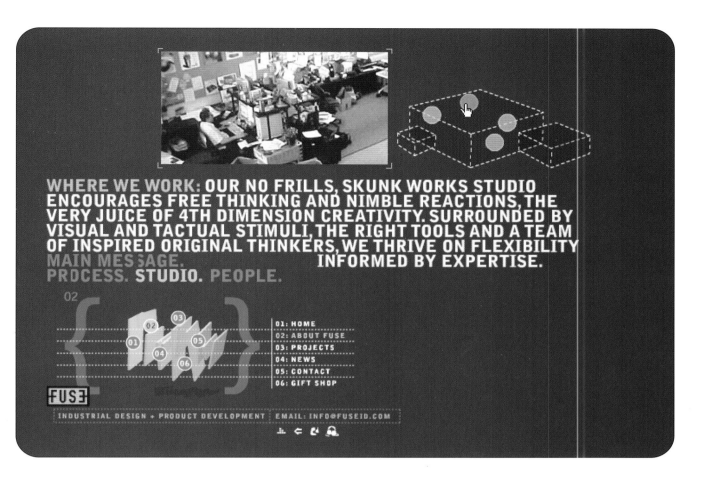

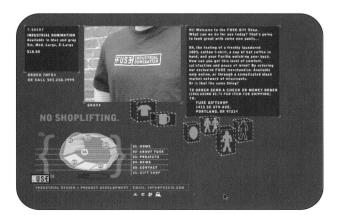

After developing a new logo and corporate ID, FUSE Industrial Design approached Opus Creative to design and produce its portfolio site. Since FUSE hadn't had a Web presence before, Opus Creative began with a clean slate.

The Opus creative team's goal was to create an awareness of the company and its capabilities as well as showcase past and current client work. The challenge was to create a living, breathing site that would entertain visitors and entice them into returning for future updates.

The designers took the "living, breathing" concept literally when creating the navigation of the site. Bright green panels—numbered to match their associated copy blocks—move in and out as if inhaling and exhaling. To add to the effect, a looping audio clip breathes in and out with the movement.

The final outcome is a site that while showcasing the portfolio and company culture of FUSE, also demonstrates the technical and design skills of Opus Creative.

UNITED STATES
www.gavinpeters.com

Project:	Gavin Peters Photography
Client:	Gavin Peters
Design Firm:	Gardner Design
Design:	Chaney Kimball
Authoring Software:	Photoshop, Dreamweaver
Specs:	775 x 225, 200KB (main movie), 85KB (photo window)
Language:	English

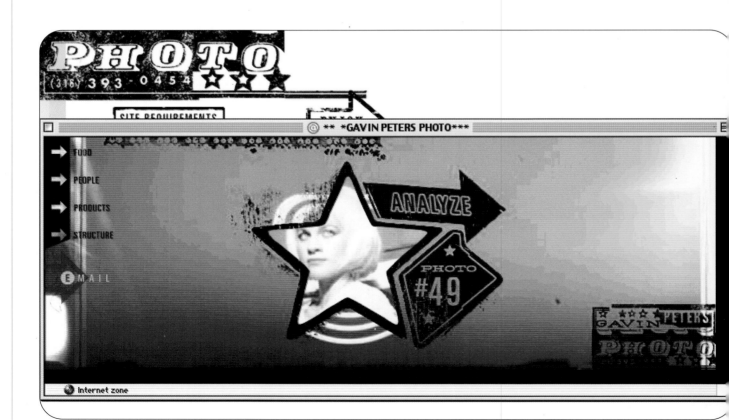

Photography sites such as Gavin Peters' portfolio are often designed conservatively to minimize distractions from the photographer's images. Because of this, photography sites are often sterile and static. The designers at Gardner Design were given more leeway by Peters, who encouraged the design firm to explore a bit with formatting and execution.

The final product is a dynamic and exciting look at the photographer's work, with a contemporary navigation and interface created to view the images. Animated headers, masked images moving behind blurred windows, and ActionScripting to affect the sliding images with a gravitylike, ease-in/ease-out technique, all working together to enhance the viewing experience. Working with the design, Peters intentionally chose photographs that would appeal to potential clients as well as complement the design of his portfolio.

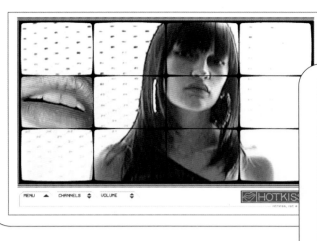

HK TV 01 is the promotional site for Hotkiss, a women's apparel manufacturer. This Flash site features a multi-screen video wall theme throughout, with multiple images of models wearing the company's designer clothing, and close-ups of the models available for view by clicking and rolling the cursor over the individual TV screens. The site is an MTV-like experience that showcases the current Hotkiss fashions and entices the viewer to explore the hidden images and content behind each TV screen.

Additional elements that make the site interesting are the multiple choices of music that can be listened to while browsing the site, downloadable video, and contests to enter. Each fashion segment incorporates different Flash-animated navigation schemes for each area of the site, such as Retailers, News, and Fashion.

UNITED STATES
www.hotkiss.com

Project:	HK TV 01
Client:	Hotkiss, Inc.
Design Firm:	Orange Voodoo
Design:	Rick Truhls, Jamie Gluck
Programming:	Rick Truhls
Photography:	Christian Webber
Authoring Software:	Photoshop, Fireworks
Specs:	700 x 400
Language:	English

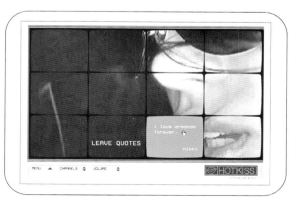

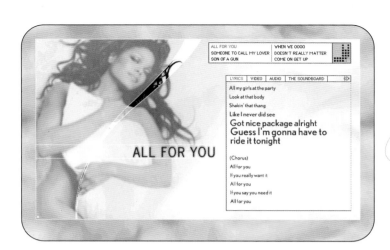

UNITED STATES
www.janet-jackson.com

Project:	Janet Jackson: All for You
Client:	Virgin Records
Design Firm:	Second Story Interactive Studios
Creative Director:	Brad Johnson
Designers:	Gabe Kean, Martin Linde
Programmers:	Seb Chevrel, Sam Ward, Martin Linde
Producers:	Aleen Adams, Julie Beeler
Developer:	Lindsey Hammond
Authoring Software:	Photoshop, HomeSite, Illustrator, SoundEdit 16, Premiere, Streamline
Programming:	Flash, ActionScript, HTML
Specs:	Varying KB size, streaming
Language:	English
Special Features:	Sound mixer, video creator

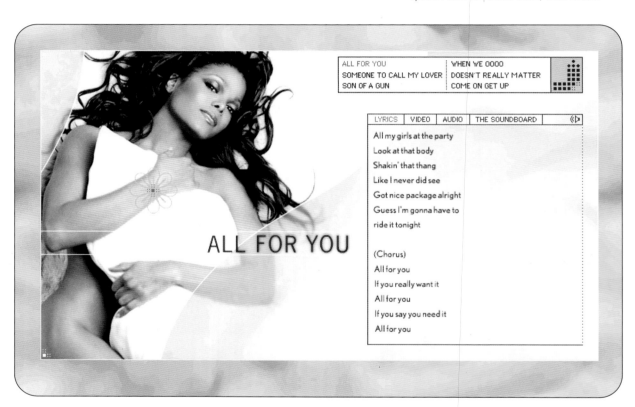

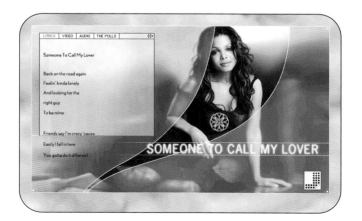

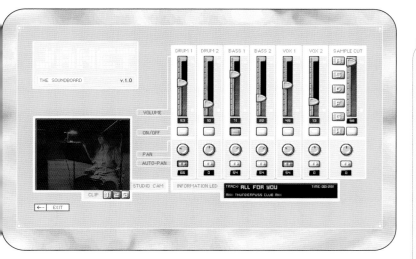

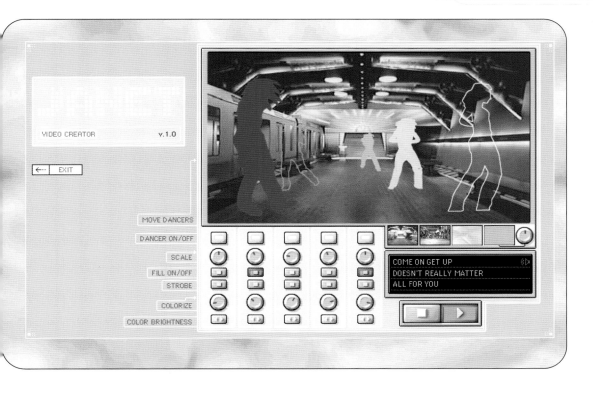

Janet Jackson: All for You is one of the many high-profile sites developed by Second Story Interactive. In the last two years, the company has produced award-winning work for many well-known clients including *National Geographic*, Eastman Kodak, Nike, and MOMA (New York City), to name just a few.

This site for Virgin Records was designed to "reflect the 'new' Janet," says Second Story creative director, Brad Johnson. She is "sexy, full of curves, and ready for fun." To convey the "sexy" elements, large, revealing JPEG images of Jackson are used as the backdrop to each area.

The experience is enhanced by animated transitions activated as the cursor rolls over the images of Jackson. This voyeuristic interaction allows viewers to pull back a translucent cover and reveal a clearer, full-color photo of the singer.

Special Flash features have been added throughout this interactive promotion: Sound Mixer, a mixing board that allows viewers to make their own club mix of the title song, "All for You"; Video Creator featuring "virtual Janets" that can be manipulated by accessing various controls on the video mixer; and scrolling lyrics that react to the viewer's mouse movements. More common elements such as videos and downloadable wallpaper images are also on the site.

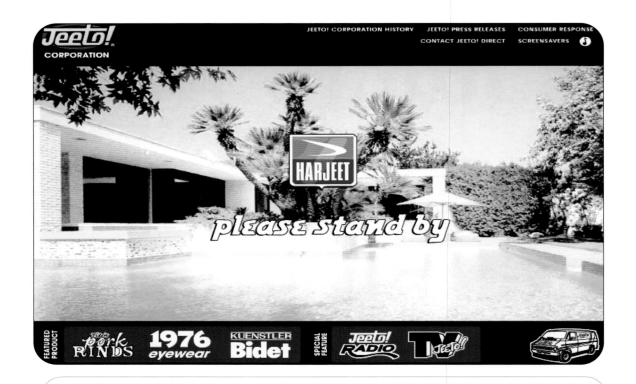

The Jeeto! Corporation Web site is a mock corporation created by two brothers, Jeffrey and Kevin Kelly. The "corporation" was created as a portfolio piece to showcase the design abilities of Jeffrey and the copywriting abilities of Kevin. The Web site is a humorous look at how branding can be used to create a famous product without the product actually existing. As an example of how well the site works, viewers can read consumer response letters that visitors to the site have e-mailed to ask where specific products (such as the Tito's Pork Rinds) can be purchased.

Other companies include Jeeto! 1976 Eyewear, Jeeto TV, Jeeto! Radio, and Kuenstler Bidet. Though the site is entirely Flash-based, the designers were conservative in the use of Flash bells and whistles, focusing instead on the content and using animated effects sparingly.

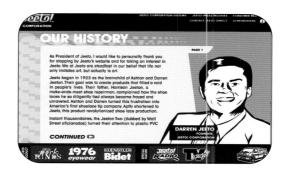

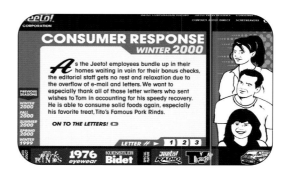

UNITED STATES
www.jeeto.com

Project:	Jeeto! Corporation
Design:	Jeffrey Kelly
Copy:	Kevin Kelly
Music:	Jake Pushinsky
Authoring Software:	Photoshop
Specs:	800 x 600
Language:	English
Special Features:	Screensavers

UNITED STATES
www.johnnyblazeny.com

Project:	Johnny Blaze New York
Design Firm:	Gr33nhous3
Design:	Michael Green
Photography:	Michael Green
Programming:	Mellanie Ruthanum
Authoring Software:	Photoshop, Illustrator, SoundEdit 16
Specs:	400 x 600, 400KB
Language:	English

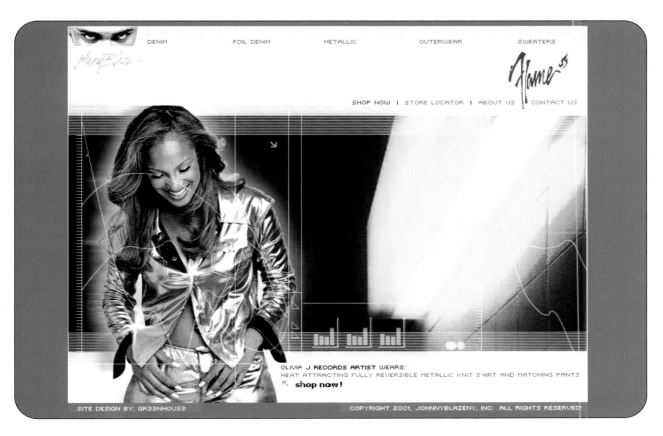

Gr33nhous3 created the Johnny Blaze Web site while keeping in mind the clothing manufacturer's urban roots, working with raster lines, techno-music design elements, and urban skylines to give the site the feel of a digital urban oasis. The site features urban youth posing in the company's fashions and offering a high degree of 'tude to the viewer.

To accompany the visuals of the models and to add to the urban hip-hop scene feel, the designers included a fast-paced techno beat that loops for several minutes before ending.

The clothing company offers its line of women's clothing in the Flame section of the Johnny Blaze site. Here, the tough attitude of the males is replaced by a group of playful and smiling female models. The Flame section of the site offers an urban youth ambience, with vocals and music by the J Records artist, Olivia. Here, too, the models are overlaid with moving vector lines and equalizer bars.

Though the entire site was designed using Flash, the visuals and accompanying music keep the viewer's mind focused on the product rather than on the bells and whistles of Flash that are sometimes overused in sites like this one.

Max-Air is an extreme-sports thrill show production company. This site, designed by Lead Dog Digital, was created with strong vertical elements to simulate actual performance events of the high-flying, high-adrenaline air- and snowboarders.

The project features a high frame rate to create the feeling of speed as type and static JPEG images stutter and flash across the screen, giving the illusion of motion graphics. The high frame rate also provides quick Flash transitions from one scene to another. Intense background music also helps to create an environment where purveyors of the sport and the more cautious (less gutsy) viewers can vicariously experience the thrill of big air. The project also features downloadable videos that can be viewed in the Windows Media Player on Macintosh or Windows PC platforms.

UNITED STATES
www.max-airshows.com

Project:	Max-Air Extreme Sports Events
Client:	Max-Air Productions
Design Firm:	Lead Dog Digital
Design:	Natalie Lam (CD), Don Eschenauer, Carl Prizzi
Illustration:	Don Eschenauer
Photography:	Max-Air
Programming:	Carl Prizzi
Production:	Carl Prizzi
Music:	Michael Denton
Authoring Software:	Photoshop, Illustrator, Premiere, Media Cleaner, Sound Forge
Specs:	715 × 550, 100KB
Language:	English

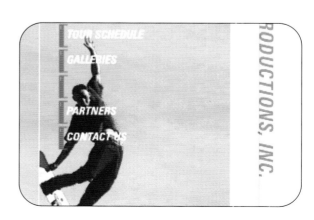

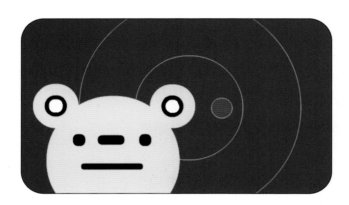

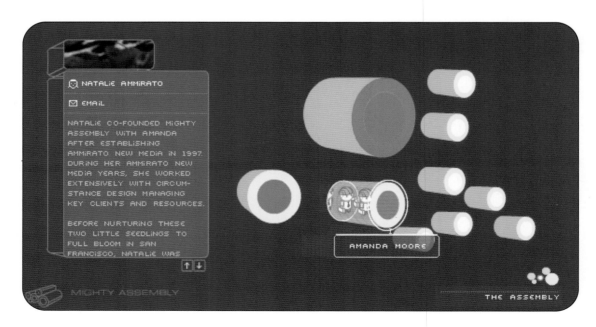

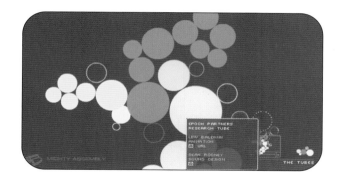

While still an up-and-coming interactive design studio in 2000, Mighty Assembly decided it was time to announce its existence with an online presence. The design team focused its attention on making the site a portfolio piece to demonstrate the company's interface design and Flash skills.

The final outcome of the site was an award-winning Flash portfolio that went from online to the printed page. In early 2002, Osborne published Mighty Assembly's *Macromedia Flash: Art, Design + Function* book. Its focus is the deconstruction—from top to bottom—of the Mighty Assembly Flash site.

One of the main elements of the site is the Tubes module navigation (right and facing page bottom). These tubes define the navigation as the main links used throughout and are at the center of the site's style both literally and metaphorically. The tubes' shape, movement, and low-tech graphic style are carried throughout other elements of the site.

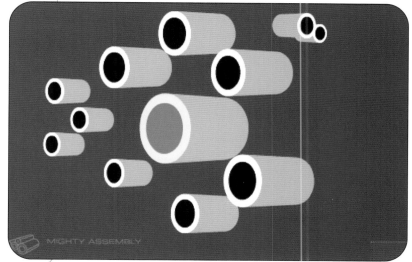

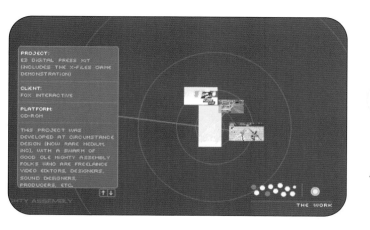

UNITED STATES
www.mightyassembly.com

Project:	Mighty Assembly portfolio
Design:	Natalie Ammirato, Mark Foltz, Fiel Valdez
Illustration:	Lew Baldwin, Mark Foltz, Grace Hsiu, George Rodgers, Scott Runcorn, Fiel Valdez
Programming:	Matt Mahnke (HTML, Flash), Sean Rooney (Flash)
Animation:	Lew Baldwin, Mark Foltz, Grace Hsiu, Amanda Moore, George Rodgers, Sean Rooney, Scott Runcorn, Fiel Valdez
Copy:	Matt Mahnke
Music/Audio:	Lew Baldwin, Amanda Moore, Sean Rooney
Authoring Software:	Photoshop, Illustrator, After Effects, GoLive, SoundEdit 16, BBEdit, Premiere, KPT, Soundhack, Swift 3D, Thonk 0+2
Specs:	600 x 325
Language:	English

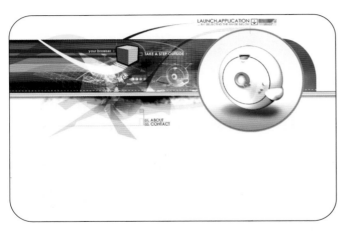

UNITED STATES
www.movtv.com

Project:	MovTV
Design Firm:	Tubatomic Studio
Design:	Alex Ogle, Aaron Hoffman, Jason Fritts
Illustration:	Ivo van de Grift, Hester van de Grift
Programming:	Alex Ogle
Production:	Alex Ogle, Aaron Hoffman
Authoring Software:	Photoshop, Illustrator, LiveStage, Cinema 4D
Specs:	80k (main MOVTV Menu), 120k (calculator), 64KB (clock), 44KB (about interface)
Language:	English

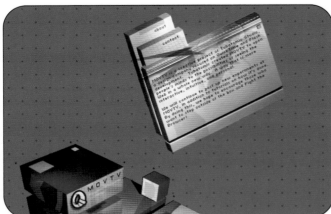

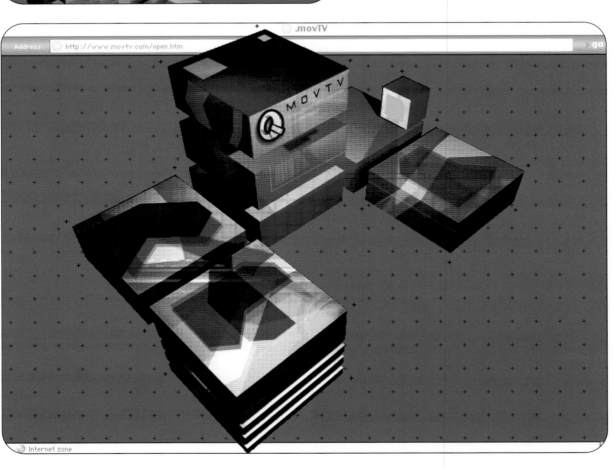

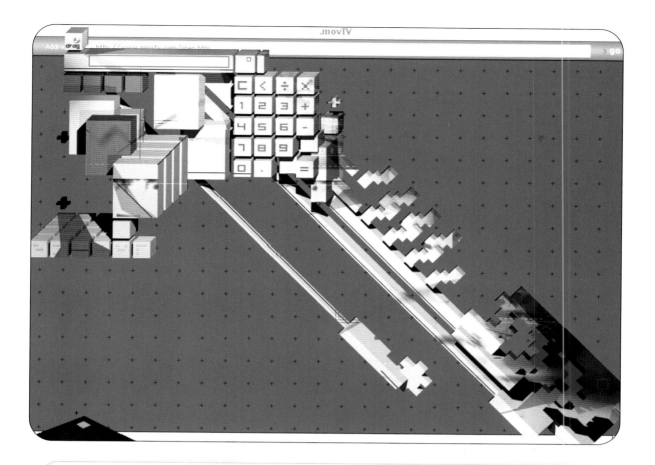

"Fight the Browser!" That's the motto Tubatomic Studio uses to present the concept and design of its new "FlashTime" application presented through MovTV. Tubatomic created MovTV—a combination of Flash and QuickTime—to explore the possibilities of thinking and designing outside the traditional Web browser. The experimental application allows a viewer to download a completely self-contained QuickTime movie that plays video, audio, and Flash animation on the user's desktop, as long as the QuickTime player is installed.

This new technology offers designers the ability to create floating interfaces that can be shaped in any way. The FlashTime interfaces are also transparent, meaning the traditional QuickTime movie that existed solely in a square frame can now be designed in any shape or size (see the calculator above) and the frame borders are transparent.

In creating MovTV, Tubatomic's designers used several different programs—Flash, QuickTime Pro, LiveStage, Cinema 4D (for any 3D work), and Photoshop. The interface "skin" is built in Photoshop, and then imported into QuickTime Pro, which allows the designers to frame the projects with the Photoshop file. All animated elements are created with Flash and then imported into QuickTime Pro. The final stage to bring it all together is LiveStage from Totally Hip Software. This software is crucial in the process because it allows the designers to write Qscript code inside of QuickTime. Without Qscript a Flash button cannot communicate with QuickTime to close the movie or control the loading process.

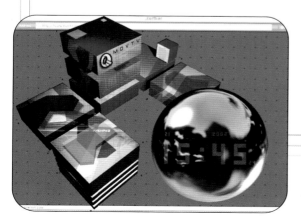

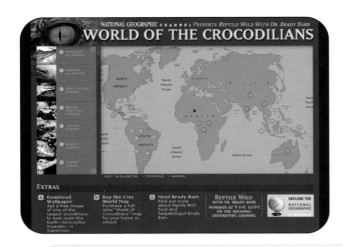

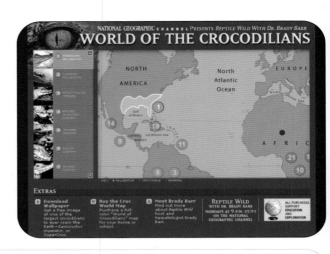

Hello Design has designed and produced several Flash projects for *National Geographic* online. As part of the promotion for a television feature on Super Croc, a 40-foot-tall (12-meter-tall) prehistoric crocodilian, Hello created the site (above) around a traditional map. As viewers navigate using the map, they are presented with an interactive experience where they can pan across or zoom into the various geographical locations of present-day crocodilians.

National Geographic also chose Hello to create an immersive interactive module that explores Australia's Great Barrier Reef (facing page). This Flash project places viewers in Australia's well-protected coral reef and allows them to learn about its inhabitants by clicking on animated sea creatures.

The third module produced by Hello illustrates the importance of the Borneo rain forest, featuring a dynamic exploration of the rain forest at night. The experience combines sounds and images of unique plants and animals in an interface surrounded by darkness. As viewers explore the site, the cursor becomes a flashlight allowing them discover hidden creatures and conservation facts as they scroll from the treetops to the rain forest floor.

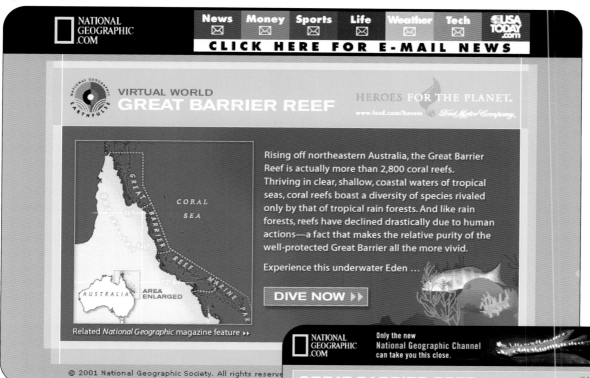

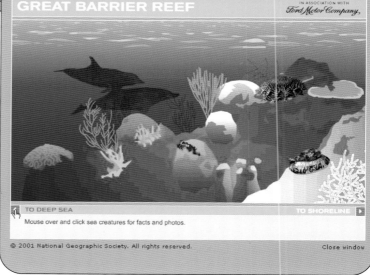

UNITED STATES
www.nationalgeographic.com

Project:	World of the Crocodilians, Rain Forest at Night, Great Barrier Reef
Client:	National Geographic Society
Design Firm:	Hello Design
Design:	David Lai (CD), Hiro Niwa (CD), Christel Leung (lead designer)
Programming:	Sandra Cheng
Production:	George Lee (project lead)
Authoring Software:	Photoshop, Illustrator, HomeSite, BBEdit
Specs:	860 x 600
Language:	English

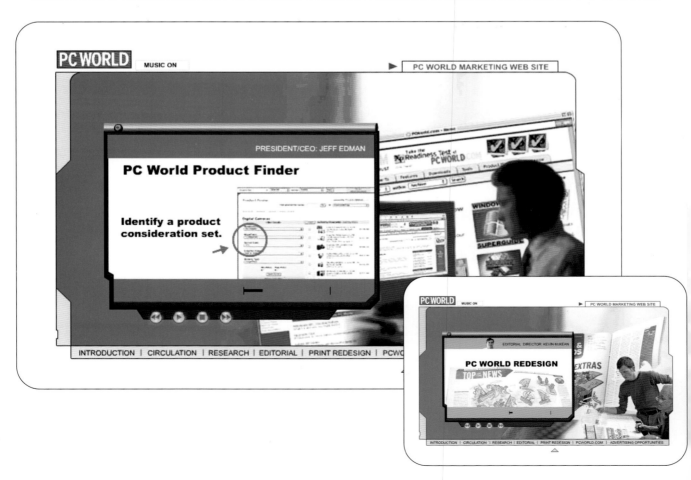

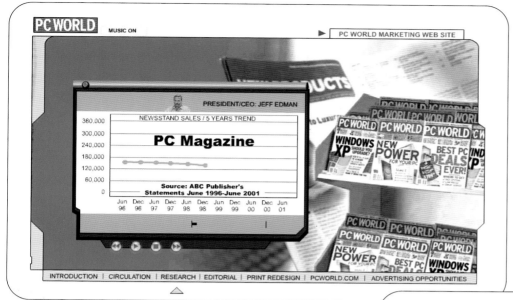

In Your Face New Media Design produced this Flash promotion for PC World Communications to be used as a sales presentation tool. The site features voiceovers by the magazine's CEO and executive editor speaking to viewers about the *PC World* magazine and the pcworld.com Web site. The project is composed of eighteen smaller Flash segments that are loaded into the main Flash interface. Each segment contains three to five minutes of audio plus animation relevant to *PC World* advertisers. The promotion was designed to be uploaded to the Web and as a stand-alone Flash project burned to a CD-ROM.

To make the viewing of each segment more streamlined, the designers added controls that allow the viewer to fast forward, pause, play, and rewind. Another element that adds to the viewing process is a progress bar that indicates in real-time how much of the segment has elapsed as it plays through to the end.

UNITED STATES
www.marketing.pcworld.com

Project:	*PC World* promotion
Client:	*PC World* Communications
Design Firm:	In Your Face New Media Design + Marketing
Design:	Daniel Donnelly
Programming:	Jesse Hall, Shoko Horikawa
Production:	Jesse Hall, Shoko Horikawa
Project Manager:	Amy Dalton (*PC World*)
Authoring Software:	Photoshop, Illustrator
Specs:	800 x 600, 228KB (main interface)
Language:	English

UNITED STATES
www.pickled.tv

Project:	Pickled.tv
Client:	Billabong USA
Design Firm:	Juxt Interactive
Design:	Todd Purgason
Production:	Brandy Lee
Programming:	Jeff Keyser, Phil Scott, Brian Drake, Anthony Thompson
Authoring Software:	Photoshop, Dreamweaver, SoundEdit 16, Fireworks, Freehand, GrooveMaker
Language:	English
Special Feature:	Wallpaper, screensavers

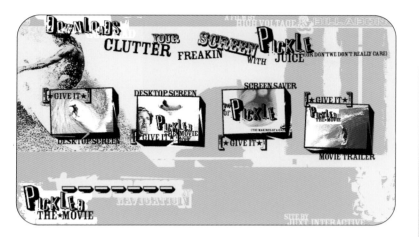

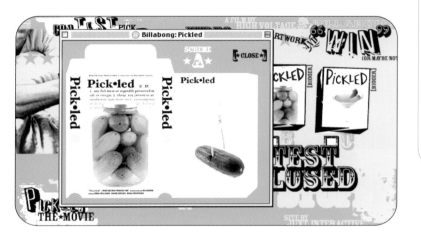

Every year, Billabong-USA makes a short promotional video that featuring its team riders. This is a key element of its marketing strategy. With Pickled, Billabong went a step further and created a film that was shot in conjunction with an extreme film series that is touring theaters around the United States. Pickled.tv was developed to promote this surf film produced by Billabong USA. The movie is a lighthearted surf film with a ridiculous plot line that centers on the drunken hallucinations of the main character.

The navigation on the Pickled site is one of the elements that stands out, among others. Throughout the project, the designers implemented voiceover by the main character, Robert Earl, to explain what users can expect when they click a button.

In Juxt Interactive's book, *FLASH deConstruction*, the authors go in-depth into the detailed ActionScripting required to make the site work as a promotional piece and to create the virtual personality of Robert Earl for the Pickled movie.

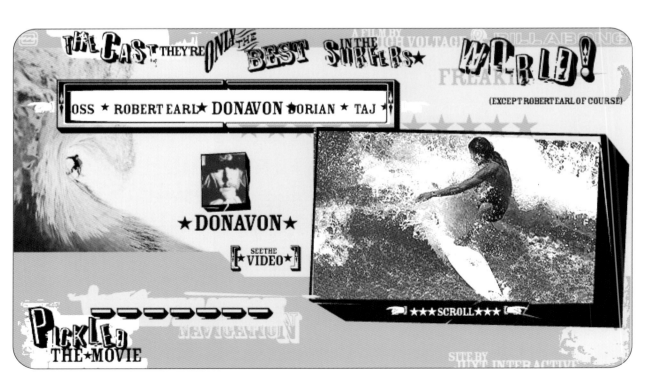

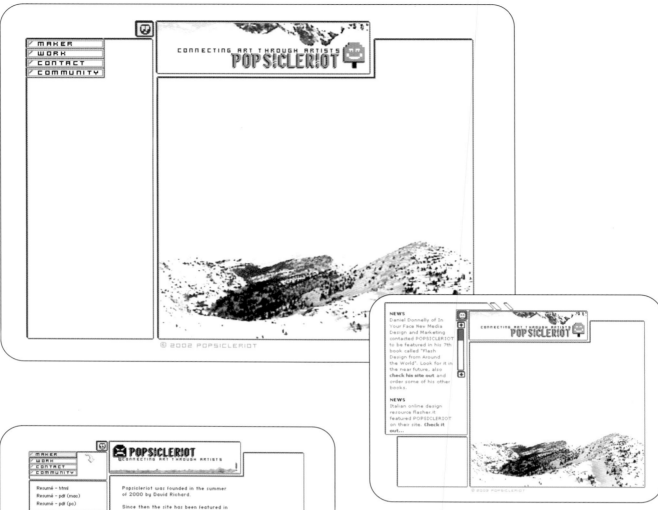

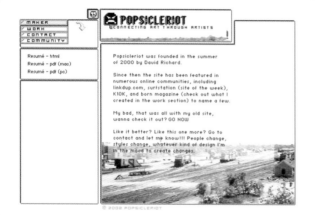

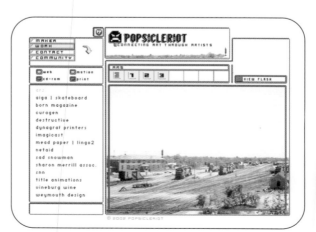

UNITED STATES
www.popsicleriot.com

Project:	Popsicleriot
Design Firm:	Popsicleriot
Design:	David J. Richard
Authoring Software:	Photoshop, Illustrator, SoundEdit 16, BBEdit
Specs:	640 x 450, 110KB
Language:	English

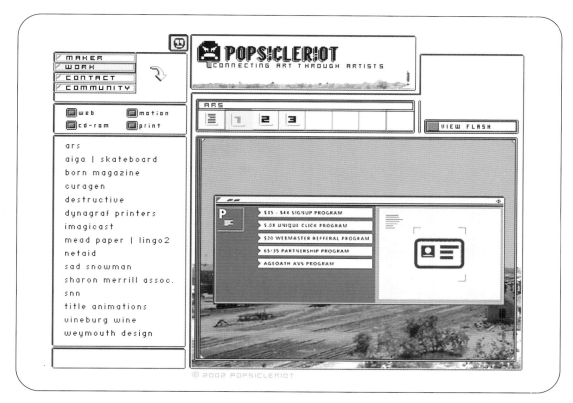

From the early concept stages, Popsicleriot designer and artist David Richard was aware that his site would be viewed not only by designers and artists but also by the general public who might be surfing to the site with slow connections. With this in mind, Richard chose to keep the design of this portfolio/artists' resource site clean and uncluttered by too many Flash animations and large background JPEGs. The site simply showcases his portfolio projects and feature artists.

An important element used to keep the project's files size low is the use of ActionScripting for creating the animations, fades, and loading of files. In areas such as the portfolio, ActionScripting was used to view the sliding images, rather than the tweening technique, which can greatly increase the file size of a project.

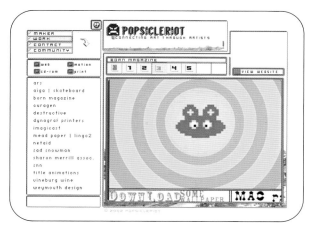

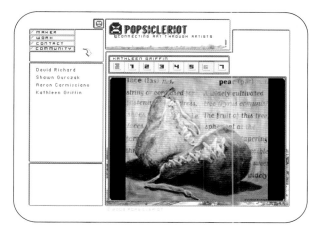

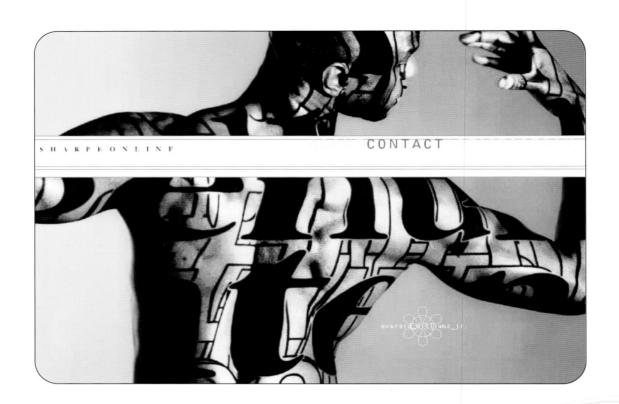

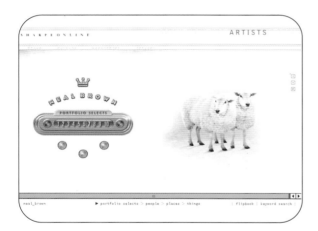

UNITED STATES
www.sharpeonline.com

Project:	Sharpeonline
Client:	Sharpe Associates Inc.
Design Firm:	120 Advertising
Design:	Ken Loh, Van Duong, Kirsten Lindquist, Ashley Pigford, Joe Suarez, John Suetton, Clement Yip
Photography:	Eric Tucker, Everard Williams, Ann Cutting, Lise Metzger, Ne... Brown, Jamey Stillings, Hugh Kretschmer, Zachary Scott
Programming:	Tim Stone, Marc Greenfield (site builder)
Production:	Philippe Safifie, Brad Serling (dir. interactive development), Steve Grant (technology project manager)
Authoring Software:	Photoshop, Illustrator, Dreamweaver, ImageReady
Language:	English
Special Features:	Stock photography

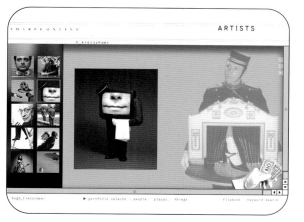

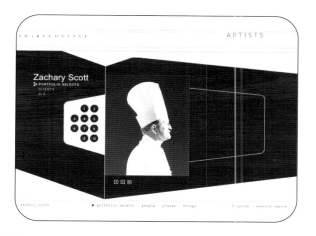

The Sharpe Associates Web site represents eight photographers whose subject matter and styles of photography cover a wide range: products, fashion, scenics, and animals.

The goal of the site is to provide potential clients with the means to easily and quickly access the portfolios of the featured artists while also highlighting certain unique traits of each individual's style. To reach this goal, Sharpe hired 120 Advertising to design and produce a site that shows a high level of sophistication while maintaining the production values and aesthetics for which Sharpe Associates is known.

What makes the Sharpe site stand out among other photographers' sites are the artistic and varied interfaces that have been designed around the each portfolio. Each has a unique look that complements the work portrayed.

All of the sections combine both HTML and Flash in their design. Flash animation is used sparingly in some sections, and different depths of implementation occur in each portfolio. Some portfolios use Flash-tweened animation for text and images, and others use Flash for the navigation buttons but HTML for the loading of photos and text.

On entering the site a random image loads in the background and a Flash-animated navigation bar loads in the middle of the screen. This navigation is then used throughout as the main navigation for the site.

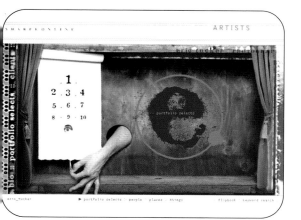

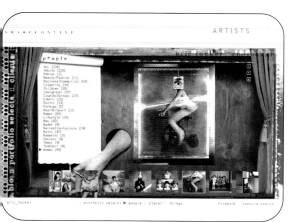

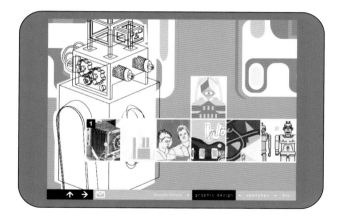

Asa Shatkin's portfolio showcases the illustrator's traditional and computer art in an eclectic collection of personal and commercial projects. The artist spent much of his life in Zambia before finally ending up in Chicago.

The main portfolio areas—illustration, graphics, and sketches—incorporate a visual, icon-based navigation system that includes a basic Flash navigation bar at the bottom of each screen with forward and backward arrows for navigation once the viewer enters a main category.

Though this site could easily have been produced with HTML or other traditional coding methods, using Flash has allowed the illustrator to create a more streamlined portfolio that incorporates animation and navigation and that will appear exactly the same on any browsers with the Flash plug-in.

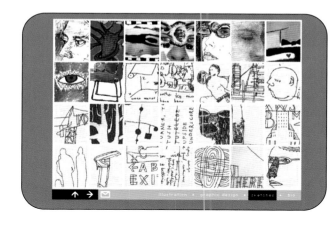

UNITED STATES
www.asashatkin.com

Project:	Illustration Portfolio
Design:	Asa Shatkin
Authoring Software:	Photoshop, Illustrator, Dreamweaver
Specs:	640 x 480, 88KB (largest file)
Language:	English

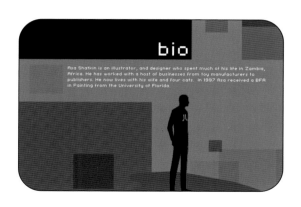

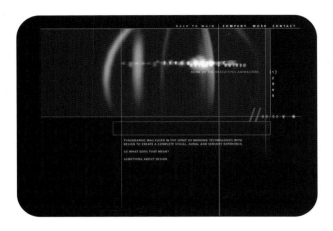

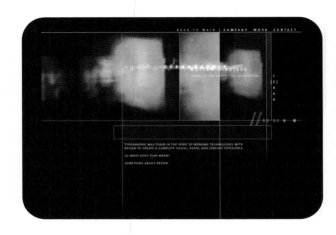

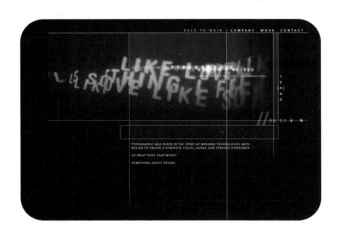

THE GETTY CENTER
ELEKTRA RECORDS
▸ MTV ONLINE
WARNER/CHAPPELL MUSIC, INC.
HEALTH CANADA
THE REMEDI PROJECT
BALANCE
AMERICAN JEWISH COMMITTEE
IMAGINARY FORCES
DIGITAL DOMAIN
CORE MAGAZINE
PLATINUM TECHNOLOGY
SONY WIRELESS
MY SIMON
GETTY RESEARCH INSTITUTE
BORN MAGAZINE
[T-26] TYPE FOUNDRY
DISCOVERY RECORDS

NOTE : THIS IS AN ABBREVIATED LIST OF WORK / CLIENTS
FOR MORE INFO. EMAIL INFO@TYPOGRAPHIC.COM

WWW.VMA.MTV.COM

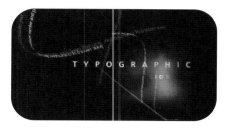

The Typographic studio focuses its design services on motion graphics, interactivity, graphics, and typography, but typography is the key word when mentioning or viewing the Typographic site. Owner and designer Jimmy Chen created the site as an experimental forum where his ideas, graphic design abilities, and internet technologies can combine into artistic explorations.

Before Flash, the Typographic site was primarily static, with a few animated GIFs thrown in. With the introduction of Flash as the new Web application of choice, Chen has been able to move the site in a new direction, focusing mainly on moving typography in a myriad collection of words, phrases, and visual narratives.

Chen uses the site as a canvas to express himself, leaving interpretation to the individuals who come to explore the site. Chen also uses the Typographic site as a sounding board for new ideas before incorporating them into his client's design and animation projects.

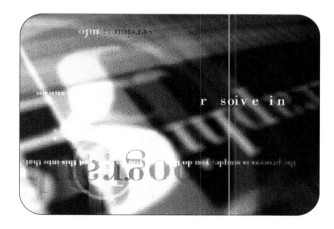

UNITED STATES
www.typographic.com

Project:	Typographic portfolio
Design Firm:	Typographic
Design:	Jimmy Chen
Authoring Software:	Photoshop, Illustrator, After Effects, Premiere
Language:	English

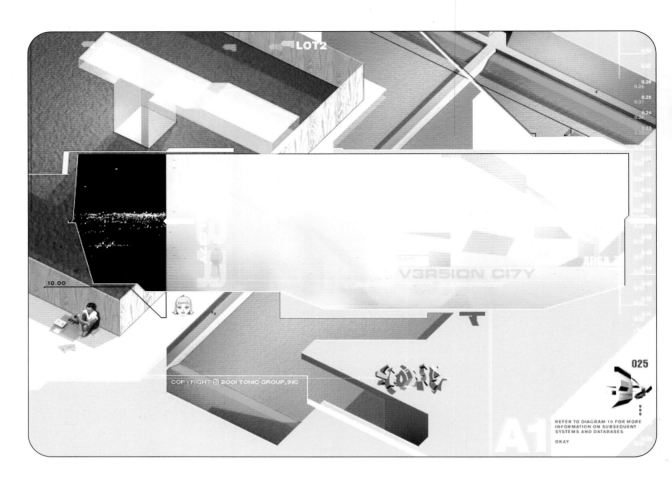

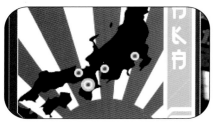

The Tonic Group's Version City Flash site is an experimental design area that is linked to the New York design firm's corporate site. The Version City site is a testing ground for Tonic Group's new ideas and a place to engage visitors with a maze of creative explorations.

The main screen for the site sets the tone for all other areas. There are no defined buttons or links to begin navigating, and the viewer is presented with a stylized aerial view of what could be a city block. Clicking on objects or icons such as the man sitting against the wall, graffiti, or moving crates, will take the viewer away: a journey to Kyoto, Japan; a subway in New York; or the open fields of a rendered landscape.

The site is completely Flash-based, but the subtle usage of animation and motion, and the interesting graphics and visual narratives help to take the viewer's attention away from the technology used to create the site, and turn it towards finding the clues and links that lead to the next level of each area.

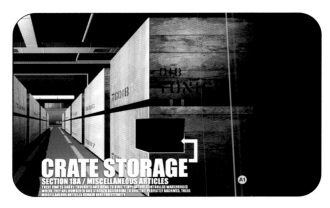

UNITED STATES
www.tonicgroup.com/versioncity

Project:	Version City
Design Firm:	Tonic Group
Design:	Chris Burr, Max Wilker
Illustration:	Chris Burr, Max Wilker
Programming:	Nico Marcellino
Authoring Software:	Photoshop, Illustrator, Bryce
Language:	English

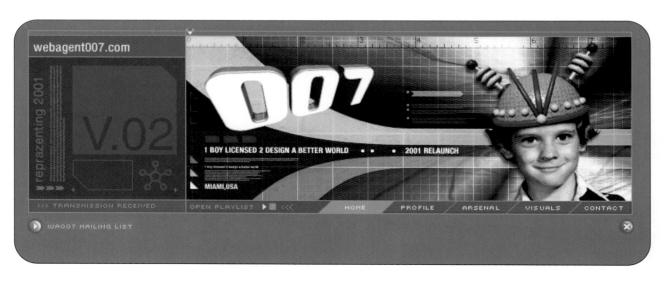

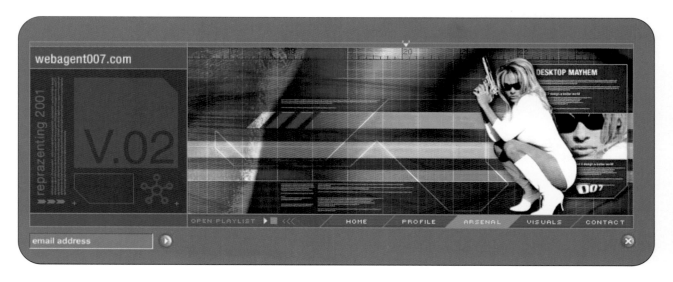

Web Agent 007 is the portfolio of Flash designer James Begera. Begera's portfolio plays upon the cliché concepts of the James Bond, Agent 007, feature film title sequence visuals, offering viewers a playful and seductive look at the designer's considerable Flash and design abilities.

The site presents the designer's work in a narrow, horizontal interface that makes use of Flash ActionScripting controls for the scrolling visuals—where the images move quickly into place while slowly coming to a stop as if controlled by gravity.

One element that increases the functionality of the site is the high frame rate used throughout the site. Setting the project's frame rate higher than the Flash program's default of twelve frames per second (fps) keeps movement—such as rollovers in the portfolio section—smooth and consistent.

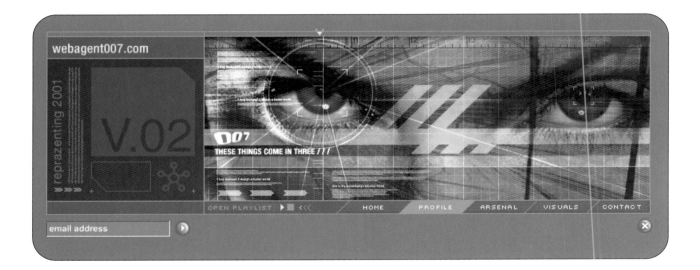

UNITED STATES
www.webagent007.com

Project:	Web Agent 007
Design Firm:	Axis 360
Design:	James Begera
Authoring Software:	Photoshop, Illustrator, FormZ, ElectricImage, Dreamweaver
Language:	English
Special Features:	Wallpapers

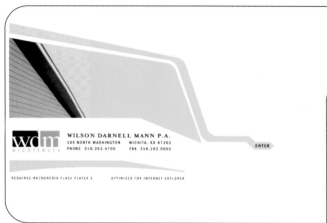

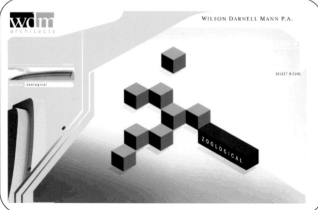

The first designs prepared for the WDM Architects site were traditional and conservative, but after reviewing those initial designs, the client surprised the designers at Gardner by asking for a nontraditional design, something "unexpected" compared to other architecture Web sites. Gardner took this as a sign to push the envelope. The result is a site that includes the angles and solid structure of architecture and also includes a sense of motion by incorporating animated type, lines, and navigation opportunities. Navigation from the main screen is by way of building-block cubes that expand as the viewer rolls the cursor over them. For continuity, this same block navigation style is incorporated in additional screens throughout the site.

The designers consciously stayed away from rectangles and instead created an interface for the site comprising boxes with multiple angles and cut-out shapes. As each screen loads, a Flash masking technique reveals the interface screen for the specific areas.

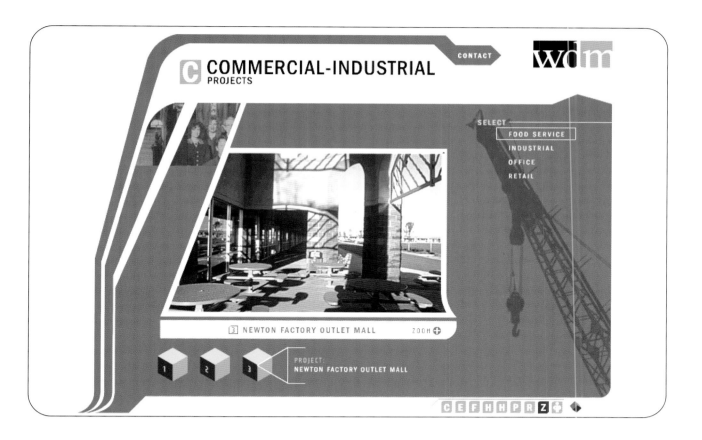

COMMERCIAL-INDUSTRIAL
PROJECTS

CONTACT

SELECT
FOOD SERVICE
INDUSTRIAL
OFFICE
RETAIL

3 NEWTON FACTORY OUTLET MALL   ZOOM ⊕

PROJECT:
NEWTON FACTORY OUTLET MALL

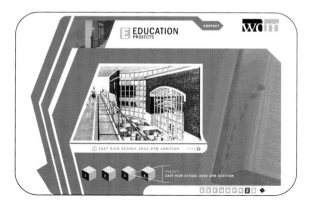

UNITED STATES
www.wdmdesign.com

Project:	Wilson Darnell Mann Architects
Client:	Wilson Darnell Mann Architects
Design Firm:	Gardner Design
Design:	Chaney Kimball
Photography:	Paul Chauncey, Steve Hauck
Programming:	Chaney Kimball
Authoring Software:	Photoshop, Dreamweaver, Freehand
Specs:	750 × 550, 120KB (main movie), 40KB (photo movies)
Language:	English

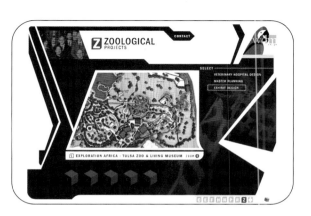

WWW.COKEBUDDY.COM • WWW.ELFADS.COM • WWW.PLAYADZ.COM • KIDSEDGE.COM • WWW.IFUNI.COM • WWW.CYBERSI.COM

Directory

AUSTRALIA
Deepend Sydney
www.deepend.com
tim@deepend.com.au
10 Charles Street
Redfern,
New South Wales 2016
61-2-9699-0046

dform(one).shift.func
www.dformishiftfunc.net
speak@dformishiftfunc.net
24/24 Sandridge Street
Bondi Beach, Sydney 2026
61-415-189-754

BELGIUM
Bubble
www.bubble.be
peter.dekens@bubble.be
Gustaaf Callierlaan 175
B-9000 Gent
32-9223-9369

Digital Age Design
www.dad.be
info@dad.be
105A Rue Colonel Bourg
1140 Evere
32-2706-0590

BRAZIL
Rumba Comunicaçao Ltda.
www.rumba.com.br
info@rumba.com.br
Carlos Steinen Street,
399 Paraiso,
Saõ Paulo 04004-012
5511-3884-3524

CANADA
Velocity Design Studio
www.velocitystudio.com
info@velocitystudio.com
104 Ashbury Court
London, Ontario N6E 3T5
519-668-1320

CZECH REPUBLIC
Deepend Prague
www.deepend.cz
info@deepend.cz
Karlovo nam. 17, budova A
Praha 2, 120 00
420-2-21986-250

DENMARK
In2Media
www.in2media.com
info@in2media.dk
Ehlersvej 21
2900 Hellerup
45-7022-1516

FRANCE
Troisième Oeil
www.3e-oeil.com
infos@3e-oeil.com
9 Rue Marchande
72000 Le Mans
33-02-43232303

Uzik
www.uzik.com
contact@uzik.com
49 rue de Clery
75002 Paris
33-01-45081640

Xcess Lab
www.xcesslab.com
phil@xcesslab.com
Technopol Izarbel
64210 Bidart
33-55-8413941

GERMANY
diffus—Buero für
Mediengestaltung
www.diffus.com
office@diffus.com
Hasenbergstrasse 95-97
70176 Stuttgart
49-711-99339131

Fork Unstable Media GmbH
www.fork.de
info@fork.de
Juliusstrasse 25
22769 Hamburg
49-40-4325480

Moccu
www.moccu.com
info@moccu.com
Christburger Str. 46
10405 Berlin
49-30-44032985

Pet Gotohda
www.petgo.de
tohda@petgo.de
Hösbacher Weg 39a
63773 Goldbach

GREECE
em(phaze)
www.emphaze.com
info@emphaze.com
56 Apostolopoulou Str.
15231 Athens
30-010-6721011

HONG KONG
ItCat Media Ltd.
www.itcatmedia.com
webmaster@itcatmedia.com
1902, Chung Nam Building,
Lockhart Road
Wan Chai
852-2865-2269

ISRAEL
Bat Sheva Graphic
www.batshevagraphic.com
info@puzzlehead.com
17 Haharoshet Street
Ramat Hasharon, 47279
972-3-5477477

ITALY
Deepend Roma SRL
www.deepend.it
design@deepend.it
Via San Bartolomeo
de'Vaccinari 80/82
00186 Roma
39-06-68309397

Micron-ASA SRL
www.micronasa.com
info@micronasa.it
Via Durban 4
00144 Roma
39-0652271-9803

JAPAN
Adwave
www.adwave.co.jp
takahashi@adwave.co.jp
2-13-3, Heijima,
Niigata-ken
Niigata-cho, 950-2004
025-230-1000

MEXICO
W Interactive Media
www.grupow.com
info@grupow.com
Paseo de los Claveles 398
Parques de La Cañada
Saltillo, Coahuila 25080
52-844-489-4400

RUSSIA
Art Lebedev Group
www.design.ru
cmart@design.ru
Box 77 c/o IPS, PMB 572,
666 Fifth Avenue
New York, NY 10103

SINGAPORE
Aretae Pte. Ltd.
www.aretae.com
portals@aretae.com
20 Raffles Place
#26-01 / 08 Ocean Towers
65-298-8859

SOUTH AFRICA
FCB Electric Ocean
www.fcbelectricocean.com
electricocean@fcb.co.za
P.O. Box 78014
Sandton 2146
27-11-301-1300

Ukubona New Media
www.ukubona.co.za
info@ukubona.co.za
5 Ravenscraig Road
Woodstock,
Cape Town 8000
27-21-448-8298

SWEDEN
Paregos Mediadesign AB
skyscraper.paregos.com
info@paregos.se
Fiskargatan 14
S-11620 Stockholm
46-8-55609390

NETHERLANDS
Grootlicht Interactive
www.grootlicht.com
info@grootlicht.com
Zijpendaalseweg 53
6814 CD Arnheim

DirecCory

PPGH JWT-Colors
www.colors.nl
w.andrea@colors.nl
Rietlandpark 301
1079 DW Amsterdam
31-020-3019494

UNITED KINGDOM
AKQA
www.akqa.com
info@akqa.com
Princess House,
38 Jermyn Street
St. James SW1Y 6DN
020-7494-9200

Less Rain
www.lessrain.com
reception@lessrain.com
Lincoln House, 33-34
Hoxton
London W16NN
44-207-729-7227

NSource
www.nsource.co.uk
info@nsource.co.uk
The Old Dairy, Lady Farm
Chelwood, Bristol BS39 4NN
01761-492800

Zentropy Partners (UK) Ltd.
www.zentropypartners.co.uk
mmayes@zentropypart-
ners.co.uk
Lynton House, 7-12
Tavistock Square
London WC1H 9LT
48-207-554-0500

UNITED STATES
Angry Monkey
www.angrymonkey.com
jpl@angrymonkey.com
San Francisco, CA 94114

Asa Shatkin Studio
www.asashatkin.com
asa@asashkatkin.com
2703 West Thomas Street
Chicago, IL 60622
773-395-2767

Axiom Studio Inc.
www.axiomstudio.com
info@axiomstudio.com
441 North 5th Street
Philadelphia, PA 19123
215-509-7686, ext. 102

Axis360
www.axis360.com
jamesb@axis360.com
13400 SW 128 Street
Miami, FL 33186
305-470-9888

Being Smart
www.beingsmart.com
information@beingsmart
.com
818-980-8155

Carbonhouse Inc.
www.carbonhouse.com
info@carbonhouse.com
3204 North Davidson Street
Charlotte, NC 28205
704-333-5600

DS9
www.dietstrychnine.com
info@dietstrychnine.com
2701 North Janssen Avenue
Chicago, IL 60614
312-446-9283

Fahrenheit Studio
www.fahrenheit.com
info@fahrenheit.com
10303 Mississippi Avenue
Los Angeles, CA 90025
310-449-7751

Gardner Design
www.gardnerdesign.net
info@gardnerdesign.net
3204 East Douglas
Wichita, KS 67208
316-691-8808

Gr33nhous3
www.gr33nhous3.com
gr33n@gr33nhous3.com
253 Prospect Place
Brooklyn, NY 11238
718-623-2381

Hello Design
www.hellodesign.com
hello@hellodesign.com
8684 Washington Blvd.
Culver City, CA 90232
310-839-4885

Jeffrey Kelly
www.jeeto.com
Los Angeles, CA

Juxt Interactive
juxtinteractive.com
info@juxtinteractive.com
858 Production Place
Newport Beach, CA 92663
949-752-5898

Lead Dog Digital
www.ldd.com
info@ldd.com
212 West 35th Street
New York, NY 10001
212-564-5070

Marc Stricklin
www.brittle-bones.com
mstricklin@mindspring.com
Birmingham, AL 35223
205-949-9494

Mighty Assembly
www.mightyassembly.com
natalie@mightyassembly.com
3178 17th Street, Studio 2
San Francisco, CA 94110
415-255-8871

OPUS:CREATIVE
www.opuscreative.com
info@opuscreative.com
2303 NW 23rd Avenue
Portland, OR 97210
503-220-0252

Orange Voodoo
www.orangevoodoo.com
rick@orangevoodoo.com
24335 El Pilar
Laguna Niguel, CA 92677
949-360-7219

Paris France
www.parisfranceinc.com
doug@parisfranceinc.com
222 NW Second, #309
Portland, OR 97209
503-225-1200

PopsicleRiot
www.popsicleriot.com
dave@popsicleriot.com
1610 Sutter Street, Suite 206
San Francisco, CA 94109
415-609-4373

Second Story Interactive
www.secondstory.com
info@secondstory.com
1104 NW 15th Avenue, #400
Portland, OR 97209
503-827-7155

Sharpe Associates Inc.
sharpela@pacbell.net
310-641-8556

Tonic Group
www.tonicgroup.com
info@tonicgroup.com
333 East 30th Street,
18th Floor
New York, NY 10016
212-679-9201

Tubatomic Inc.
www.tubatomic.inc
info@movtv.com
1136 Englewood Avenue
Chattanooga, TN 37405
423-364-4208

Typographic
www.typographic.com
info@typographic.com
351 South Cochran Avenue
Los Angeles, CA 90036
323-935-3375

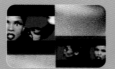

Glossary

Actions
Actions make a movie respond to events in particular ways. This makes a movie interactive.

ActionScript
Flash object-oriented programming language. Use ActionScripts to add interactivity to specific events.

Animation
The process of taking a series of static pictures—called frames or panels—and stringing them together in a timed sequence giving the appearance of continuous motion. Flash offers two forms of animation, tweened animation and frame-by-frame animation.

Antialiasing
A graphic technique used to blur and smooth diagonal edges and abrupt color changes along the edge of a graphic or piece of text.

Bandwidth
The data-carrying capacity of a data communications channel, such as within a cable, DSL, or modem connection.

Bandwidth Profiler
Allows the user to view downloading performance in a .SWF file. Use the Bandwidth Profiler in the Flash Player to see how much data is sent for each frame in the movie.

Bezier curve
To create curved segments using the Subselect tool. Slope and length of each curve can be changed using anchor points and handles.

Bitmap graphic
A graphic image that is composed of a pattern of dots or pixels. The individual pixels are stored as data on a computer.

Browser
The software tools the user runs to "browse" the Internet.

Character panel
Used to edit the font's size, color, kerning, leading.

Checkbox
Turns on and off the designated setting. When checked, the setting is on, and when unchecked, the setting is off.

Close icon or Close box
Lets you close the dialog box, window, panel, or application currently showing.

Controller
A floating dialog box that controls playback. ncludes Stop, Rewind, Step Back, Play, Step Forward, Go To End.

Custom keys
Customized Shortcuts for Flash commands and functions.

Dithering
Simulating a color by placing pixels in close proximity to each other.

Drop-down list
Displays an expanded hierarchical list of options that complements the selection. A highlighted triangle pointing down indicates a drop-down list.

Effect panel
Used to create color tints and transparency effects for vector graphics.

Event sound
A sound file that must download completely before it begins playing and that continues playing until prompted to stop.

External image editor
A program that you use outside the Flash environment to modify images.

Fill
A solid shape. Can be accompanied by a stroke.

Fill panel
Use to select a fill color and design linear and radial gradients.

.FLA file
The native Flash file format; the format you use to save your work when creating and editing a movie.

Flash lessons
Part of the instructional media provided by Macromedia with Flash. Interactive lessons that allow users to practice on examples that introduce you to Flash's core features. Can be found under Help menu.

Flash player format (SWF)
The main file format for distributing Flash content.

Flip
The act of turning an object over across its horizontal or vertical axis without moving its relative position on the Stage.

Frame
A single complete graphic image that is displayed chronologically in the timeline. A single frame makes up a static image, while a series of frames make up an animation.

Frame-by-frame animation
Animation created using an individual image for each frame.

Frame panel
Used to set motion and shape tweens and their properties. Also used to label frames.

Frame rate
The number of animation frames to be displayed every second, usually expressed as fps, or frames per second.

GIF (Graphics Interchange Format)
A compression graphics file format developed by CompuServe and characterized by small file sizes and a maximum palette of 256 colors.

GIF animation
An animation that is created or exported as a GIF image.

Gradient
A transition from one color to another so that the intervening colors shade from the starting point to the ending point.

Grid
Lines that appear behind the artwork, allowing the user to position objects precisely.

Group
Two or more drawing objects combined so that you can edit or move them as a single unit.

Guide layer
Assists in holding objects that aid as reference points for placing and aligning objects on the Stage.

HTML (HyperText Markup Language)
The most popular coding method for defining documents on the World Wide Web.

Info panel
Used to edit an objects size, location, and check registration points.

Instance
An occurrence of a Flash element. When a symbol is placed on the Stage, an Instance of that symbol is created.

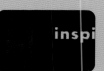

GLOSSARY

Instance panel
Used to recall information about symbols and instances in your movie.

JPEG (Joint Photographic Experts Group)
A graphic file type featuring adjustable compression and the ability to display millions of colors.

Kerning
Adjusts the spacing between pairs of letters.

Keyframe
A frame in an animation that marks a key point of change or action.

Layer
A level or plane where a graphic or graphics can reside.

Library
Where you store and organize created symbols and imported files.

Linear gradient
A gradient that follows a straight line.

Loop
The cycle of animation from start to finish.

Magic wand
A tool used to select groups of pixels in a bitmapped image based on a color or range of colors.

Mask layer
This layer hides and exposes sections of the linked layer that lies directly below.

Modifier
Additional actions of tools on the Toolbar. For example, when you draw a rectangle using the Rectangle tool, you can select the rectangle, and the modifiers for Smoothing, Straightening, Rotating, and Scaling become available.

Motion Guide Layer
Allows you to create a path along which an animation occurs.

Motion path
A drawn path that an animated object follows.

Motion tween
Tweening that changes position, size, rotation, skew, color, and tint of images.

Mouse event
Any movement of the mouse button, possibly triggering a mouse action such as clicking or rollover.

Mouse event actions
Actions assigned to a button that react to a mouse event such as a rollover.

Movie clip
A symbol selection used in Flash to describe an animated element.

Onion skinning
A preview mode that allows you to select a frame and then see the contents of surrounding frames in a dimmed, wire-frame mode.

Pixel
A small rectangle filled with color referred to as a dot-as in dots per inch or dpi.

Playhead
The red controller bar that moves through the Timeline showing the current frame displayed on the stage.

PNG (Portable Network Graphics)
A graphic file format that supports transparency in Flash.

Projector or Standalone Projector
Software that allows a movie to be played without using the Flash Player software.

Publish
Creates a Flash Player file (SWF) and an HTML document that puts the Flash Player file into a browser window

QuickTime
A digital video-and-audio standard developed by Apple and popular for Internet use.

Radial gradient
A gradient that changes from the center of a circle and finishes at the circle's outer edge.

Rich media
Term describing advanced technology used in graphic design, going beyond static images or animated GIFs.

Rollover
An area on a Web page that triggers an event when the user moves the cursor over it.

Scene
Used to organize a movie's subject matter.

Shape tween
Creates an effect similar to morphing, making one shape appear to change into another shape over a fixed period of time.

Shared library
Used to link to library items as external assets. You can create font symbols to include in shared libraries, as well as buttons, graphics, movie clips, and sounds.

Shockwave
An animation and authoring file type established by Macromedia(tm). Shockwave differs from Flash in that bitmap images are used instead of vector graphics, making Shockwave better suited to those with fast Internet connections.

Stage
The blank rectangular area where movies are created and played.

Streaming
The flow of data from a server to the visitor's own computer. Streaming allows for an animation to start right away while the rest of the file downloads in the background.

Symbol
A graphic with a series of instructions that can be duplicated, modified, and reused to help keep file sizes small and more easily editable throughout a file or files.

Text box
The bounding box that surrounds created or selected text, allowing the user to manipulate the type using the handle on the box.

Timeline
The area that holds each frame, layer, and scene that makes up the movie.

Transparency
An image attribute that allows one color to be transparent, showing underlying layers or objects.

Tweening
In tweened animation, a beginning and ending keyframe is created and Flash fills in the in-between frames. The beginning keyframe and ending keyframe contain a significant event.

resources

About: Animation
http://animation.about.com

ActionScripts.org
www.actionscripts.org

A List Apart
www.alistapart.com

Altermind
www.altermind.org/v6tutorials.htm

Arabic typography
www.arabictypography.com/flash.html

Art's Web Site
www.artswebsite.co

Beatnik
www.beatnik.com

Best german Sites
http://bestflashsites.de

BrainJar
www.brainjar.com

Brendan Dawes' Headshop
www.brendandawes.com/headshop

Canfield Studios
http://canfieldstudios.com/flash4

Computer Arts Tutorials
www.computerarts.co.uk/tutorials

Concept 4 Web
www.concept4web.com

Crazy Raven
www.crazyraven.com

D-art
www.d-art.ch

Deconcept
www.deconcept.com

Designer Wiz
www.designerwiz.com

Digital Web Magazine
www.digital-web.com

Echo Echo
www.echoecho.com/flash.htm

EgoMedia
www.egomedia.com

Extreme Flash
www.extremeflash.com

Extreme Zone
www.extremezone.com/pzero/en/home.html

Fig Leaf
http://chattyfig.figleaf.com

Flahoo
www.flahoo.com

Flash 4 All
www.flash4all.de

Flash 5 Actionscript!
www.flash5actionscript.com

Flash Academy
www.enetserve.com/tutorials/

Flash Central
www.flashcentral.com

Flash CFM
www.flashcfm.com

Flash Challenge
www.flashchallenge.com

Flash Core
www.flashcore.com

Flash DB
www.kessels.com/FlashDB/

Flash deConstruction
www.juxtinteractive.com/deconstruction/

Flash Enabled
www.flashenabled.com

Flasher
www.flasher.ru

Flasher l
www.chinwag.com/flasher

Flash Factory
www.flash-factory.ch

Flash Film Maker
www.flashfilmmaker.com

Flash Forge
www.goldshell.com/flashforge

Flash Freaks
www.flashfreaks.nl

Flash Fruit
www.flashfruit.com

Flash Geek
www.flashgeek.com

Flash Gen
www.flashgen.com

Flash Guru
www.flashguru.co.uk/

Flash Heaven
www.flashheaven.de/englisch.htm

Flash House
www.flashhouse.net

Flash Jester
www.flashjester.com

Flash Links
www.flashlinks.de

Flash Lite
www.flashlite.net

Flash Magazine
www.flashmagazine.com

Flash Move
www.flashmove.com

Flash online studeren
www.sip.be/flash

Flash Opensource
www.fortunecity.com

Flash Pagina
http://flash.pagina.nl/

Flash Planet
www.flashplanet.com

Flash Pro
www.muinar.com/flashpro

Flash Pro: The Netherlands
www.flashpro.nl

Flash Skills
www.flashskills.com

Flash Tek
www.flashtek.com

Flash Thief
www.flashthief.com

Flash Web Links
www.flash-web-links.de

Flash Xpress
www.flashxpress.net

Full Screen
www.fullscreen.com

Geckoarts
www.geckoarts.com/

Geomagnet
www.geomagnet.com

Help4Flash
www.help4flash.com

Intuitiv Media
www.intuitivmedia.com

Jessett: Creating a Web Site
www.jessett.com

killersound
www.killersound.com

Kilowatt Design
www.kilowattdesign.com

Kirupa Flash Tutorials
www.kirupa.com

LINKZ
www.north-support.com/thelinkz

Moock
http://moock.org/webdesign/flash

Motion Culture
www.motionculture.org

Nuthing But Flash
http://nuthing.com

Open SWF
www.openswf.org/

resources

Philter's Flash
http://philterdesign.com

Photoshop Web guide
www.photoguide.co.za/flash/

Phresh
www.phresh.de

Pope de Flash
www.popedeflash.com

Pro Flasher
www.proflasher.com

Quintus
www.come.to/qfi

Quintus Flash Usability
www.quintus.org/use

Risorse Flash
www.risorseflash.it

Screen Weaver
http://screenweaver.com

Shock Fusion
www.shockfusion.com

Site Point
www.sitepoint.com

Spoono
www.spoono.com/tutorials/flash

Sticky Sauce
www.stickysauce.com

Stylus Inc.
www.stylusinc.com/website/flash_sql.htm

SWF Studio
www.northcode.com

Swiff Tools
www.swifftools.com

Swift Tools
www.swift-tools.com

Swift 3D
www.swift3d.com

Swifty Utilities
http://buraks.com/swifty

Swish
http://swishzone.com

The Linkz
www.thelinkz.com

Training Tools
www.trainingtools.com

Tree City
www.treecity.co.uk

Ultra Shock
www.ultrashock.com

Vecta 3D
www.ideaworks3d.com

Virtual-FX
www.virtual-fx.net

Web Pros Now
www.webprosnow.com

MAGAZINES

Computer Arts
www.computerarts.co.uk

Create Online
www.createonline.co.uk

Critique Magazine
www.critiquemag.com

Digital Animator
www.animator.com

E.n.z.o.
www.enzo.co.kr

Het Grafisch Weekblad
www.gw.nl/

How Now
www.howdesign.com

IDN World
www.idnworld.com

NeoMu
www.neomu.com

Ningen
www.ningen.com